FIX YOUR

VOLKSWAGEN

Larry Johnson

Executive Technical Editor,
Motor Service Magazine
Member, Society of Automotive Engineers
Certified General Automobile Mechanic by
National Institute for Automotive Service Excellence

SOUTH HOLLAND, ILLINOIS
THE GOODHEART-WILLCOX COMPANY, INC.
Publishers

2

INTRODUCTION

Some books on servicing and repairing Volkswagen cars cover theory and fundamentals of operation. Others go into explicit detail for servicing VWs of one model year. Still others give step-by-step repair procedures for certain assemblies or specific systems.

"Fix Your Volkswagen" takes something from each of these approaches, blending solid service information with basic theory where necessary or in full detail when it is required in the scope of repair.

Helpful explanatory material often precedes the service procedure for the benefit of VW owners tackling a given service operation for the first time. Procedures shown and described are typical. Many time and labor saving shop kinks used by top-flight Volkswagen mechanics are included.

Be sure to give special attention to the specification tables just ahead of the index in the back of the book. Service data contained in these tables goes back to 1954 Beetle models. Vital statistics and service specifications for Beetles and other lines of late model VW cars are also compared. While the modern Basic Beetle appears to be much the same vehicle first introduced in the U.S. in 1949, there have been a great number of mechanical changes. These specification tables further establish that fact.

By way of warning, note that it is customary for all automobile manufacturers to have alternate sources of supply for batteries, generators, ignition distributors and other units. Therefore, parts and assemblies of different makes may be found on cars built in the same model year. Also design improvements in brakes, suspension or other systems could result in a running change during a given production year. If this occurs, late production vehicles could differ slightly from those built early in the model year.

"Fix Your Volkswagen" covers the Beetle, Super Beetle, Squareback and Fastback or Type 3, 411 and 412 or Type 4 models. The purpose of this book is to provide selected service information for owners who want to do all or part of their own Volkswagen maintenance and service, and for experienced mechanics contemplating Volkswagen service and repair work.

Larry Johnson

3

CHANGES IN THE 1973 VOLKSWAGEN

Volkswagen has adopted the name "Basic Beetle" for the 111 model to distinguish it from the Super Beetle, 113 model. Appearance-wise, the basic model has larger round taillights, a new dashboard with improved ventilation outlets, redesigned front seats and reinforced front and rear bumpers. An inertia-type front seat belt system is a carry-over from late 1972 models. This combination lap/shoulder belt allows freedom of movement, but emergency-locking reactor locks the belt and restrains the occupant when the car is braking or cornering hard. The intake air preheating system is improved as well as the air cleaner with a new dry-type air filter. Other changes include: diaphragm-type clutch, larger transmission bearings and softer mountings for the transmission and differential. The automatic stick shift transmission has a "Park" position for 1973.

The new Super Beetle features a curved windshield, larger round taillights and reinforced bumpers. The dashboard is built farther forward with a high-level instrument cluster and rocker switches instead of knobs. Bucket seats and inertia-type seat belts are standard equipment. A diaphragm-type clutch replaces the coil spring unit.

CONTENTS

CHANGES ON 1973 SQUAREBACK, TYPE 3, TYPE 4 MODELS

The Type 3 series (Basic Compact, Sedan and Squareback) has new, reinforced bumpers, stronger transmission bearings, repositioned hand brake lever and increased computer diagnosis capabilities.

In the Type 4 series, the model name has been changed from 411 to 412. Restyled from the windshield forward, this series has stronger bumpers, larger taillights and radial steel-belted tires. Rear doors have child-proof locks, disc brakes have thicker pads, and the front and rear suspension has been revised.

The 412 series utilizes inertia reel 3-point safety belts for the driver and front seat passenger. If either fails to fasten his belt once the ignition is "on" and the car is in gear, a warning light on the dashboard and a buzzer are activated. Rear seats are equipped with retractable belts.

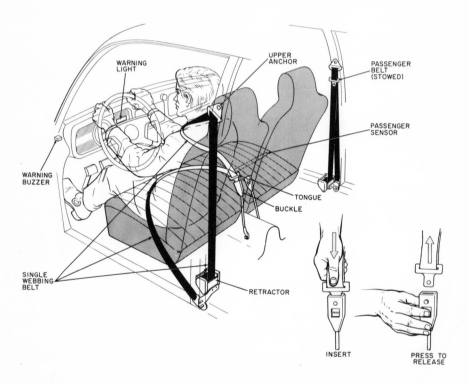

The 2-door sedans are available with 4-speed manual transmission having larger diameter synchronizers. The 4-door sedans and station wagons are equipped with VW's 3-speed automatic transmission as standard equipment.

Engine changes include modified camshaft timing for smoother idle and a nickel-plated muffler.

TUNING
for Best Economy and Performance

A Volkswagen car is a precision-built piece of machinery, regardless of model line, model year or body style. However, like all machinery, it must be maintained properly if you expect to obtain optimum overall performance and maximum service life from its carefully engineered components.

The latest Basic Beetle model, for example, weighs over 1800 lbs. and can be powered at speeds up to 80 mph by an air-cooled, horizontally opposed 4-cylinder engine only half the size of current U.S. 6-cylinder

Fig. A-1. Most assemblies and components requiring maintenance services are within easy reach under the engine hood of a Volkswagen.

engines. Today's VWs will accelerate from 0 to 60 mph in 19.5 seconds. They will operate under normal conditions at 25 miles per gallon of gasoline.

In order to receive the benefits of maximum fuel economy and highest performance, your Volkswagen engine must be tuned up regularly, carefully, completely and accurately. The rule-of-thumb tune-up interval is once every 10,000 to 12,000 miles. However, driving conditions, driving habits and miles-driven-per-month are variables that must be considered.

As far as efficiency of engine operation is concerned, the need for a tune-up is indicated by hard starting, engine miss, loss of power or poor fuel mileage. Anyone having a reasonably good assortment of metric-sized hand tools and some mechanical inclination can do his own tune-ups.

If you feel so inclined, you will find that the compact engine is quite accessible, Fig. A-1. Air cleaner, ignition distributor, spark plugs, generator, V-belt and valve covers are within easy reach. Compression pressure should be checked first to assure the engine is tuneable.

Fig. A-1A. Compression tester is a valuable diagnostic tool. Compression pressure readings help to establish whether or not the engine is tuneable.

HOW TO CHECK COMPRESSION

Compression, ignition and carburetion have great influence on engine performance. Therefore, tune-up service procedures related to these factors should be performed in the order mentioned. However, it may be impossible, for example, to obtain a satisfactory carburetor adjustment if compression and/or ignition are not up to specifications.

So the first step in the VW tune-up procedure is to check compression pressure. Compression is the amount of pressure built up in each engine cylinder as the piston moves outward from the crankshaft and compresses the air-fuel charge into the relatively small combustion chamber area. Unless compression is at or near maximum pressure and approximately equal in all cylinders, satisfactory engine performance cannot be obtained.

Tuning For Best Economy, Performance

To make a compression test:
1 - Run the engine until it is warm. This will allow sufficient time for a film of oil to form a seal between the pistons, rings and cylinder walls.
2 - Stop the engine.
3 - Remove the spark plug connectors one at a time, marking each connector - and the engine - with chalk or grease pencil to identify connector-to-plug location.
4 - Remove all four spark plugs.
5 - With the throttle wide open, place a compression gauge (see Fig. A-1A) in each spark plug hole in turn and crank the engine by means of the starter.
6 - Make note of each cylinder's highest pressure reading in cylinder number order.

Engines with the following compression ratios should have the respective compression pressures shown:

Ratio	Range (lbs.)	Min. Pressure (lbs.)	Max. Variation (lbs.)
6.0:1	85-107	65	20
6.6:1	100-114	65	20
7.1:1	100-128	65	20
7.3:1	107-135	85	14
7.5:1	114-142	100	14
7.7:1	135-156	114	14
7.8:1	120-150	100	14
8.2:1	128-156	114	14

Compression readings lower than those specified indicate leakage at the engine valves or past the piston rings. If total mileage on the engine is less than 50,000 miles, the compression loss probably is due to maladjusted or defective valves.

EASY WAY TO ADJUST VALVES

If compression pressure readings are within limits, continue with the engine tune-up job by checking and adjusting valve clearance as required. Valve clearance is the gap allowed for the expansion of operating parts. It is measured by placing a feeler gauge of specified thickness between the end of the valve stem and the adjusting screw in the rocker arm.

If insufficient valve clearance is provided, the valves will stay open too long and operate at excessively high temperatures. This could result in early failure of valves and seats due to burning.

On the other hand, if valve clearance is excessive, valve action will be noisy. The valve will not remain open long enough to allow the full air-fuel charge to enter the combustion chamber, or provide time for the burned charge to pass into the exhaust system.

Access to the valve covers and valve assemblies on most models is from under the rear fenders. Use the jack provided with your car to jack up the right side first. Complete the valve clearance adjustments on that side of the engine, then repeat the car jacking and valve adjusting procedures on the left side.

The valve cover is held in place by a wire bail or retaining spring. To remove the bail, insert a breaker bar handle or wheel cover remover through the center hoop of the bail. Pull down on the breaker bar until the bail drops free.

Valve clearance can be adjusted by means of a screw and locknut in the rocker arm, Fig. A-2. Clearance must be checked when the engine is cold and the piston in the corresponding cylinder is at top dead center. Specifications for the various VW engine applications are given in charts immediately preceding the index in the back of the book.

Fig. A-2. Loosen lock nut with wrench and turn adjusting screw with screwdriver.

Adjust the valves in 1, 2, 3, 4 cylinder order. On late model engines, the cylinder arrangement is shown by numbers on the engine cover plates.

On all Volkswagen engines, the cylinders are numbered from front to rear. Standing at the rear of your VW, the cylinder farthest from you on the right is cylinder No. 1. The cylinder closest to you on the right is No. 2. The one farthest forward on the left is No. 3, and the cylinder closest to you on the left is No. 4, see Figs. C-1 to C-2B.

To prepare the engine for adjustment of both valves of cylinder No. 1:

1 - Remove distributor cap.

2 - Turn engine by using a socket wrench and breaker bar on crankshaft pulley nut, or turn V-belt by hand.

3 - Turn engine until firing end or rotor aligns with mark on rim of distributor base.

4 - Also note that timing mark on crankshaft pulley is in line with vertical joining faces of crankcase, Fig. A-3.

5 - Both valves for cylinder No. 1 should be closed and rocker arms should have clearance at valve stem ends and push rods.

Tuning For Best Economy, Performance

Fig. A-3. Location of timing mark on pulley. If pulley has two marks on it, use left-hand mark for valve adjustment.

Proceed with the actual valve clearance adjustment as follows:

1 - Insert feeler gauge blade of correct thickness between adjusting screw and valve stem end of each valve of cylinder No. 1.

2 - If blade slides smoothly between contact surfaces with a slight drag, clearance is correct.

3 - If clearance is too small or too large, loosen locknut on adjusting screw, turn adjusting screw with a screwdriver to obtain correct clearance. Then hold adjusting screw with screwdriver and tighten locknut.

4 - Recheck clearance and readjust if necessary.

5 - Turn crankshaft 180 deg., moving distributor rotor counterclockwise

Fig. A-4. Turn crankshaft to move rotor 90 deg. to reposition engine for valve adjustment.

90 deg. and placing engine in position for checking clearance of valves of cylinder No. 2, Fig. A-4. Repeat steps 1, 2, 3, and 4.

6 - Turn crankshaft another 180 deg. for checking clearance of valves of cylinder No. 3, and once again for checking valves of cylinder No. 4.

7 - Clean and reinstall valve covers on cylinder heads, using new gaskets. Push wire bails into place on valve covers.

ACCESS TO THE BATTERY

The battery is the source of electrical power for your VW, so it deserves careful attention, cleaning, inspection and testing early in the tune-up. Also, later tests of ignition system performance and charging system output rely on the use of a fully charged battery.

The battery is located under the right rear seat in Beetle, Type 3 and Squareback models, Fig. A-4A. It is under the driver's seat on all 411 and 412 (Type 4) models, Fig. A-4B.

To check and perform simple battery services, merely lift up the back seat on cars having the battery located in this area. If the battery must be removed for recharging or replacement, take the seat out of the car, fold the right rear floor mat out of the way, push out the bottom of the kickboard and remove it.

Fig. A-4A. Battery in VW Beetle and Type 3 cars is located under rear seat at right. Note removable plastic cover over positive terminal.

Fig. A-4B. Battery is under driver's seat on 412 models. Access is made easy by moving seat up and back before releasing locking lever.

Next, loosen the cable clamp nuts, spread the clamps and lift them from the posts. Remove the ground cable first and install it last when disconnecting the cables from the battery. This helps avoid drawing a spark and possibly causing a battery explosion.

Remove the nut and washer securing the battery hold-down plate. Make sure all battery filler caps are tight. Carefully tilt the battery toward the front of the car and slide it back and out of the battery well.

Getting at the battery on 411 and 412 models is a bit more difficult. Move the driver's seat to the rear of its track and raise the seat as high as possible. Adjust the backrest to its most forward position and get out of the car. Reach under the front edge of the seat and pull the locking lever toward the driver's side of the car. Tip the seat to the rear to provide access to the battery.

Reverse this procedure after completing the battery service job. When lowering the seat to normal driving position, make sure that the locking lever pin engages firmly in the height-adjusting support.

BASIC BATTERY MAINTENANCE

First things first, keep sparks or an open flame away from the top of the battery. Fumes from the cells could cause the battery to explode and cause serious injury.

Clean the top of the battery, cable clamps and posts with water. Take care that none of the foreign matter enters the battery cells. Moisture and dirt will create a path for electrical leakage that could cause the battery to discharge.

If corrosion has built up on the battery cable clamps or hold-down, clean off as much corrosion as possible. Treat the area with a solution of baking soda and water. After this solution has had a chance to "work," wash it off with clean water.

To be sure of good connections, remove the cable clamps from the battery posts, negative cable first. Clean the inside of the clamps and side surfaces of the posts to a bright finish with a special wire-brush tool or very fine sandpaper. Reinstall the cable clamps on the battery posts, positive cable first, and tighten them securely.

To test the battery, consult the battery service portion of the chapter on "Simplified Electrical Service."

NORMAL CONDITION   CARBON FOULING

BURNING   OIL FOULING

Fig. A-5. Appearance of spark plug electrodes and insulators reveals engine condition.

SIMPLIFIED IGNITION TUNE-UP

The first step when tuning the ignition system is to make sure that the spark plugs are in satisfactory condition. If the plug is good, the insulator will be free of deposits and usually will be a light amber color at the firing end. If the insulator and electrodes are covered with deposits, the firing end usually can be cleaned by means of special spark plug cleaning equipment. In an emergency the electrodes can be cleaned by scraping with a thin-bladed knife. If the side electrode is grooved or if the center electrode is rounded, voltages higher than normal are required to jump the gap, and misfiring will occur. Replace the plugs.

Deposits on the insulator result from burning of the air/fuel mixture in the combustion chamber and may be broadly classified as carbon fouling and lead fouling. Oil fouling may occur in badly worn engines, Fig. A-5.

Carbon fouling results primarily from extended low speed operation and when the carburetor air/fuel adjustment is excessively rich. Carbon fouling is usually a relatively soft black soot which is easily removed.

Lead fouling results from the tetraethyl lead used in the gasoline to reduce the tendency of the engine to "ping." In many cases it is barely visible. Spark plugs with lead fouling will operate satisfactorily at low and medium speeds, but will miss when full load or high speed is attempted. This results from the higher temperatures melting the accumulation of lead salts, thus increasing their electrical conductivity so that the plug is shorted out and misfiring results. In some cases of lead fouling it is possible to burn off the deposits. Operate the engine at a speed just below the point where missing will occur, then gradually increase the speed until full throttle operation can be obtained.

When checking spark plugs, always make sure they are the correct type for the application. Any of the following plugs are acceptable for use in the applications shown.

	Type 1, 3 1968-73	Type 4 1968-73	Type 1 Pre-1968
Bosch	W 145T1	W 175T2	W 175T1
Beru	145/14	175/14/3	175/14
Champion	L-88A	N-88	L10S, L85, L95Y

The types of plugs listed in the accompanying table are for normal driving. However, if the car is to be driven at high speeds for prolonged periods, a "colder" plug should be used. Or, if the car is to be used exclusively in slow speed, stop and go, city driving, a "hotter" plug is recommended.

Different types of spark plugs are needed for different types of driving because the temperature of the firing end of the spark plug varies greatly with varied operating conditions. Prolonged high speed operation will produce higher plug temperatures than traffic driving. Spark plugs, therefore, are designed so that the firing end of the plug is hot enough to burn off any carbon deposits, but not so hot that the insulator or electrodes will be burned.

This is accomplished by increasing or decreasing the distance the heat must travel from the tip of the spark plug to metal surrounding the plugs. This is known as the heat range of the spark plug, Fig. A-6. A long path for the heat will produce a "hot" plug, while a short path permits the heat to escape more quickly and the plug is known as a "cold" plug. "Hot" plugs are used for slow speed operation, while "cold" plugs are used in full load high speed operation.

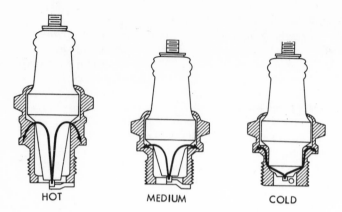

Fig. A-6. Heat flow paths in cold and hot type spark plugs.

| HOT | MEDIUM | COLD |

GAPPING THE PLUGS

Armed with the correct set of spark plugs for the application, adjust the side electrode closer to or farther from the center electrode. Special bending tools are available for the purpose. Either gauges of flat strip or round wire are available, Fig. A-7. However, the wire type is preferred because more accurate gauging is possible when the electrodes are worn. When edges of the electrodes become rounded, discard the spark plug or file the electrodes until surfaces are flat and true. Late model engines call for .028 in. gap, Fig. A-8. Check specifications.

The rule-of-thumb recommendation for spark plug replacement is 12,000 miles. All plugs should be fitted with new gaskets. Thread the plugs in carefully by hand, then use a wrench to seat them firmly in place, Fig. A-9. Crush the gasket but do not overtighten the plug or the electrode gap will change markedly.

Fig. A-7. A wire gauge is recommended for checking spark plug gap.

TIPS ON DISTRIBUTOR SERVICE

Many different models of ignition distributors have been utilized in Volkswagen engines, and several types of spark advance mechanisms have been employed. In 1954 and 1955, both centrifugal and vacuum devices were installed. From 1956 to 1970, distributors in all Beetle engines were equipped with vacuum advance only. In 1971, a double vacuum unit was used in conjunction with a centrifugal advance. In Fastback and Squareback engines through 1968, a vacuum advance distributor was original equipment. Starting in 1969, combined vacuum and centrifugal units provide automatic spark advance.

Fig. A-8. Spark plug gap specification is .028 in. on late model engines.

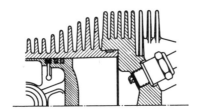

Fig. A-9. Tighten spark plugs enough to crush gasket. Do not over tighten.

To test distributor operation, disconnect a spark plug wire and - with engine running - hold the end of the wire about 1/4 in. from the cylinder head or other metal engine part. A good, vigorous spark 1/4 to 3/8 in. long should jump from the end of the wire to the engine if the distributor is in good condition. Failure to obtain a good spark indicates some defect in the distributor or some other part of the ignition system.

Inspect the condition of the breaker points. They should contact each other (in the closed position) over their entire area, Fig. A-10. Their contacting surfaces should be smooth and free from pitting with no metal transferred from one contact to the other. The points should be clean, gray metallic color. If they have a burned or smoky appearance, the condenser probably is defective and both condenser and points should be replaced.

Also check the rotor and the distributor cap. The rotor should have a firm push fit on the end of the distributor shaft and its firing end should not be eroded. In addition the contact button on top of the rotor must be in good condition.

Before examining the distributor cap, it is advisable to remove the high tension wires so the cap can be cleaned in a cleaning solution. But before removing the wires, mark the distributor cap tower for No. 1 spark plug wire so that the wires can be replaced in the correct order. The firing order of the Volkswagen is 1-4-3-2. The high tension wires are placed in the towers in a similar sequence. Facing the engine, the cylinder farthest from you on your right is No. 1

Fig. A-10. Contact points should meet squarely as at extreme left. Transfer of metal from one point to other indicates condenser of incorrect capacity. Condenser and points should both be discarded.

Examine the distributor cap carefully for cracks and evidence of arcing between firing points. Also inspect the interior of the cap towers (wells) for corrosion. If a cap is cracked or has been burned as the result of arcing, replace it with a new cap. If the wells are corroded, clean them with fine sandpaper rolled on a pencil.

REPLACING HIGH TENSION IGNITION WIRES

Defective ignition cables will cause misfiring by permitting the high tension ignition current to jump through the insulation to some part of the engine. In many cases the sound or "snap" of the jumping spark can be heard. Another test is to operate the engine in a dark garage and observe the ignition wires for any sparks or glowing which is known as "Corona Effect." Still another test is to disconnect the wires from the spark plugs and examine them carefully for worn spots where the insulation has been chafed by rubbing against the engine. Also try bending the cable in a tight loop. If fine cracks appear in the insulation, install new wiring.

Replacement of high tension wires is simple on older Volkswagen engines having copper core ignition cables. To avoid errors in re-assembly, replace them one at a time. Or, mark the distributor cap towers with the number of the cylinder served by each spark plug wire, then remove all the wires.

Cut replacement cables to the same length as the original cables, then install the boots and connecting clips on the ends of the cables. This is accomplished by pressing the pointed tang of the clip into the cable so it firmly contacts the strands of wire. Bend the sides of the clip against the cable insulation.

Then force the ends of the cables into the wells of the distributor cap and push the boots down over the outside of the wells. Be sure the cable ends "bottom" in the wells to avoid arcing and subsequent corrosion within the wells.

On engines having resistor type spark plug cables (VW 1960 and later, all Type 3 and Type 4 engines), the cables must be handled with care to avoid damage or poor connection to the synthetic core. Special spark plug connectors and cable connectors screw into the cable ends to insure perfect contact between the synthetic core and connector. When screwing the connector in place on a new cable, squeeze the cable with a pair of pliers at the place where the connector fits to keep from pushing the synthetic core out of the cable.

REPLACING IGNITION BREAKER POINTS

Replacing the ignition breaker points is a relatively simple procedure because the distributor is readily accessible on the left side of the engine. Unsnap the clips on each side of the distributor cap and remove the cap. The rotor is a push fit on the end of the distributor shaft; pull it from the shaft.

Determine the condition of the breaker points by moving the breaker arm back so the surface of both the movable point and the stationary point can be seen. If the breaker points are badly pitted or have a smoky appearance, replace the points rather than attempt to recondition them by filing with a breaker point file. Filing can be used in an emergency, but

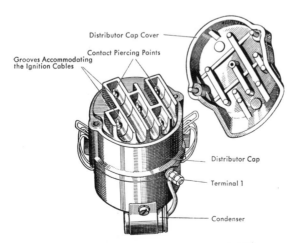

Distributor Cap Cover

Contact Piercing Points

Grooves Accommodating
the Ignition Cables

Distributor Cap

Terminal 1

Condenser

Fig. A-11. Early type distributor with cap removed to show placement of cables.

considerable skill is required to keep the surfaces of the breaker points smooth and parallel to each other for maximum life and performance.

On earlier distributors with horizontally placed high tension wires, Fig. A-11, remove low tension wire from terminal post on side of distributor body, Fig. A-12. Loosen inner nut and lift out breaker arm spring with arm attached. At this point note proper position of insulator to assure correct reinstallation, then remove lock screw and take out stationary point assembly.

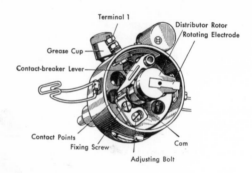

Terminal 1

Distributor Rotor
Rotating Electrode

Grease Cup

Contact-breaker Lever

Contact Points
Fixing Screw

Cam

Adjusting Bolt

Fig. A-12. Contact point arrangement of earlier distributors.

Install new breaker point assembly on pivot post and hook spring end over terminal post. Tighten inner nut, connect low tension wire to terminal post and reinstall outer nut. Place new stationary point assembly over adjusting screw and install lock screw.

On later type distributors, the procedure is somewhat different:

1 - Remove wire from terminal post on side of distributor.

Fig. A-13. Take care to insure that connections of primary circuit are insulated: 1—Condenser. 2—Cable entry. 3—Cable. 4—Insulation on breaker arm spring.

2 - Remove spring clip and washer from breaker arm pin.

3 - Disconnect breaker arm spring and insulator from terminal on breaker plate and remove breaker arm.

4 - Remove breaker point lock screw.

5 - Remove screw of vacuum pull rod bracket.

6 - Lift off breaker arm.

Replace parts in reverse order, making sure insulator is properly placed to avoid possibility of a short circuit, Fig. A-13.

ADJUSTING BREAKER POINTS

1 - Crank engine until fiber block on breaker arm rests on highest point of cam lobe.

2 - Loosen lock screw of stationary breaker point.

3 - Turn eccentric adjusting screw until correct gap of .016 in. is obtained. Check with a feeler gauge. On later distributors, insert screwdriver tip between two lugs on contact plate and slot in stationary point carrier, Fig. A-14. Twist screwdriver to obtain .016 in. gap. Tighten lock screw.

4 - Recheck gap.

WARNING: After contact points have been adjusted, it is absolutely necessary to readjust ignition timing. A change of .004 in. in size of gap changes ignition timing by about 3 deg. of crankshaft angle.

Fig. A-14. Adjustment of breaker point gap on late model distributors.

SETTING IGNITION TIMING

The procedure for timing engines built prior to 1968 models is as follows:

1 - Crank engine until mark on crankshaft pulley lines up with vertical crankcase joining faces, Fig. A-15, and distributor rotor arm is in position for firing on No. 1 cylinder (see mark on rim of distributor base). If pulley has two marks on it, right-

Fig. A-15. To position engine properly for timing or distributor installation, align timing mark on pulley with joint formed by crankcase halves.

hand mark (in direction of rotation) is for 10 deg. advance. Left-hand mark is for 7.5 deg. advance with low octane fuel.

2 - Pull vacuum hose off distributor advance unit.

3 - Loosen clamp screw of distributor retainer.

4 - Connect one lead of test lamp to terminal 1 at distributor and other to ground.

5 - Switch on ignition.

6 - Rotate distributor body clockwise until contact points are closed, then turn it slowly counterclockwise until breaker points just start to open as indicated by test lamp.

7 - Tighten clamp screw of distributor retainer, Fig. A-16.

Timing procedure is similar for all models, but be sure to check specifications for timing setting. On 1968-70 models with exhaust emission controls or an electronic fuel injection system, ignition timing is 0 deg. TDC with vacuum hose disconnected from distributor advance unit

Fig. A-16. To set ignition timing on late model engines, loosen distributor clamp (arrow) and turn distributor by hand until timing mark on pulley or fan aligns with reference mark on housing.

and with engine at normal operating temperature.

On all 1971-1973 Beetle and Type 3 engines, Fig. A-16, set timing to 5 ATC at 900 rpm with vacuum hoses connected. Setting timing on these late model engines requires the use of a stroboscopic timing light. On 1971-1973 Type 4 engines, set timing at 27 BTC at 3500 rpm. Align red notch in fan pulley with mark on fan housing.

OVERHAULING THE DISTRIBUTOR

After many thousands of miles of operation, it may be necessary to completely overhaul the distributor.

Fig. A-17. Location of mark on distributor housing.

The first step is to remove the distributor from the engine: Disconnect high tension cable connecting ignition coil to distributor and remove distributor cap. Then crank engine until rotor arm is in position for firing on No. 1 cylinder (see mark on rim of distributor base, Fig. A-17). This is necessary so distributor can be reinstalled in its original position and avoids necessity of retiming engine. Be sure that engine is not cranked after distributor is removed from engine.

Disconnect primary lead from side of distributor housing. Then loosen distributor clamp screw which is located below distributor housing. Pull distributor assembly up and out of engine cylinder block.

Next disassemble distributor: Remove rotor and contact points as previously described. Remove condenser and insulated terminal stud assembly. Drive out pin which fastens driving coupling or driving dog to distributor shaft, Fig. A-18. Pull coupling or driving dog from shaft, then lift shaft out top of distributor housing. Remove advance weight springs and/or vacuum advance unit. Remove cam and advance weights on distributors so equipped.

After disassembly, wash all parts in a cleaning solvent and thoroughly inspect for defects. Check shaft for wear and "fit" in bearings of distributor body. If there is more than .005 in. play or side movement, parts should be replaced. In addition, make sure shaft is not bent. Mount shaft in V-blocks and check run-out with a dial indicator: .002 in. is maximum. Reassemble distributor in reverse order.

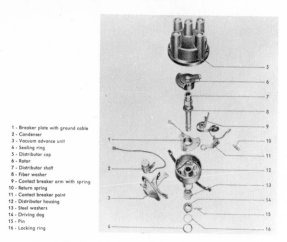

1 - Breaker plate with ground cable
2 - Condenser
3 - Vacuum advance unit
4 - Sealing ring
5 - Distributor cap
6 - Rotor
7 - Distributor shaft
8 - Fiber washer
9 - Contact breaker arm with spring
10 - Return spring
11 - Contact breaker point
12 - Distributor housing
13 - Steel washers
14 - Driving dog
15 - Pin
16 - Locking ring

Fig. A-18. Exploded view of distributor (ZV JU4R3).

TESTING MECHANICAL AND VACUUM ADVANCE

Advance weights used in ignition distributors should not be worn and should be free of burrs and have a free fit on pins. Surfaces of distributor cam on all distributors should be smooth and show no evidence of wear. On late model distributors, Fig. A-18A, check return spring, insulation of low tension connection, and "fit" of spark advance pull rod on stud on distributor plate.

To test mechanical and vacuum advance of distributor, place distributor assembly on a test stand. Seldom is any difficulty found with mechanical advance, except for rusted-in-position weights due to lack of lubrication. If diaphragm of vacuum advance is good, but advance curve is incorrect, an adjustment can be made on late model distributors by altering tension of the breaker plate return spring, Fig. A-18A.

HOW TO REPLACE IGNITION CONDENSER

The need for replacing ignition condensers is generally indicated by a smoked or burned appearance of the ignition breaker points. Special testers are available for testing ignition condensers, but most mechanics replace the condenser when new points are installed. Simply remove the single screw holding the condenser on the outside of the ignition distributor or on the distributor plate. Then detach the pigtail clip from the insulated terminal, Figs. A-18A and A-18B.

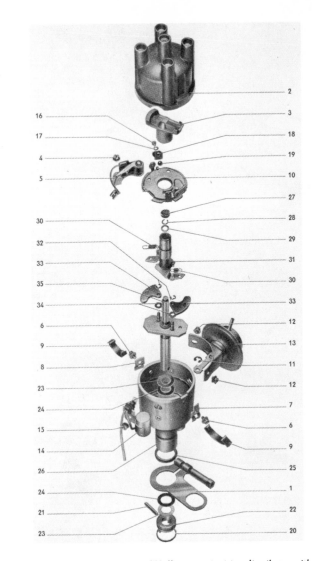

1—Bracket.
2—Cap.
3—Rotor.
4—Contact screw.
5—Breaker points.
6—Screw.
7—Tab with boss.
8—Tab.
9—Retaining clip.
10—Breaker plate.
11—Clip for pull rod.
12—Screw.
13—Vacuum unit.
14—Condenser.
15—Screw.
16—Screw.
17—Spring washer.
18—Ball retaining spring.
19—Ball.
20—Circlip.
21—Pin.
22—Driving dog.
23—Shim.
24—Fiber washer.
25—Rubber sealing ring.
26—Distributor body.
27—Felt washer.
28—Circlip.
29—Thrust ring.
30—Return spring.
31—Cam.
32—Circlip.
33—Centrifugal weight.
34—Washer.
35—Drive shaft.

Fig. A-18A. Exploded view reveals parts that make up typical Volkswagen ignition distributor with centrifugal and vacuum advance.

FIx Your Volkswagen

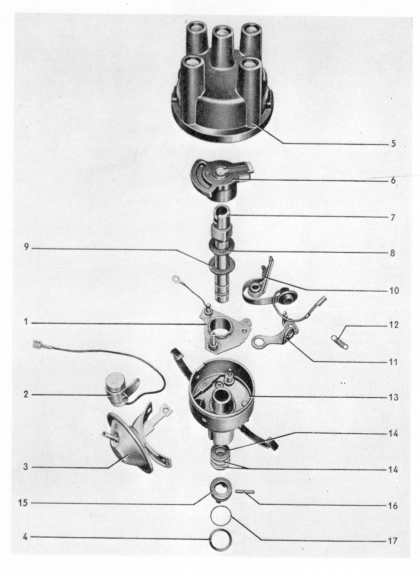

1—Breaker plate with ground cable.	9—Fiber washer.
2—Condenser.	10—Breaker arm with spring.
3—Vacuum unit.	11—Breaker point.
4—Sealing ring.	12—Return spring.
5—Cap.	13—Distributor housing.
6—Rotor.	14—Steel washers.
7—Drive shaft.	15—Driving dog.
8—Shim.	16—Pin.
	17—Circlip.

Fig. A-18B. Volkswagen ignition distributor with vacuum advance.

INSTALLING DISTRIBUTOR

To reinstall the distributor: Turn rotor to mark on distributor housing which indicates firing position on No. 1 cylinder. Then start driven end of distributor down into cylinder block and push distributor into position. It may be necessary to turn rotor slightly in order to get coupling or driving dog to engage.

If for some reason the engine was cranked while the distributor was out of the engine, it will be necessary to completely retime the ignition: First position piston in No. 1 cylinder at end of compression stroke. On "Beetle" engines built before Aug., 1967, offset slot in drive pinion should

Fig. A-19. When aligning distributor drive pinion on Fastback/Squareback/Type 3 engines, offset slot of pinion must be at approximately 60 deg. angle to crankcase joint with smaller segment of pinion toward oil cooler.

be approximately crosswise to longitudinal axis of engine with its small segment facing pulley. On later engines with exhaust emission control, slot should face front stud for attaching fuel pump with small segment facing pulley. Timing mark on pulley should align with joint in crankcase. On Type 3 engines, slot in drive pinion must be positioned at 60 deg. angle to crankcase joint, with smaller segment of pinion toward oil cooler. Type 4 engine calls for offset slot to be at an angle of 12 deg. from longitudinal center line of engine, with smaller segment of pinion away from center line. Then install distributor as previously described.

ADJUSTING CARBURETOR FOR ECONOMY

After making sure compression, ignition and tappet clearance are correct and satisfactory, adjust the carburetor. Jets are of the fixed type; only a volume control screw and engine idling speed need to be adjusted. All adjustments should be made with the engine at normal operating temperature.

1 - Condenser	8 - insulator
2 - Oil drilling	9 - Hexagon screw
3 - Return spring	10 - Condenser cable
4 - Ground connection	11 - Breaker arm
5 - Pull rod	12 - Breaker point
6 - Low tension cable	13 - Retaining screw
7 - Breaker arm spring	14 - Pins and adjusting slot

1 - Primary connection	8 - Pull rod
with cable	9 - Fixed point
2 - Securing screw	10 - Adjusting slot
3 - Leaf spring	11 - Threaded rod
4 - Hexagon head screw	12 - Spring
5 - Stop bracket	13 - Leaf spring for breaker
6 - Breaker arm	plate
7 - Breaker arm spring	14 - Breaker plate

Fig. A-20. Typical distributor of late type with condenser mounted on distributor plate.

Fig. A-21. Typical distributor of late type with externally mounted condenser.

On 1965 and older Volkswagen engines: Warm up engine, then shut it off. Turn in volume control screw until it seats lightly, then back it out approximately 3/4 turn, Fig. A-22. Handle this preliminary setting gently, otherwise screw or seat or both will be ruined.

Next start engine and turn idling speed adjustment screw in or out until approximate idling speed of 500-550 rpm is attained. Turn volume control screw in until engine tends to stall, then turn screw out (approx. 1/4 turn) until maximum engine speed is attained and engine runs

Fig. A-22. Adjustment of volume control screw.

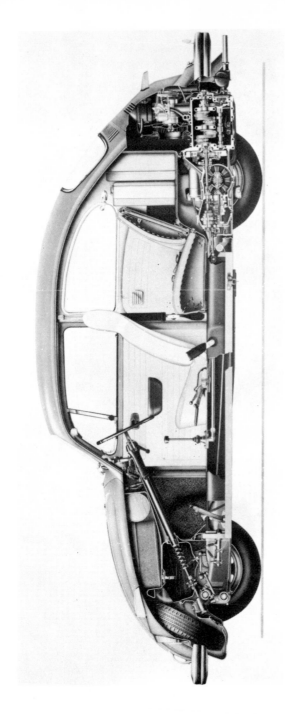

Late model Volkswagen Sedans incorporate "1600" rear engine, double-jointed rear axles, dual brake system, collapsible steering column, raised bumpers, safety windshield and built-in head-rests on front seatbacks. A "Stick Shift" torque converter transmission is optional.

Fig. A-23. *Adjustment of idle control screw.*

smoothly, Fig. A-22. Finally, readjust idling speed to desired 500-550 rpm, Fig. A-23.

On 1966 and 1967 Volkswagen engines, adjust engine idling speed 700 to 800 rpm. On 1968-1970 Volkswagen engines, adjust engine idling speed 800 to 850 rpm.

On 1971-1973 models, set engine idle speed to 900 rpm by turning the bypass air screw. Do not adjust the volume control screw, since this air-fuel mixture adjustment is preset at the factory for each individual car. If 900 rpm cannot be set, ignition timing may be incorrect. Check and reset timing, if necessary.

On 1966 and 1967 Fastback and Squareback twin carburetor engines, proceed as follows: Warm up engine, then shut it off. Turn out engine idle speed screw until throttle valve closes, then screw it in 1/2 turn. Turn in volume control screw until it seats lightly, then back it out 1 1/2 turns. Repeat these adjustments on other carburetor, Fig. A-24.

Fig. A-24. *Adjustment of twin carburetors is a delicate balancing operation featuring careful setting of: 1—Idle speed adjusting screw; 2—Volume control screw.*

Tuning For Best Economy, Performance

Start engine and disconnect accelerator cable rod at three-arm lever. Set idling speed adjustment screws to obtain 800 to 900 rpm. Turn in volume control screws until rpm begins to fall off. Turn them out until engine runs smoothly, then turn them an additional 1/4 turn. Recheck idling speed adjustment. Connect accelerator cable rod to three-arm lever.

On all engines, check carburetor performance by speeding up the engine momentarily, then releasing the accelerator pedal quickly. If the engine stalls, the mixture should be enriched a trifle by backing out the volume control screw, perhaps 1/16 of a turn, until sudden releasing of pedal after acceleration does not cause stalling.

If performance is still unsatisfactory, refer to TROUBLE SHOOTING at end of Chapter on Carburetors and Fuel Systems as well as the general Trouble Shooting section in the last chapter.

TUNING ENGINES WITH EXHAUST CONTROLS

Late model engines are equipped with exhaust emission controls which make tune-up tests and adjustments more critical. Ignition timing and engine idle speed specifications have been changed, and the new carburetor equipped with throttle positioner and altitude corrector calls for special settings.

To adjust 1968-1969 Volkswagen engine with exhaust controls:
1 - Make sure that engine, ignition and fuel systems are in good condition.
2 - If distributor was removed, it must be reinstalled with shaft turned 30 deg. to left (one tooth) and with small segment of drive pinion facing pulley.
3 - With engine warm and running at 850 rpm, loosen distributor clamp screw and connect timing light to ignition system.
4 - Pull vacuum hose from vacuum advance unit on distributor and plug hose.
5 - Direct beam of timing light at mark on pulley and turn distributor until TDC mark is in line with crankcase joint.
6 - Turn off engine and tighten distributor clamp screw.
7 - Start engine, recheck timing at 850 rpm, and connect vacuum hose to distributor at same time. Timing must not change more than 3/16 in.
8 - Speed engine to 3,000 rpm, briefly, and check timing. Mark should move approximately 2 in. to left if distributor is in good operating condition.

To set carburetor:
1 - With engine warm, adjust idle speed to 850 rpm.
2 - Turn volume control screw to right until speed drops off, then turn screw to left until engine runs at peak rpm.
3 - Readjust idle speed to 850 rpm, if necessary.

ADJUSTING THE CONTROLS

In addition to conventional distributor and carburetor adjustments, engines with exhaust controls may require precise setting of the altitude corrector and throttle positioner. This assembly holds the throttle valve open on deceleration to help promote better combustion of the air-fuel mixture. On 1968-1969 Beetle engines, Fig. A-25, adjust these controls as follows:

1 - With engine warm and choke valve open, connect a tachometer to the ignition system.

2 - Run engine and turn altitude corrector adjusting screw clockwise until pull rod of throttle positioner moves inward and butts stop washer against housing. Tachometer should read between 1,600 and 1,700 rpm.

3 - If engine speed is higher than 1,700 rpm, lengthen pull rod; if speed is lower than 1,600 rpm, shorten pull rod.

4 - Tighten locknuts, then turn adjusting screw on altitude corrector counterclockwise until engine speed is 850 rpm.

5 - Increase idle speed to 3,000 rpm, release throttle lever and time return to 1,000 rpm. It should take 3 to 4 sec.

6 - If time is less than 3 sec., turn altitude corrector adjusting screw clockwise; if time is more than 4 sec., turn adjusting screw counterclockwise.

7 - Tighten the lock screw and recheck the throttle closing time. If the throttle positioner cannot be adjusted, replace it with a new assembly.

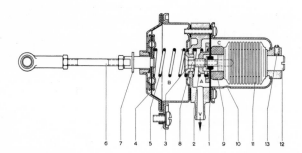

Fig. A-25. Throttle Positioner: A and B—Vacuum chambers; C—Housing; V—Vacuum; 1—Diaphragm; 2—Spring; 3—Valve; 4—Diaphragm; 5—Spring; 6—Pull rod; 7—Stop washer; 8—Drilling; 9—Plastic foam filter; 10—Hole; 11—Altitude corrector; 12—Adjusting screw; 13—Lock screw.

To set up a 1970-1973 VW engine with exhaust emission controls:

1 - Make sure that engine, ignition and fuel systems are in good condition.

2 - If distributor was removed, see that slot in distributor drive

points right to left, and that it is offset to rear of car. Note whether notch on pulley is in line with split in crankcase. Place a chalk mark on the notch.

3 - Install distributor with firing tip of rotor pointing to No. 1 cylinder mark on rim of distributor body.

4 - Install hold-down clamp, leaving mounting bolt slightly loose. Attach distributor cap to distributor.

5 - Connect green vacuum hose to front adapter of vacuum advance unit. Connect black hose to rear adapter, Fig. A-25A.

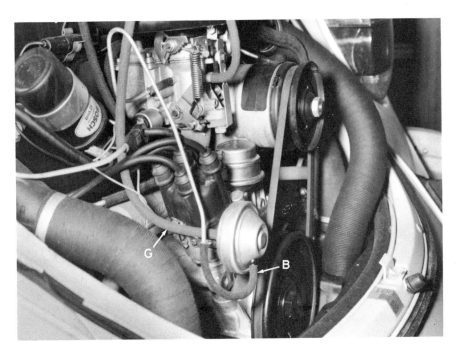

Fig. A-25A. Late model VW engines utilize a dual diaphragm vacuum advance unit on the ignition distributor. See that the vacuum hoses are connected as indicated by arrows: B—Black, G—Green.

6 - Install green primary wire on coil terminal.

7 - With engine warm and running at 900 rpm (850 on 1970 models), check initial ignition timing with a stroboscopic timing light. Timing is correct when mark on pulley is in line with split in crankcase.

8 - If timing is incorrect, rotate distributor until mark and split are in line. Tighten distributor mounting bolt.

9 - Readjust engine idle rpm, if necessary, by means of bypass air screw. Do not turn timing screw or volume control screw. These

are preset and should not be changed.

10 - Pull green vacuum hose from vacuum advance adapter. See that mark on pulley moves approximately 5/8 in. to the left, which indicates satisfactory vacuum advance unit operation.

To adjust throttle valve positioner on 1970-1973 engines, Fig. A-26:

1 - Connect tachometer to ignition system.

2 - With engine running, pull throttle valve positioner lever back against its adjusting screw. Tachometer reading should be between 1450 and 1650 rpm.

3 - If engine speed is high or low, turn adjusting screw to obtain 1450 to 1650 rpm.

Fig. A-26. New throttle valve positioner has two parts connected by a hose: operating part (1) attached to carburetor, and control part (2) at left side of engine compartment.

4 - To test throttle valve closing time, pull throttle valve lever back until tachometer reads 3000 rpm.

5 - Using a watch with sweep-second hand, release throttle valve lever and see how long it takes for engine speed to drop back to 900 rpm (850 rpm on 1970 models).

6 - Closing time must be between 2 1/2 and 4 1/2 seconds. If not, loosen setscrew on remote control unit, Fig. A-26, and turn adjusting screw clockwise to increase closing time or counterclockwise to decrease closing time.

7 - Recheck closing time. If it is between 2 1/2 and 4 1/2 seconds, tighten setscrew and road test car.

OTHER SERVICE NEEDS

In addition to the various services covered in this chapter, a complete engine tune-up includes: Battery, starter and generator tests; cooling system maintenance service; air cleaner service; fuel filter cleaning; positive crankcase ventilation system service. On cars equipped with electronic fuel injection, this system needs attention. Consult chapters related to these subjects for full details.

Air cleaners are major service items since heated intake air system was incorporated to improve cold running and help reduce emissions.

Beetle engine for 1972 features improved engine air intake and intake manifold preheating to help reduce exhaust emissions and to assure smoother engine warm-ups after cold weather starts. Compression ratio is down from 7.5 to 1 to a new ratio of 7.3 to 1 to permit engine to run on unleaded fuel.

CARBURETOR, FUEL SYSTEM

As is the case with most rear-engine automobiles, the Volkswagen gasoline tank is located at the front end of the car under the hood. A filtering screen is utilized at the fuel outlet at the bottom of the tank.

In order to clean this screen, it is necessary to remove the tank. Older models have a fuel control valve and filter mounted on the outside of the tank at the fuel outlet. This filter is readily accessible for cleaning from under the car or through an inspection hole in the body.

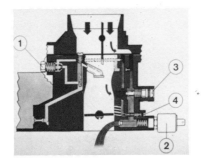

Fig. B-1. The 34 PICT 3 carburetor is used on Volkswagen Beetle engines in 1971–1973. New idle bypass circuit includes: 1–Pilot jet. 2–Electromagnetic cutoff valve. 3–Bypass air screw. 4–Volume control screw.

A mechanically operated·fuel pump is mounted on the engine and supplies fuel under pressure to the carburetor. An electric fuel pump is used in conjunction with the electronic fuel injection system which was introduced on 1968 Fastback and Squareback engines.

Solex carburetors are used on all carburetor-equipped Volkswagen engines. A model 28 PC1 was used prior to 1961; model 28 PICT with automatic choke, Figs. B-5 and B-6, from 1961 to 1965; model 30 PICT 1 in 1966 and 1967; model 30 PICT 2 with throttle positioner in 1968 and 1969; model 30 PICT 3 in 1970; model 34 PICT 3 in 1971 to 1973, Fig. B-1.

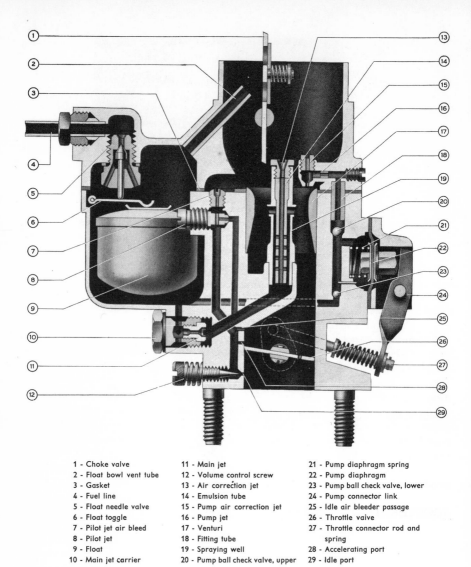

1 - Choke valve	11 - Main jet	21 - Pump diaphragm spring
2 - Float bowl vent tube	12 - Volume control screw	22 - Pump diaphragm
3 - Gasket	13 - Air correction jet	23 - Pump ball check valve, lower
4 - Fuel line	14 - Emulsion tube	24 - Pump connector link
5 - Float needle valve	15 - Pump air correction jet	25 - Idle air bleeder passage
6 - Float toggle	16 - Pump jet	26 - Throttle valve
7 - Pilot jet air bleed	17 - Venturi	27 - Throttle connector rod and
8 - Pilot jet	18 - Fitting tube	spring
9 - Float	19 - Spraying well	28 - Accelerating port
10 - Main jet carrier	20 - Pump ball check valve, upper	29 - Idle port

Fig. B-2. Solex 28 PC1.

Two down-draft Solex 32 PDSIT carburetors were used on 1966 and 1967 Fastback and Squareback engines. The electronic fuel system eliminated the use of carburetors after the 1967 model year.

OPERATING PRINCIPLES

A model 28 PC1 is used to illustrate typical systems operations: During normal operation (high speed, part-load circuit), fuel flows from the float bowl through the main jet into the spraying well and is pulled out through a row of radial outlet holes by the vacuum created in the venturi, Fig. B-2. The amount of the vacuum depends on venturi size, engine speed and throttle opening. The restriction (waist) of the venturi surrounding the outlet holes in the spraying well speeds up the air drawn in by the engine. Thus the amount of throttle opening determines the force of the vacuum, permitting varying amounts of air/fuel mixture to be pulled from the spraying well or discharge arm. When the throttle opening increases, the fuel level in the spraying well decreases and air is sucked in through the correction jet. This air passes through holes in the emulsion tube and mixes with the fuel coming from the main jet. Thus, a foamy mixture passes out through the holes in the spraying well into the venturi, where it meets the main high velocity air current by which it is atomized. The proportion of air increases with the speed. This insures proper proportions of air and fuel required for varying operation conditions.

LOW SPEED CIRCUIT

When the throttle is closed, or slightly open, the idling and low speed circuit performs the function of furnishing the air/fuel mixture. Air speed is low and such a small volume of air passes through that very little vacuum develops in the venturi. This means that the spraying well or discharge arm centered in the venturi will not feed fuel with a closed or slightly open throttle. Therefore, the pilot jet and the pilot jet air bleed produce the mixture at idling speed. This fairly rich mixture is pulled from the idle port by a high vacuum existing on the lower side of the throttle valve. The mixture flows past the tapered point of the volume control screws, mixes with the air escaping around the throttle valve to produce a leaner air/fuel mixture, and passes on into the engine.

ACCELERATING CIRCUIT

There are two accelerating ports drilled in the wall of the carburetor throat near the throttle valve. When the throttle valve is gradually opened, a nearly constant air/fuel mixture ratio is maintained during the shift from the low speed to the high speed circuit. As the edge of the throttle valve swings past the accelerating ports, a sufficient quantity of air/fuel mixture is pulled out by the high velocity air current passing through the space between the edge of the throttle valve and the wall of the carburetor throat.

About 0.4 in. above the accelerating ports is an idle air bleeder passage which leans out the mixture when the throttle valve is suddenly closed. In order to assure a proper function of this bleeder passage, the idling speed adjustment must be correct.

The accelerator pump is linked to the throttle, Fig. B-3. When the throttle is closed, the spring-loaded diaphragm returns to its original position and the pump chamber in front of the diaphragm is filled with fuel sucked in from the float bowl. When the throttle valve is opened, the movement is transmitted to the diaphragm through the linkage, forcing the fuel up the passage and out through the discharge nozzle into the mixing chamber. The upper ball check valve is lifted by the fluid pressure while the lower ball check valve prevents the fuel from escaping back into the float bowl.

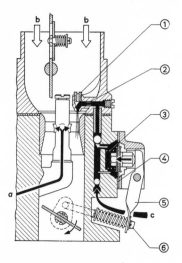

Fig. B-3. a—Fuel from the main jet. b—Primary air. c—Fuel from float bowl. 1—Pump discharge nozzle and air correction jet. 2—Pump jet. 3—Diaphragm spring. 4—Diaphragm. 5—Pump connector link. 6—Throttle connector rod and spring. (28PC1 illustrated.)

This delivery of additional fuel as the throttle is opened momentarily enriches the mixture and causes the engine to pick up speed quickly. The accelerator pump jet in the discharge nozzle meters the flow of fuel discharged into the mixing chamber. The accelerator pump enriches the mixture only in the low and intermediate speed range, as the spring on the throttle connector rod takes up any further movements of the throttle when the diaphragm has reached its foremost position. The pump chamber is refilled with fuel only before the throttle nearly closes.

POWER CIRCUIT

When the throttle is wide open, the accelerator pump passage admits an added flow of fuel to discharge through the pump nozzle. This extra fuel is drawn into the mixing chamber by suction on the discharge nozzle. At part throttle positions, the mixture is only slightly enriched because suction is controlled by the air correction jet in the discharge nozzle. Suction increases with the amount of throttle opening, so that a progressive supply of extra fuel is given to secure added engine performance.

IDLING ADJUSTMENT

The carburetor is tested at the factory and adjusted to produce the best consumption-to-performance ratio. Any change in its setting by replacing the jets or the venturi with other than the prescribed sizes should be avoided. In general, excessive fuel consumption is not due to any malfunctioning of the carburetor. With the idling mixture being overrich, the engine tends to stall when suddenly braking and the consumption will be excessively high in the speed range up to 28 mph. A properly adjusted idling speed is the first requirement for satisfactory operation of the carburetor. All idling adjustments should be carried out with the engine at operating temperature as described in the Chapter on Tune-Up.

CARBURETOR CLEANING

Dirt in the carburetor will cause all sorts of trouble. (See "Carburetor Trouble Shooting" in this chapter.) All jets and passages in the Solex carburetor may be readily reached for cleaning after removal of the air cleaner and carburetor bowl cover.

Clean all carburetor components in special carburetor cleaning solvent. Blow out the jets, valves and passages with compressed air. Never use a pin or a piece of wire since this will damage the jets.

INSPECTION AND ASSEMBLY TIPS

1 - Check needle valve for leaks.
2 - Examine needle valve gasket for correct condition and see to it that it is properly installed to prevent leaks.
3 - Check choke valve spring and clearance of choke valve shaft.
4 - Inspect choke poppet valve for perfect sealing and make sure that it opens easily.
5 - Check pump diaphragm for leaks. Replace if necessary.
NOTE: Carburetor "flat spot" when suddenly opening throttle generally indicates a leaky pump diaphragm.
6 - Dip float in hot water. If air bubbles appear, float is leaky and must be replaced. Leaky floats must not be soldered, as this would result in an increase of the weight.

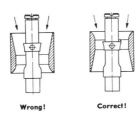

Wrong!   **Correct!**

Fig. B-4. In installing venturi, be sure restriction of inner diameter is at the top.

7 - Install venturi. Be sure that restriction of inner diameter (waist) of venturi is at the top, Fig. B-4.
  Do not overtighten retaining screw.

8 - Check clearance of throttle valve shaft. Excessive clearance causes ingress of secondary air which has detrimental effect on the starting and idling operation of engine. If necessary, fit bushings to throttle valve shaft to take up clearance.

9 - Inspect tip of volume control screw. Renew if tip is bent or broken off. Volume control screw must be made of brass.
  Inspect tapped hole and seat of volume control screw for damage. Remove tip of old control screw if it has broken off.

10 - The word "oben" on the float toggle lever must face upwards.

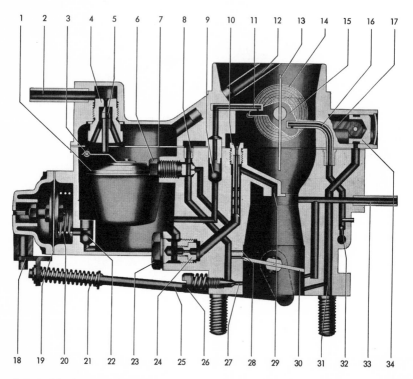

Fig. B-5. Model 28PICT with automatic choke. 1—Float. 2—Fuel line. 3—Float lever. 4—Float needle valve. 5—Float needle. 6—Pilot jet. 7—Gasket. 8—Pilot air drilling. 9—Ball check valve in power fuel system. 10—Air correction jet with emulsion tube. 11—Power fuel tube. 12—Float bowl vent tube. 13—Choke valve. 14—Bimetal spring. 15—Operating lever. 16—Accelerator pump discharge tube. 17—Piston rod. 18—Pump lever. 19—Pump diaphragm. 20—Diaphragm spring. 21—spring. 22—Ball check valve for accelerator pump. 23—Main jet carrier. 24—Main jet. 25—Pump connector rod. 26—Volume control screw. 27—Idle port. 28—Bypass port. 29—Discharge arm. 30—Throttle valve. 31—Vacuum drilling. 32—Ball check valve in accelerator pump drilling. 33—Vacuum connection. 34—Vacuum piston.

SPECIAL FEATURES, AUTOMATIC CHOKE

Among special carburetor features which appear on later model Volkswagen engines are the automatic choke, electromagnetic pilot jet and throttle positioner. Another innovation related to carburetion is the air cleaner setup that permits preheated air to enter the carburetor.

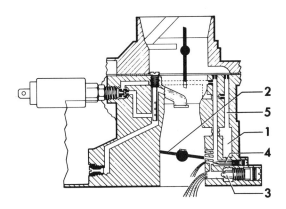

Fig. B-6. Carburetor 30 PICT 3 has an air bypass drilling (1) which allows air for idling to bypass throttle valve (2). Other features: air bypass screw (3); volume control screw (4); fuel drilling (5).

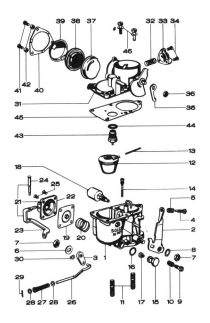

Fig. B-7. 30PICT 1 details.

1 — Body
2 — Throttle lever
3 — Pump intermediate actuating lever
4 — Slow idle adjusting screw
5 — Adjusting screw spring
6 — Throttle spindle washer
7 — Throttle spindle end nut
8 — Toothed washer
9 — Volume control screw
10 — Control screw spring
11 — Flange stud
12 — Float
13 — Float toggle spindle
14 — Air correction jet
  with emulsion tube
15 — Main jet carrier
16 — Carrier washer
17 — Main jet
18 — Idle cutoff valve
19—25 — Accelerating pump assembly
26—30 — Pump control rod assembly
31—34 — Float chamber cover assembly
35 — Intermediate lever
36—42 — Choke assembly
43 — Float needle valve
44 — Needle valve washer
45 — Float chamber cover gasket
46 — Assembly screws

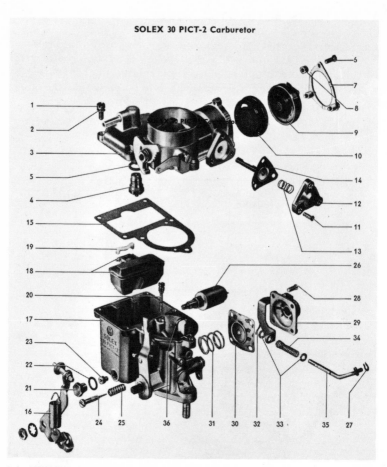

SOLEX 30 PICT-2 Carburetor

Fig. B-8. 30PICT 2 Downdraft Carburetor: 1–Cover screw. 2–Spring washer. 3–Float chamber cover assembly. 4–Float needle valve. 5–Washer. 6–Screw. 7–Retaining ring. 8–Spacer. 9–Choke unit. 10–Plastic cap. 11–Screw. 12–Diaphragm cover. 13–Diaphragm spring. 14–Vacuum diaphragm. 15–Gasket. 16–Return spring. 17–Carburetor body. 18–Float and pin. 19–Bracket. 20–Air correction jet. 21–Plug. 22–Plug seal. 23–Main jet. 24–Volume control screw. 25–Spring. 26–Pilot jet cutoff valve. 27–Circlip. 28–Screw. 29–Pump cover. 30–Pump diaphragm. 31–Diaphragm spring. 32–Cotter pin. 33–Washer. 34–Spring. 35–Connecting rod. 36–Injector tube.

The automatic choke is designed to enrich the air/fuel mixture to suit engine temperatures when starting and during cold engine operation. It progressively weakens the enrichment as the engine warms up. The action of the automatic choke also controls the position of the fast idle cam to provide increased idle speed until the engine reaches normal operating temperature.

The key to choke operation is the bimetal coil which controls the position of choke valve shaft and therefore the opening and closing of the choke valve itself. As the bimetal coil heats up, a vacuum piston in the choke assembly overcomes the tension of the coil and the choke valve gradually opens. When the choke valve is wide open, a stop lever drops to the low step on the fast idle cam and the air/fuel mixture becomes normalized for proper operation of the idling system.

ELECTROMAGNETIC PILOT JET

The electromagnetic pilot jet, or idle cutoff valve in Figs. B-7 to B-11, is installed on later carburetors to eliminate the possibility of the engine "running on." The pilot jet incorporates a needle-type cutoff valve which closes the jet and shuts off the supply of fuel as soon as the ignition is switched "off." When the ignition is turned "on," the needle is withdrawn and fuel flows through the jet.

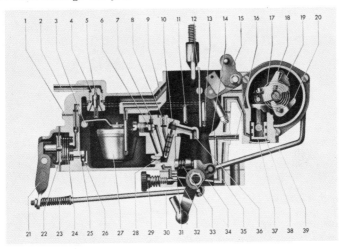

Fig. B-9. Solex 32 PDSIT Carburetor consists of: 1—Gasket. 2—Fuel pipe. 3—Float pin. 4—Float needle valve. 5—Float needle. 6—Pilot jet. 7—Pilot air bleed drilling. 8—Air correction jet. 9—Vent passage for float chamber. 10—Emulsion tube with ventilation jet. 11—Power fuel pipe. 12—Choke valve. 13—Injector tube. 14—Venturi. 15—Relay lever. 16—Vacuum connection. 17—Bimetal coil. 18—Intermediate lever. 19—Fast idle cam. 20—Stop lever. 21—Pump lever. 22—Pump diaphragm. 23—Connecting rod spring. 24—Diaphragm spring. 25—Ball pressure valve. 26—Ball suction valve. 27—Float. 28—Main jet. 29—Volume control screw. 30—Connecting rod. 31—Idling mixture port. 32—Bypass port. 33—Idle adjustment screw. 34—Throttle valve. 35—Vacuum drilling. 36—Discharge arm. 37—Vacuum piston. 38—Piston rod. 39—Operating rod.

CARBURETOR WITH THROTTLE POSITIONERS

Late model Volkswagen engines utilize carburetor and distributor settings designed to give more complete combustion of the air/fuel mixture and thereby reduce the amount of hydrocarbons and carbon monoxide in the exhaust gases. Also contributing to emission control on

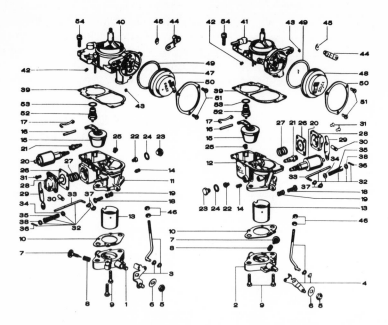

Fig. B-10. Exploded view of Solex 32 PDSIT Carburetor: 1 and 2—Throttle body. 3—Throttle lever. 4—Throttle lever with intermediate rod. 5—Throttle spindle end nut. 6—Washer. 7—Volume control screw. 8—Volume control screw spring. 9—Fixing screw. 10—Insulating gasket. 11 and 12—Float chamber body. 13—Choke tube. 14—Choke tube fixing screw. 15—Float. 16—Float toggle spindle. 17—Float toggle holder. 18—Slow running adjustment screw. 19—Slow running adjustment screw spring. 20—Idle cutoff valve. 21—Idle jet. 22—Main jet. 23—Screw plug. 24—Screw plug washer. 25—Air correction jet. 26—Diaphragm. 27—Diaphragm spring. 28—Pump cover. 29—Pump lever. 30—Spindle. 31—Pump cover fixing screw. 32 through 38—Pump control rod assembly. 39—Float chamber cover gasket. 40 through 45—Float chamber cover assembly. 46—Hex nut. 47 and 48— Choke housing cover assembly. 49—Insulating washer. 50—Choke housing cover clamp. 51—Fixing screw. 52—Float needle valve. 53—Float needle valve washer. 54—Float chamber cover attaching screws.

deceleration is a throttle positioner, Fig. B-12, which works in conjunction with the altitude corrector to balance the forces of intake manifold vacuum and atmospheric pressure.

In operation, manifold vacuum increases on deceleration to create suction in chamber A. Diaphragm 7, in turn, is drawn to the left, opening valve 5 and exposing chamber B to greater vacuum draw. Diaphragm 2 is pulled to the right, moving pull rod 1 which opens the throttle valve of the carburetor via the damper lever.

As manifold vacuum drops, atmospheric pressure enters housing C through hole 9. This relieves the suction on the diaphragms and the return spring 6 releases the diaphragms, permitting the pull rod to close the throttle valve.

The altitude corrector compensates for changes in atmospheric pressure. It is installed with a slight preload, which can be adjusted at screw 12 if necessary. The action of the throttle positioner can be adjusted by means of a clevis and lock nut on the rod.

To improve operating conditions when starting a cold engine, an appliance was introduced on 1961 models, and refined later, which causes warm air intake to the carburetor. The warm air is drawn from

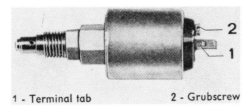

1 - Terminal tab   2 - Grubscrew

Fig. B-11. Electromagnetic pilot jet prevents "run-on" by shutting off supply of fuel when ignition is turned "off."

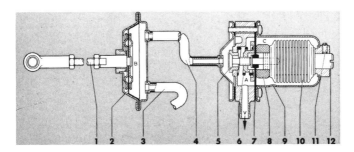

Fig. B-12. Late-type throttle valve positioner: A and B—Vacuum chambers. C—Housing. V—Vacuum. 1—Pull rod. 2—Operating diaphragm. 3—Hose to carburetor. 4—Hose connecting vacuum chambers. 5—Valve. 6—Spring. 7—Control diaphragm. 8—Filter. 9—Drilling. 10—Altitude corrector. 11—Lock screw. 12—Adjusting screw.

a heater junction box by way of a flexible pipe and intake tube to the air cleaner. On earlier models a flap valve with a balance weight at the intake tube is operated by the flow of air. The preheated air can be cut off if desired by fixing the valve in the closed position, Fig. B-13.

The air cleaner on 1967-1968 Volkswagen engines is fitted with two air intake pipes having weighted flaps and two flexible pipes attached,

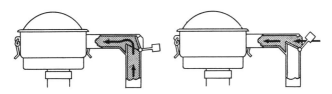

Fig. B-13. Left. How warm air is fed to carburetor when idling or at low speed. Right. Air flow at medium and high speed ranges.

which route heated air to the carburetor. At temperatures over 50 deg. F. (+10 deg. C.), the flaps should be held open by jamming the levers under the ridge of the intake pipes.

The air cleaner on 1969 and 1970 Beetle engines has only one air intake, fitted with a warm air control flap. In 1971 models, a thermostat in the air cleaner controls the flow of warm air to the carburetor.

In 1972, and again in 1973 Beetle engines, the air cleaner and heated air controls were modified to help reduce exhaust emissions. When servicing these late model air cleaners, be sure to mark hoses as they are disconnected to insure correct reinstallation later.

The air cleaner used on Fastback and Squareback twin-carburetor engines is connected to a warm air control box which utilizes a flap to control entry of fresh air or preheated air.

CARBURETOR TROUBLE SHOOTING

Complaint	Cause	Correction
1 - Engine fails to start (with fuel in tank, ignition ok, and choke closed)	a - Choke inoperative	a - Free vacuum diaphragm or choke valve shaft
	b - Bimetal spring unhooked or broken	b - Reconnect spring; replace ceramic plate
	c - Ceramic plate broken	c - Replace ceramic plate; note marks
	d - Float needle sticking; carburetor flooding	d - Clean or replace needle and seat
2 - Engine idles unevenly or stalls	a - Idling adjustment incorrect	a - Readjust volume control screw
	b - Pilot jet blocked	b - Clean jet
3 - Engine "runs on" when ignition is switched off	a - Idling mixture too rich or idle rpm too high	a - Readjust volume control screw
4 - Flat spot in transfer from idling to normal running	a - Accelerator pump dirty	a - Clean accelerator pump; test action
	b - Torn diaphragm	b - Replace diaphragm
	c - Idling adjustment incorrect	c - Readjust volume control screw

Complaint	Cause	Correction
5 - Engine runs continually at fast idle	a - Automatic choke malfunction	a - Check choke heater element and connections
6 - Engine misfires, cuts out or lacks power	a - Fuel starvation	a - Clean carburetor b - Increase fuel pump pressure, if necessary c - Clean fuel tank and cap
7 - Engine runs unevenly at idle speed; emits black exhaust smoke	a - Excessive pressure on float needle valve b - Float leaking c - Float needle valve does not seat	a - Reduce fuel pump pressure b - Replace float c - Clean or replace needle valve
8 - Engine stalls when accelerator pedal is released suddenly	a - Idling mixture too rich or linkage maladjusted	a - Readjust volume control screw or throttle valve positioner
9 - Excessive fuel consumption	a - Jet sizes not matched b - Excessive pressure on float needle valve c - Float leaking d - Float needle valve does not seat e - Automatic choke malfunction	a - Install correct set of jets b - Reduce fuel pump pressure c - Replace float d - Clean or replace needle valve e - Repair or replace choke components
10 - Banging in exhaust when car over-runs engine	a - Idling mixture too lean	a - Turn volume control screw approximately 1/8 turn counterclockwise
11 - Poor idling on exhaust control cars	a - Clogged crankcase ventilation system	a - Clean air cleaner; clean ventilation system
12 - Engine idles too fast on exhaust control cars	a - Throttle valve sticking b - Throttle valve positioner maladjusted	a - Free throttle valve lever and pull rod b - Adjust positioner as prescribed

Complaint	Cause	Correction
13 - Back-firing when a coasting on exhaust control cars	a - Throttle valve positioner maladjusted	a - Adjust or replace positioner as required

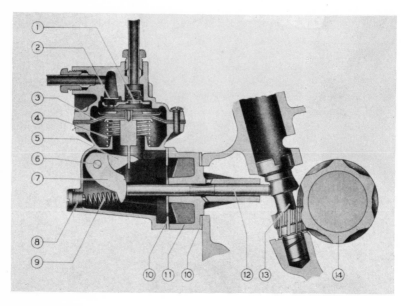

Fig. B-14. Solex fuel pump, sectional view. 1—Delivery valve. 2—Suction valve. 3—Diaphragm. 4—Diaphragm spring. 5—Rocker arm link. 6—Rocker arm pin. 7—Rocker arm. 8—Spring retaining plug and gasket. 9—Rocker arm spring. 10—Gasket. 11—Intermediate flange. 12—Push rod. 13—Distributor drive shaft. 14—Distributor drive gear.

FUEL PUMP SERVICE

Fuel is fed to the carburetor by a Solex-diaphragm pump which is attached to the crankcase. It is operated mechanically by a push rod that rides an eccentric on the distributor drive shaft. The flow of fuel delivered by the pump is automatically regulated as the fuel is used up from the float bowl.

On older engines, the pump is located below and to the left of the distributor, and the push rod operates in a horizontal plane. On later engines, the pump is mounted above and to the right of the distributor, and the push rod operates in a vertical plane.

The fuel pump consists of the cover, containing suction valve and delivery valve, and the pump body, incorporating the rocker mechanism. The diaphragm and spring are situated between the cover and the body. The diaphragm consists of several layers of special flexible clothlike material that is not affected by the fuel and two protectors which are riveted to the diaphragm pull rod.

As the distributor drive shaft revolves, the eccentric causes the push rod to move against the rocker arm which pulls the diaphragm downward against the diaphragm spring. This movement creates a vacuum above the diaphragm which lifts the suction valve off its seat so that fuel can be drawn in. When the push rod moves away, the loaded diaphragm spring pushes the diaphragm upward, forcing the fuel in the pump through the delivery valve and into the carburetor. This process is repeated at every turn of the eccentric (once every two revolutions of the engine).

The pump pressure depends on how much the spring is compressed during the pump suction stroke. This pressure is balanced by the buoyancy of the carburetor float, which causes a corresponding pressure at the needle valve seat. As fuel rises in the float bowl, the needle is forced up with greater pressure. Thus the pressure in the fuel line and pump chamber increases, while the pump working stroke decreases. With normal engine operation, the diaphragm is moved only a fraction of an inch.

A hole is provided for bleeding the chamber below the diaphragm. This hole also permits the draining of fuel which might have entered the lower chamber.

The pump requires no regular service attention, since its moving parts are lubricated by oil from the crankcase. However, on late engines through 1965, the fuel filter under the pump cover should be cleaned every 3,000 miles; on 1966 and later models, every 6,000 miles.

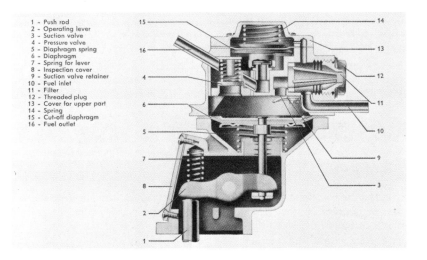

1 – Push rod
2 – Operating lever
3 – Suction valve
4 – Pressure valve
5 – Diaphragm spring
6 – Diaphragm
7 – Spring for lever
8 – Inspection cover
9 – Suction valve retainer
10 – Fuel inlet
11 – Filter
12 – Threaded plug
13 – Cover for upper part
14 – Spring
15 – Cut-off diaphragm
16 – Fuel outlet

Fig. B-15. Late type fuel pump for Beetle engine has fuel cutoff diaphragm (15).

Fig. B-16. Fuel pump used on late model engines is fitted with a recleanable filter located at fuel intake port.

Starting with 1967 models, the filter was located at the fuel intake port, Fig. B-16. This fuel filter also calls for cleaning at 6,000 mile intervals, or at time of tune-up.

CHECKING PUMP PRESSURE

On older engines, the pump pressure should amount to 1.30 - 1.85 lbs. sq. in. with the needle valve closed and the engine running at 1,000 - 3,000 rpm. The minimum amount of fuel delivery is 10.2 cu. in. per minute. On later engines, pressure should be 2.8 lbs. sq. in., delivery capacity, 24 cu. in. per minute. On Fastback and Squareback engines with twin carburetors, maximum pressure should be 4.5 lbs. sq. in., delivery capacity, 24 cu. in. per minute. To check the fuel pump pressure, connect a suitable pressure gauge between the pump and the carburetor.

The pump pressure is determined by the correct adjustment of the push rod stroke and the diaphragm spring tension. Adjustment of the push rod stroke is affected by adding or removing flange gasket.

ADJUSTING STROKE OF FUEL PUMP

Place intermediate flange, push rod and two gaskets, which should be in perfect condition, on fuel pump mounting studs. The lug on the intermediate flange must face upwards. The convex end of the push rod must be at the eccentric of the distributor drive pinion.

The push rod stroke of about 0.16 in. is determined by the eccentric on the distributor drive shaft. On pumps operated by a horizontal push rod, the stroke should move within a range of 1.14 and 1.34 in., measured from the fuel pump contact flange (incl. gaskets) to the projecting push rod end. On pumps with a vertical push rod, the stroke should move from .3 to .5 in., measured with a depth gauge.

Rotate the engine to check the pump stroke. The stroke can be adjusted by fitting an appropriate number of gaskets to the intermediate flange. Do not fit less gaskets than required, as this would have a detrimental effect on the diaphragm and the drive mechanism.

If the stroke adjustment does not give the desired result, replace the diaphragm spring. With the pump pressure too high, the intermediate turns of the spring may be brought further together, and with the pump pressure too low they may be stretched apart.

If the pressure is too high, flooding and dilution of the engine oil will result. If it is too low, insufficient fuel will be delivered and engine performance will be affected.

ELECTRONIC FUEL INJECTION

Beginning with 1968 Fastback and Squareback models, an electronic fuel injection system replaced the twin carburetors previously used. The system was devised to help meet the need for exhaust emission control since it senses engine requirements and maintains a metered flow of fuel and air to the cylinders according to the demands of varied operating conditions. VW 411 and 412 models also utilize fuel injection.

In operation, Fig. B-17, current is supplied to a control unit (4) via a main relay (3) and to an electric fuel pump (1) via a pump relay (2). A time switch in control unit activates fuel pump for 1 to 1-1/2 seconds after ignition is turned on to permit buildup of fuel pressure. Fuel injectors (6) are kept under constant pressure (28 lbs. sq. in.), so amount of fuel injected depends on length of time injectors are kept open, and it is metered according to engine requirements. Control unit opens injectors in pairs (cylinders 1 and 4; 2 and 3).

Various sensors (5, 7, 10 and 11) send information concerning engine speed, load and temperature to control unit which determines how long fuel injectors will remain open. The ignition distributor houses trigger contacts that signal to control unit when and where fuel is to be injected. A throttle valve switch (10) cuts off supply of fuel on deceleration.

HOW FUEL AND AIR SYSTEMS WORK

An electrically driven fuel pump forces fuel into the pressure line, through a filter to the ring main. The pressure regulator connected to the ring main maintains pressure at approximately 28 lbs. sq. in., and surplus fuel can flow back to the tank through a return line. The ring main feeds fuel to the electromagnetic injectors by way of fuel distributor pipes.

An intake air distributor in the system keys the air supply to four intake manifolds and to the four cylinders of the engine. The amount

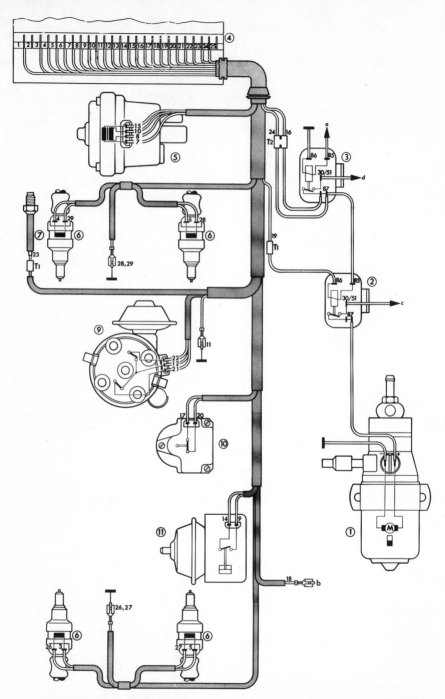

Fig. B-17. Diagram depicts main components of electronic fuel injection system: 1–Electric fuel pump. 2–Pump relay. 3–Main relay. 4–Electronic control unit. 5–Pressure sensor. 6–Injectors. 7–Temperature sensor. 9–Distributor with trigger contacts. 10–Throttle switch. 11–Pressure switch.

of air required by the fuel injection system is controlled during vehicle operation by a throttle valve in the intake air distributor. Since the throttle valve is connected to the accelerator pedal, it is completely closed during idling and intake air must pass through an idling circuit that includes adjusting screw which controls engine idling speed.

Fig. B-18. Trigger contacts are replaceable in ignition distributor used on fuel injection engines in Type 3/Type 4 Volkswagens. Contacts are located in lower section of ignition distributor. They are designed to determine when fuel is to be injected into a selected pair of cylinders.

Fig. B-18A. To adjust idle speed: turn adjusting screw clockwise (a) for slower rpm; or counterclockwise (b) for faster rpm. Turn lock nut clockwise (c) to tighten. Engine must be at normal operating temperature. Idling speed is 850 rpm, or 925 with automatic transmission.

The idling circuit supplies sufficient air at normal operating temperatures. However, at lower temperatures, more air is required and an auxiliary air regulator provides it. This regulator is a rotary valve in an auxiliary air line from the air cleaner and its on-off positions are controlled by a device that senses oil temperature.

FUEL INJECTION SYSTEM MAINTENANCE

Volkswagen's electronic fuel injection system testing can be carried out in 19 electrical, hydraulic and dynamic test stages. However, some simple checks and maintenance steps can be performed by one not having elaborate equipment or great technical skill.

The fuel system should be checked for leaks or pinched lines, especially at the tank, pump, filter and pressure regulator, Fig. B-17. The fuel filter should be replaced every 6,000 miles: Pinch the fuel hose between filter and tank with a clamp. Also clamp hose between "Y" connector and pump. Remove old filter, install new filter with arrow facing pump, remove clamps.

The air system calls for cleaning the air cleaner at regular intervals, every 6,000 miles or in keeping with dusty conditions that prevail: Clean reservoir and refill with SAE 30W engine oil to red line. Align red arrows on upper and lower parts on reassembly. Correctly install rubber boot on air cleaner intake and elbow on intake air distributor, Fig. B-19. Connect auxiliary air hose to air cleaner.

Trigger contacts in ignition distributor are not adjustable. The two contacts are mounted on a holder in the lower part of the distributor. Two screws hold the assembly in place. Replacement is simply a matter of pulling out the old unit and putting in the new one, Fig. B-18.

Electrical connections are of prime importance in maintaining the electronic fuel injection system. All push-on connectors must be seated firmly - on the pump, pump relay, pressure sensor, distributor (trigger contacts), etc.

Set engine idle speed: Adjust idling air adjusting screw, Fig. B-18A, with engine at normal operating temperature. Back off lock nut, turn adjusting screw clockwise (slower) or counterclockwise (faster) to obtain 850 rpm.

FUEL PUMP TROUBLE SHOOTING

Complaint	Cause	Correction
1 - Pump leaky at joining faces; loss of fuel	a - Slotted screws insecure b - Diaphragm cracked	a - Tighten screws b - Renew diaphragm
2 - Diaphragm leaks at rivets; loss of fuel	a - Diaphragm damaged by unskilled assembly	a - Renew diaphragm
3 - Diaphragm material leaky; loss of fuel	a - Diaphragm material damaged by solvent substance in fuel	a - Renew diaphragm
4 - Excessive pump stroke; overstraining the diaphragm	a - Pump incorrectly installed; gasket too thin	a - Correctly install pump; check diaphragm
5 - Pump pressure low	a - Pump incorrectly installed, gasket too thick b - Spring pressure low	a - Correctly install pump b - Renew spring or, if necessary, stretch it

Carburetor, Fuel System

Complaint	Cause	Correction
6 - Pump pressure excessive; float needle valve forced down	a - Pump incorrectly installed, gasket too thin b - Spring pressure excessive	a - Correctly install pump b - Renew spring or, if necessary, bring intermediate turns closer together
7 - Insufficient fuel delivery	a - Valves leaky or sticking	a - Renew valves and valve seats, or renew top half of pump
8 - Electric fuel pump inoperative	a - Pump wiring or relay faulty b - Pump defective	a - Tighten connections; replace wiring or relay b - Replace pump

Fig. B-19. Improved electronic fuel injection system on late Fastback and Squareback models, has modified air cleaner and intake air distributor with new cold starting valve and temperature sensor that measures temperature of intake air and replaces oil temperature sensor formerly installed in crankcase. Assembly includes: A—Bellows on intake pipe. B—Crankcase breather hose. C—Auxiliary air control valve hose. D—Intake air distributor. E—Air cleaner top part. F—Clips. G—Alignment arrows. H—Weighted flap. J—Fuel hose.

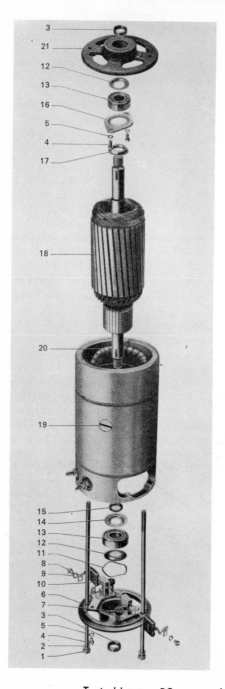

1—Housing bolt.
2—Lock washer.
3—Spacer ring.
4—Fillister head screw.
5—Lock washer.
6—End plate (commutator end).
7—Brush spring.
8—Fillister head screw.
9—Lock washer.
10—Carbon brush.
11—Lock washer.
12—Dished washer.
13—Ball bearing.
14—Splash shield.
15—Thrust washer.
16—Retaining plate.
17—Splash shield.
18—Armature.
19—Pole shoe screw.
20—Field coil.
21—End plate (fan end).

Typical late-type DC generator for Beetle models.

Simplified
ELECTRICAL SERVICE

Volkswagen's electrical system is simple yet capable of handling every need of a modern automobile. A 6-volt battery and DC generator-operated electrical system is used on all "Beetle" and Fastback and Squareback models through 1966. The 12-volt system was introduced on 1967 models in both lines. Details are shown in accompanying diagrams, Figs. C-1 to C-2B.

These diagrams are typical and may vary in some details from a particular car because of changes in electrical units as well as variations between different body types. Later models, for example, incorporated an emergency flasher, headlight dimmer switch in the turn signal lever, and dual back-up lights. The 12-volt electrical system introduced a more powerful battery and starting motor, an early cut-in generator and 2-speed windshield wiper motor. An electronically controlled fuel injection system became standard equipment on Fastback and Squareback models in 1968. The system was modified in later model years, for Type 3 and Type 4 Volkswagens.

While accurate testing of the various electrical units requires special equipment, there are many simple tests which do not require such equipment and which will quickly tell where the trouble is located. Having determined the trouble, it is a simple matter to replace the defective unit.

BATTERY AND STARTING SYSTEM

Basically, the electrical system consists of: Battery; starting motor; generator and regulator; ignition switch, coil, distributor and spark plugs; lighting system; electrical accessories; instruments and connecting wires. On models so equipped, the electronic fuel injection system adds more electrical circuitry.

The battery stores energy in chemical form and converts it to electrical energy when an external switch is closed and a circuit is completed. The battery discharges current to the cranking and ignition systems to start the engine. Then, as engine speed increases and

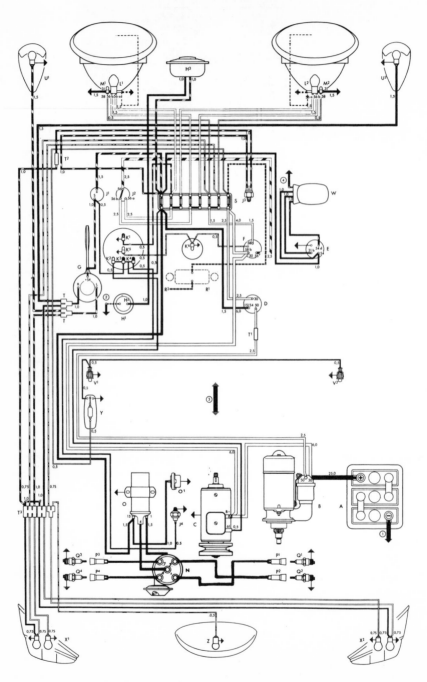

Fig. C-1. Wiring diagram of 6-volt electrical system used on Volkswagen Beetle models from August, 1961.

Simplified Electrical Service

generator output exceeds battery voltage, the generator takes over the task of supplying current to the electrical equipment and it also recharges the battery.

Since the battery is common to all of the engine's basic electrical circuits, it should be checked first when electrical problems arise.

A - Battery

B - Starting Motor

C - Generator

D - Ignition/Starter Switch

E - Windshield Wiper Switch

F - Light Switch and Instrument
    Panel Lighting

G - Flashing Indicator Switch (self-cancelling)

H^1 - Horn Half-ring

H^2 - Steering Column Connection

H^3 - Horn

J^1 - Flasher Relay

J^2 - Dimmer Switch

J^3 - Stop Light Switch

J^4 - Oil Pressure Switch

K^1 - High Beam Indicator Light

K^2 - Generator Control Light

K^3 - Flashing Indicator Control Light

K^4 - Oil Pressure Warning Light

K^5 - Speedometer Light

K^6 - Fuel Gauge Light

L^1 - Bifilament Bulb for Headlight, Left
    or Sealed-Beam Insert, Left

L^2 - Bifilament Bulb for Headlight, Right
    or Sealed-Beam Insert, Right

M^1 - Parking Light, Left

M^2 - Parking Light, Right

M^3 - Parking Light, Sealed-Beam Insert, Left

M^4 - Parking Light, Sealed-Beam Insert, Right

N - Ignition Distributor

O - Ignition Coil

O^1 - Automatic Choke on Carburetor

P^1 - Spark Plug Connector for Cylinder 1

P^2 - Spark Plug Connector for Cylinder 2

P^3 - Spark Plug Connector for Cylinder 3

P^4 - Spark Plug Connector for Cylinder 4

Q^1 - Spark Plug for Cylinder 1

Q^2 - Spark Plug for Cylinder 2

Q^3 - Spark Plug for Cylinder 3

Q^4 - Spark Plug for Cylinder 4

R^1 - Radio

R^2 - Aerial Connection

S - Fuse Box (eight fuses)

T - Cable Connector

T^1 - Connector, single

T^2 - Connector, double

T^3 - Connector, triple

U^1 - Flasher Light, Left

U^2 - Flasher Light, Right

V^1 - Door Contact Switch, Left

V^2 - Door Contact Switch, Right

W - Windshield Wiper Motor (3 connections)

X^1 - Indicator, Stop and Tail Light, Left

X^2 - Indicator, Stop and Tail Light, Right

Y - Interior Light

Z - License Plate Light

(1) - Battery Ground Strap

(2) - Horn ring to Steering Column Flange Ground
    Strap

(3) - Ground Strap between Transmission and
    Frame

(4) - Ground Strap between Windshield Wiper
    Motor and Body

Key to wiring diagram shown in Fig. C-1.

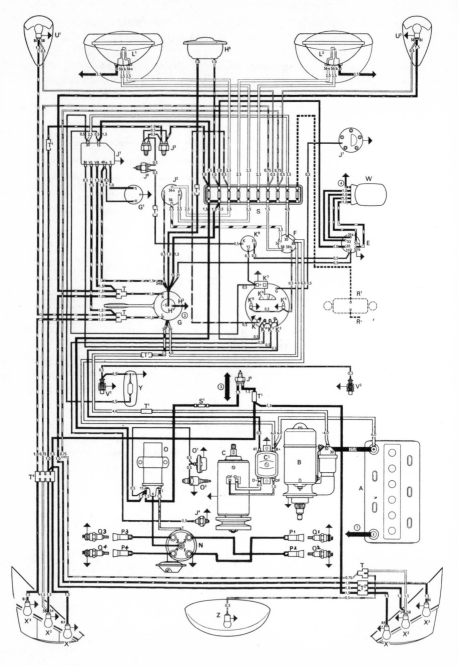

Fig. C-2. Wiring diagram of 12-volt electrical system used on Volkswagen
Beetle models from August, 1967.

Type 1 Sedan and Convertible

A — Battery
B — Starter
C — Generator
C¹ — Regulator
E — Windshield wiper switch
F — Light switch
G — Turn signal switch, dimmer switch and ignition / starter switch
G¹ — Emergency flasher switch
H¹ — Horn half ring
H² — Steering column connection
H³ — Horn
J¹ — Turn signal and emergency flasher relay
J² — Dimmer relay
J³ — Brake light switch (2×)
J⁴ — Oil pressure switch
J⁵ — Back-up light switch
J⁶ — Warning switch for brake system
J⁷ — Fuel gauge sender unit
K¹ — High beam warning light
K² — Generator charging warning light
K³ — Turn signal warning light
K⁴ — Oil pressure warning light
K⁵ — Speedometer lights
K⁶ — Fuel gauge light
K⁷ — Vibrator for fuel gauge
K⁸ — Brake warning lamp with test button
L¹ — Sealed beam unit, left
L² — Sealed beam unit, right
N — Distributor
O — Ignition coil
O¹ — Automatic choke
O² — Electro-magnetic pilot jet
P¹ — Spark plug connector, No. 1 cylinder
P² — Spark plug connector, No. 2 cylinder
P³ — Spark plug connector, No. 3 cylinder
P⁴ — Spark plug connector, No. 4 cylinder

Q¹ — Spark plug for No. 1 cylinder
Q² — Spark plug for No. 2 cylinder
Q³ — Spark plug for No. 3 cylinder
Q⁴ — Spark plug for No. 4 cylinder
R¹ — Radio
R² — Aerial connection
S — Fuse box
T — Cable adapter
T¹ — Cable connector, single
T² — Cable connector for horn under front luggage compartment lining
T³ — Cable connector, triple
T⁴ — Multiple cable connector
U¹ — Front turn signal and parking light, left
U² — Front turn signal and parking light, right
V¹ — Door contact switch, left
V² — Door contact switch, right
W — Windshield wiper motor
X¹ — Back-up lights
X² — Brake and tail lights
X³ — Turn signal lights
Y — Interior light
Z — License plate light

① — Battery to frame ground strap
② — Horn ring to steering coupling ground cable
③ — Transmission to frame ground cable
④ — Wiper motor to body ground strap

Black dotted line = optional extras or service installation

Key to wiring diagram shown in Fig. C-2.

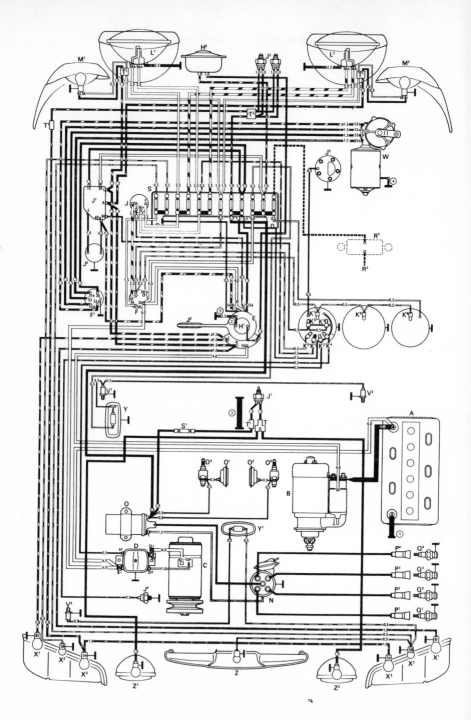

Fig. C-2A. Wiring diagram for 12-volt electrical system used on Volkswagen Type 3, 1600 models.

Wiring diagram VW Type 3, 1600

A — Battery
B — Starter
C — Generator
D — Regulator
E — Turn signal switch with ignition / starter lock
F — Light switch
F¹ — Windshield wiper switch
H¹ — Horn half ring
H² — Horn
J — Hand dimmer relay
J¹ — Turn signal / emergency flasher
J² — Hand dimmer switch
J³ — Brake light switch
J⁴ — Oil pressure switch
J⁵ — Fuel gauge sender unit
J⁶ — Emergency flasher switch
J⁷ — Back-up light switch
K¹ — High beam warning light
K² — Generator charging warning light
K³ — Turn signal warning lights
K⁴ — Oil pressure warning light
K⁵ — Parking light warning light
K⁶ — Speedometer light
K⁷ — Fuel gauge light
K⁸ — Clock light
L¹ — Sealed beam unit, left
L² — Sealed beam unit, right
M¹ — Parking light and turn signal light, left
M² — Parking light and turn signal light, right
N — Distributor
O — Ignition coil
O¹ — Automatic choke, left
O² — Automatic choke, right
O³ — Electro-magnetic pilot jet, left
O⁴ — Electro-magnetic pilot jet, right

P¹ — Spark plug connector, No. 1 cylinder
P² — Spark plug connector, No. 2 cylinder
P³ — Spark plug connector, No. 3 cylinder
P⁴ — Spark plug connector, No. 4 cylinder
Q¹ — Spark plug for No. 1 cylinder
Q² — Spark plug for No. 2 cylinder
Q³ — Spark plug for No. 3 cylinder
Q⁴ — Spark plug for No. 4 cylinder
R — Radio
R² — Aerial connection
S — Fuse box
S¹ — Back-up light fuse
T¹ — Cable connector, single
T² — Cable connector, double
V¹ — Door contact switch, left
V² — Door contact switch, right
V³ — Luggage compartment light switch
W — Windshield wiper motor
X¹ — Turn signal lights
X² — Tail lights
X³ — Brake lights
Y — Interior light
Y¹ — Luggage compartment light
Z — License plate light
Z¹ — Back-up light, left
Z² — Back-up light, right

① — Battery to frame ground strap
② — Horn half ring to steering coupling ground cable
③ — Transmission to frame ground strap
④ — Windshield wiper motor to body ground strap
⑤ — Front axle to frame ground cable

Key to wiring diagram shown in Fig. C-2A.

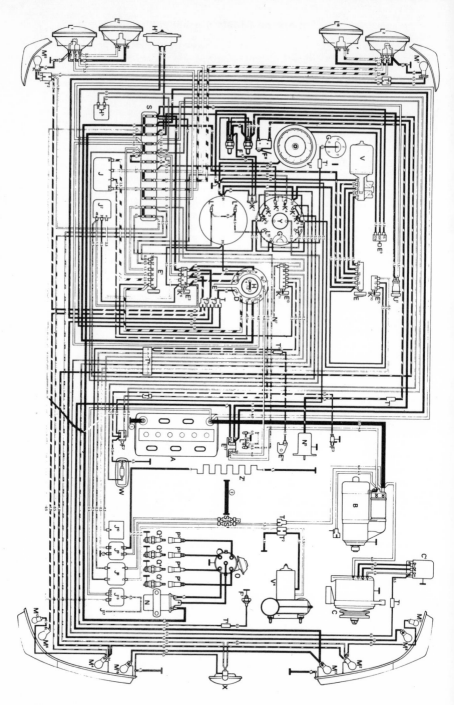

Fig. C-2B. Wiring diagram of 12-volt electrical system used on Volkswagen 411 models.

Wiring Diagram VW 411

A - Battery
B - Starter
C - Generator
C¹ - Regulator
D - Starter/ignition switch
E - Windshield wiper switch
E¹ - Lighting switch
E² - Turn signal switch (dimmer switch)
E³ - Emergency warning light switch
E⁹ - Fan motor switch
E¹³ - Heater switch
E¹⁵ - Switch for heatable rear window
E¹⁶ - Switch for heater
E¹⁷ - Starter inhibitor switch and back-up light switch
F - Stop light switch
F¹ - Oil pressure switch
F² - Door contact switch, front left
F³ - Door contact switch, front right
F⁸ - Kick-down switch
G - Sender for fuel gauge
G¹ - Fuel gauge
H - Horn lever
H¹ - Horn
H⁵ - Buzzer for ignition key warning equipment
J - Dimmer relay
J² - Emergency light relay
J⁸ - Heater relay
J⁹ - Heated rear window relay
J¹⁰ - Safety switch (relay)
J¹⁶ - Power supply relay
J¹⁷ - To fuel pump relay
K¹ - High beam warning lamp
K² - Charging warning lamp
K³ - Oil pressure warning lamp
K⁴ - Parking light warning lamp
K⁵ - Turn signal warning lamp
K⁶ - Emergency light warning lamp
K⁷ - Dual brake circuit warning lamp
K¹⁰ - Heated rear window warning lamp
K¹¹ - Heater warning lamp
L¹ - Sealed-beam unit left, low and high beam
L² - Sealed-beam unit right, low and high beam
L⁶ - Bulb for speedometer lighting
L¹⁰ - Instrument lighting

L¹³ - Bulb for high beam left
L¹⁴ - Bulb for high beam right
L¹⁷ - Sealed-beam unit left, high beam
L¹⁸ - Sealed-beam unit right, high beam
L¹⁹ - Bulb for selector lever console
M² - Bulb for tail/stop light, right
M⁴ - Bulb for tail/stop light, left
M⁵ - Bulb for turn signal/parking light, front left
M⁶ - Bulb for turn signal, rear left
M⁷ - Bulb for turn signal/parking light, front right
M⁸ - Bulb for turn signal, rear right
M¹¹ - Bulb for side marker, rear right
M¹² - Bulb for side marker, rear left
M¹⁶ - Bulb for back-up light, left
M¹⁷ - Bulb for back-up light, right
N - Ignition coil
N⁵ - Kick-down solenoid
N⁷ - To temperature feeler
O - Distributor
P¹ - Plug connector for No. 1 cylinder
P² - Plug connector for No. 2 cylinder
P³ - Plug connector for No. 3 cylinder
P⁴ - Plug connector for No. 4 cylinder
Q¹ - Plug for No. 1 cylinder
Q² - Plug for No. 2 cylinder
Q³ - Plug for No. 3 cylinder
Q⁴ - Plug for No. 4 cylinder
S - Fuse box
S¹ - Heater fuse
S² - Back-up light fuse
T - Cable adaptor
T¹ - Cable connector, single
T² - Cable connector, double
T⁶ - Cable connector, 8 point
T²⁰ - Central socket
U¹ - Cigarette lighter
V - Windshield wiper motor
V² - Fan motor, front
V⁴ - Warm air fan
W - Interior light
X - License plate light
Y - Clock
Z¹ - Heated rear window
① - Ground cable from battery to frame
② - Ground cable from transmission to frame
④ - Steering coupling ground cable

Key to wiring diagram shown in Fig. C-2B.

It is not unusual to find a starting battery in good condition but because of dirty connections and high resistance in the circuit, the cranking speed is very low and starting is difficult.

To insure quick starting under all conditions, all battery connections must be clean and tight. This applies not only to the cable-to-post connections at the battery, but also to the battery ground connection on the engine and to the connection at the starting switch. Also be sure that the cable or strap that connects the engine to the frame is in good condition, and makes good electrical connection at both ends.

HOW TO TEST BATTERY

A quick test of the starting battery is to crank the engine. If the engine turns over at a rapid speed, the battery can be considered to be in good condition.

However, this is only a rough test. It is much better to test the battery with a hydrometer.

Check the condition of a starting battery with a hydrometer, but not immediately after water has been added to bring the electrolyte to the desired level. Take the readings before the water is added in order to

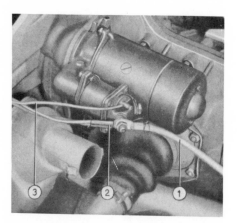

Fig. C-3. External connections on starter solenoid.

obtain a representative sample of the electrolyte. If the hydrometer reading is in excess of 1.225, the battery is in fair to good condition. If the reading is less than 1.225, the battery is in poor condition and should be recharged or replaced. The readings for each of the cells of the starting battery should be approximately the same.

If an open circuit voltage tester is used to test the storage battery, cells in good condition will give a reading of 2.2 volts each. If the reading is 2.0 volts or less, the battery requires attention.

BATTERY SERVICE KINKS

The battery posts are stamped + and -, with the positive post the thicker of the two. The negative post is grounded.

For best results, remove the battery cable clamps and clean the posts and clamps thoroughly. If the clamps are oxidized to the posts, use a special pulling tool to remove them. Clean the posts with a post-cleaning wire brush, reinstall the clamps, and coat the terminals with petrolatum.

Remember too, that efficient battery operation is possible only if the connecting wiring is in good condition and making clean, tight contact. This includes ground connections, which should be removed, scraped or buffed clean and bright on both contact surfaces. Then reinstall securely.

It is also important that the top of the battery be kept clean and dry, otherwise there will be a leakage of current which may seriously affect starting, particularly during cold weather operation.

Batteries should be filled with sufficient quantity of distilled water to bring the level of the electrolyte up to the top of the split ring in each cell. Ordinary tap water can be used, but for maximum battery life distilled water is preferred.

SIMPLIFIED STARTER SERVICE

Difficulty with the starting system is usually caused by a defective starting battery or in the electrical connections rather than with the starting motor itself. So if the starting motor fails to crank the engine or cranks it over very slowly, make sure the connections to the battery and starter are clean and tight and that the starter mounting bolts are tight.

To engage the gear drive, a starter solenoid operated by a switch is used. Heavy contacts within the solenoid, in turn, connect the starting motor and the starting battery. If the starting motor does not rotate when the switch is turned on, use a heavy wire to bypass the large terminals on the starter solenoid, Fig. C-3. This will short out the starter solenoid and current will be supplied directly from the battery to the starting motor. If the starting motor still fails to rotate, it indicates that the motor is defective and should be rebuilt or replaced.

In case either the motor or solenoid is at fault, remove the assembly, Fig. C-4. The solenoid is readily removed from the starter motor without disassembly of motor, Fig. C-5.

Note in Fig. C-5 that the solenoid shaft attaches to a shifting fork on the drive pinion assembly. Thus when the solenoid shaft moves to engage the contacts, the pinion gear is shifted into mesh with the flywheel ring gear. The pinion gear is fitted with an overrunning clutch to avoid damage when the engine starts and drives the pinion at high speed.

Volkswagen "Beetle," Fastback and Squareback models through 1966 were fitted with 6-volt starting motors. In 1967, the 12-volt electrical

Fig. C-4. Arrows indicate attachment bolts for removal of starter and solenoid assembly.

Fig. C-5. Slight in-and-out movement of starter shifting fork will facilitate removal of solenoid.

system was introduced. Service is basically the same. If anything, however, clean and tight connections are more critical on the 12-volt starting motor - at the battery posts, solenoid terminals and all ground connections.

In keeping with good preventive maintenance practice, the brushes and commutator should be inspected every 6,000 miles. This is readily accomplished by removing the end cap or inspection covers on the starting motor, Figs. C-6 to C-8.

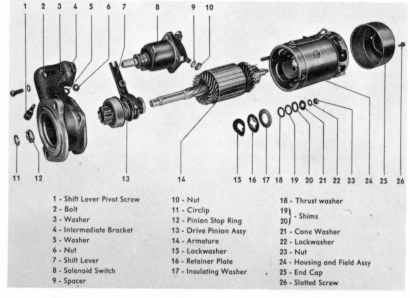

1 - Shift Lever Pivot Screw	10 - Nut	18 - Thrust washer
2 - Bolt	11 - Circlip	19 ⎱
3 - Washer	12 - Pinion Stop Ring	20 ⎰ - Shims
4 - Intermediate Bracket	13 - Drive Pinion Assy	21 - Cone Washer
5 - Washer	14 - Armature	22 - Lockwasher
6 - Nut	15 - Lockwasher	23 - Nut
7 - Shift Lever	16 - Retainer Plate	24 - Housing and Field Assy
8 - Solenoid Switch	17 - Insulating Washer	25 - End Cap
9 - Spacer		26 - Slotted Screw

Fig. C-6. Exploded view of starting motor used on early "Beetle" models, locates and identifies all components.

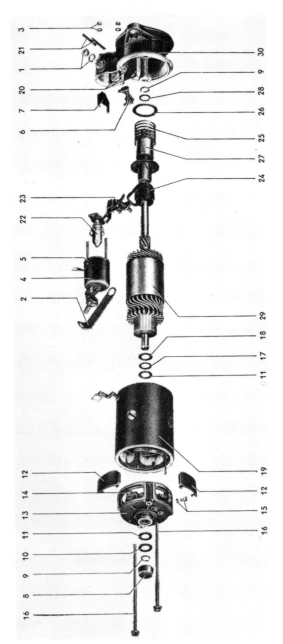

Fig. C-7. Alternate Starting Motor: 1—Hex nut and spring washer. 2—Connecting strip. 3—Hex nut and spring washer. 4—Solenoid housing and windings. 5—Insulating disc. 6—Profiled seal. 7—Insulating plate. 8—Cap. 9—Circlip. 10—Steel washer. 11—Bronze washer. 12—Inspection cover. 13—Commutator end plate. 14—Brush holder and brushes. 15—Screw and spring washer. 16—Housing screws. 17—Dished washer. 18—Steel washer. 19—Housing and field windings. 20—Spring clip. 21—Pivot pin. 22—Solenoid core. 23—Linkage. 24—Connecting bushing. 25—Spring. 26—Intermediate washer. 27—Drive pinion. 28—Dished washer. 29—Armature. 30—Intermediate bearing.

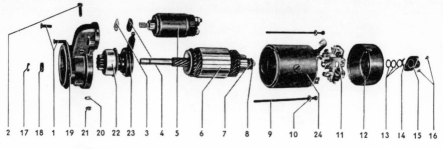

1 - Securing screws	9 - Housing screws	17 - Circlip
2 - Bearing bolt	10 - Washer	18 - Stop ring
3 - Support washer	11 - Brush holder	19 - Intermediate bracket
4 - Rubber seal	12 - End plate	20 - Spring washer
5 - Solenoid	13 - Shims	21 - Nut
6 - Armature	14 - Lockwasher	22 - Drive pinion
7 - Steel washer	15 - End cap	23 - Shift lever
8 - Synthetic washer	16 - Screws	24 - Housing

Fig. C-8. Alternate starting motor construction.

Inspect brushes for wear and make sure that they slide freely in the brush holders, Fig. C-9. If the brushes are worn down half their length, particularly if the flexible connector shows on the contact face, they must be replaced. Also replace brushes which are oil saturated or have loose flexible connectors.

Check tension of brush springs and replace any that are weak.

If the commutator is oily or gummed, clean with a cloth dampened with solvent. Do not flush out with solvent, which might carry dirt or fluid into the adjacent bearing.

If the commutator surface is rough and pitted, or shows burned spots, the starting motor should be overhauled by someone with special equipment and knowledge.

STARTING MOTOR TROUBLE SHOOTING

Complaint	Cause	Correction
Starter does not operate when button is pressed or ignition key is turned to starting position	Switch on the lamps when testing: a - Lights do not burn. Loose cables or poor ground connection. Battery run down	a - Check battery cables and connection. Test voltage of battery
	b - Lights go out when button is pressed or key is turned to starting position. Insufficient current due to loose con-	b - Clean battery terminals and cable clamps, clean and tighten connections between battery, starting motor and ground

Simplified Electrical Service

Complaint	Cause	Correction
	nections or corroded terminals	
	c - Lights go dim when button is pressed or key is turned to starting position. Battery run down	c - Charge battery
	d - Lights stay bright when button is pressed or key is turned to starting position. Make a jumper contact between terminals 30 and 50 at starting motor: If starter operates, there is an open circuit in cable 50 to starter button or to ignition switch, or in cable 30 to lighting switch, or starter button or ignition switch is defective	d - Eliminate open circuits, replace defective parts
	e - Lights stay bright and plunger in solenoid switch is pulled when button is pressed or key is turned to starting position. Disconnect battery cable from terminal 30 at starting motor and connect it to terminal stud of connector (contact) blade. If the starting motor operates, the contacts of the solenoid switch are worn or dirty	e - Replace solenoid switch

Complaint	Cause	Correction
Starting motor does not operate when battery cable is directly connected with terminal stud of connector (contact) blade	a - Brushes sticking	a - Clean brushes and guides of brush holders
	b - Brushes worn	b - Replace brushes
	c - Weak spring tension. Brushes do not make contact	c - Replace springs
	d - Commutator dirty	d - Clean commutator
	e - Commutator rough, pitted or burned	e - Recondition starting motor
	f - Armature or field coils defective	f - Overhaul starting motor
Sluggish or slow action of the starting motor	a - Battery run down	a - Charge battery
	b - Insufficient current flow due to loose or corroded connections	b - Clean battery terminals and cable clamps, tighten connections
	c - Brushes sticking	c - Clean brushes and guides of brush holders
	d - Brushes worn	d - Replace brushes
	e - Commutator dirty	e - Clean commutator
	f - Commutator rough, pitted or burned	f - Recondition starting motor
	g - Armature or field coils defective	g - Overhaul starting motor
Starting motor is heard to operate, but cranks engine erratically or not at all	a - Drive pinion defective	a - Replace drive pinion
	b - Flywheel gear ring defective	b - Replace flywheel or remachine gear ring
Drive pinion does not move out of mesh	a - Drive pinion armature shaft dirty or damaged	a - Overhaul starting motor
	b - Solenoid switch defective	b - Replace solenoid switch

ELECTRICAL GENERATOR

The electric generating system on the Volkswagen is provided with a voltage regulator which is designed to maintain the starting battery in a fully charged condition. The design is such that when the battery is fully charged, the charging rate is reduced to a minimum. When the battery is low in charge, the voltage regulator will automatically increase the current flowing into the starting battery to restore it to a fully charged condition.

The generator is located on top of the engine and is driven by a belt from a pulley on the crankshaft. It supplies the current necessary to keep the starting battery in charge and also to operate the ignition and lighting systems. It should give satisfactory service for at least 25,000 miles of operation, at which time it will probably require new brushes. In addition, the commutator will probably require sanding with fine sandpaper in order to remove any roughness.

*Fig. C-9. Brushes are readily inspected after end cap
is removed from starting motor on older models.*

GENERATOR TROUBLE SHOOTING
WITHOUT TESTING EQUIPMENT

The first test in checking a generator is to start the engine and observe the red indicator light on the instrument panel. This lamp may light up when the engine is going slowly, but it should go out above idling speed. If no charge is indicated, the first point to be examined is the belt driving the generator. A loose belt will cause a generator to perform erratically and, of course, an extremely loose belt or one that is broken will result in no current being produced at all.

Another way to check a generator without the use of testing equipment is to remove the steel band or covers on the generator, Fig. C-10, and examine the inside. If it is speckled with drops of solder, it indicates that the generator has been overloaded and the resulting high temperatures have melted the solder used to connect the ends of the armature wires to the commutator. On generators having smaller inspection ports and no

Fig. C-10. With cover band removed, brushes and
brush springs are readily accessible.

cover, the thrown solder will be evident on the inside of the generator
housing in the ported area. When that condition is found, the armature or
preferably the entire generator should be replaced, Fig. C-11.

Also examine the commutator and brushes. Commutators in good
condition will have a slightly purplish color and will be smooth and
without ridges. Commutators that are slightly scratched should be sand-
ed with a fine sandpaper. To do this pass a strip of the sandpaper over
the end of a flat piece of wood. Then with the armature revolving, the
sandpaper is pressed against the commutator. Do not use emery paper
for this operation.

The brushes should press firmly against the commutator. If they are
worn to half their original length, they should be replaced, Fig. C-10.

Fig. C-11. Generator used on later models charges even when engine
is idling or car is moving slowly in start-and-stop traffic.

Simplified Electrical Service

To make an accurate and conclusive test of a generator, a voltmeter should be employed. Since the amount of the charging current depends on the state of charge of the battery, the on-car test is made at the regulator terminal. Disconnect cable from terminal B+ (51) at the regulator, Fig. C-12. Connect the positive lead of a voltmeter to terminal B+ (51) at the regulator and ground the negative lead.

Start engine and increase speed gradually from idle to 1895-2200 rpm. On 6-volt systems, the voltmeter reading should jump from 0 to 6-7 volts at slightly above idling speed, and then constantly read between 7.4 and 8.1 volts (specifically 8.1 volts at 68 deg. F.) if the regulator is correctly set. On 12-volt systems, the voltmeter reading should be from 12-13 volts at slightly above idling speed. At 1900 rpm, it should read from 13.6 to 14.4 volts.

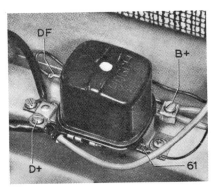

Fig. C-12. Close-up view of generator regulator on early Fastback and Squareback models shows location of terminals.

GENERATOR, REGULATOR SERVICE

Before making any changes in the voltage regulator, make sure that all electrical connections in the charging circuit are clean and tight and the generator is in good operating condition.

It should be remembered that when the generator and voltage regulator are operating correctly, that a heavy charge will be indicated only when the battery is in need of charging. Then as the battery is fully charged, the voltage regulator will automatically reduce the charging rate to two or three amperes.

In many cases, voltage regulators only require adjustment and cleaning of the contacts. However, to adjust a voltage regulator, accurate voltmeters and ammeters are required, and the procedure for making the tests and adjustments will accompany such testing equipment. The contact points of the voltage regulator can be cleaned by sliding a strip of linen or lintless bond paper tape between the contacts. If the contacts are badly pitted, it is usually advisable to replace the regulator.

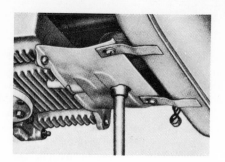

Fig. C-13. Remove thermostat mounting screw as shown, then unscrew thermostat from connecting rod.

When checking the generator and voltage regulator, it is also important to make sure that the fan belt is adjusted to the correct tension.

To remove generator from older "Beetle" engines for replacement or service off the car, it must be removed with the fan housing - and reinstalled as an assembly.

1 - Disconnect battery ground cable and remove lead wires from regulator.
2 - Take off air cleaner and carburetor.
3 - Remove fan belt and generator mounting strap.
4 - Unsnap distributor cap and pull off spark plug connectors.
5 - Detach heater hoses from fan housing and remove thermostat, Fig. C-13.
6 - Unscrew fan housing mounting screws and lift assembly from engine, Fig. C-14.

Fig. C-14. With mounting screws, lead wires, hoses and fan belt detached, lift fan housing and generator from engine.

7 - Remove screws from fan housing cover and withdraw generator and fan from housing.
8 - Remove fan nut, fan spacers, hub and Woodruff key.
9 - Unscrew generator through bolts and remove fan housing cover.
10 - Service generator as required, then reassemble in fan housing and reinstall assembly in reverse order, Fig. C-14.

Fig. C-15. On Beetle models built after August, 1966, generator and fan housing cover can be removed after taking off air cleaner, carburetor, cooling air thermostat, warm air hoses and disconnecting fan.

Fig. C-16. On reinstallation, generator and fan housing cover must be installed with cooling air intake slot (upper arrow) facing downward. Allow .080 in. gap at housing when reconnecting fan.

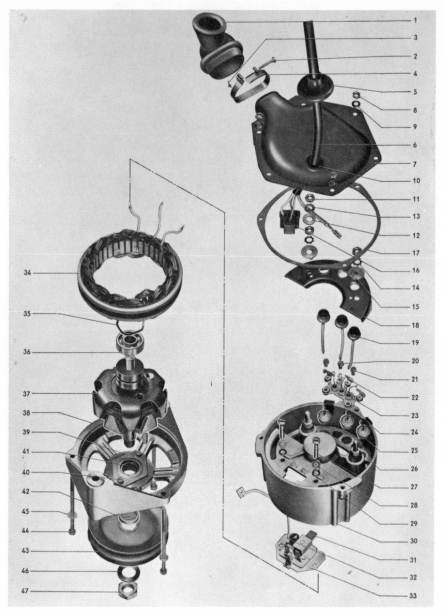

Fig. C-16A. Alternator assembly for Model 411, Type 4 Volkswagen. An alternator manufactured in the U. S. will appear on late production 1973 Beetle engines.

Simplified Electrical Service

1 – Elbow.
2 – Screw for hose clip.
3 – Threaded portion.
4 – Hose clamp.
5 – Rubber grommet.
6 – Wiring harness.
7 – Intake cover.
8 – Hex nut.
9 – Lock washer.
10 – Rubber grommet.
11 – Hex nut.
12 – Washer.
13 – Washer.
14 – Star washer.
15 – Contact disc.
16 – Three pin plug.
17 – Intake cover gasket.
18 – Positive diode carrier.
19 – Positive diodes.
20 – Fillister screw.
21 – Connection screw for stator winding.
22 – Exciter diode carrier.
23 – Exciter diodes.
24 – Seal.
25 – Negative diodes.
26 – Pin for positive diode carrier.
27 – Screw for brush holder.
28 – Washer.
29 – Spring washer.
30 – Generator housing.
31 – Carbon brush.
32 – Brush retaining spring.
33 – Brush holder.
34 – Stator.
35 – Spring washer.
36 – Ball bearing, slip ring.
37 – Claw-pole rotor.
38 – End plate.
39 – Bearing end plate.
40 – Fillister screw.
41 – Drive end ball bearing.
42 – Intermediate ring.
43 – Pulley.
44 – Housing bolt.
45 – Washer.
46 – Washer.
47 – Nut.

Key to alternator assembly in Fig. C-16A.

GENERATOR TROUBLE SHOOTING

The red generator lamp lights up when the ignition is switched on and should go out when the engine has been started and the speed increases.

Complaint	Cause	Correction
Generator lamp does not light with ignition switched on	a - Battery discharge	a - Charge battery
	b - Battery defective	b - Renew battery
	c - Bulb burned out	c - Renew bulb
	d - Corroded or loose battery terminals	d - Clean or tighten terminals respectively
	e - Loose connections or broken cables	e - Tighten or repair cables respectively
	f - Ignition switch defective	f - Renew ignition switch
	g - Generator brushes do not make contact with commutator	g - Make the brushes to move freely or renew brushes. If necessary, renew the brush springs

Complaint	Cause	Correction
Generator lamp does not go out or flares up when engine is accelerated	a - Drive belt loose	a - Adjust belt tension or renew belt
	b - Regulator faulty	b - Renew regulator
	c - Charging cables loose or disrupted	c - Check cables and connections
	d - Generator faulty	d - Check generator
Generator lamp goes out only at high speed	a - Generator faulty	a - Check generator
	b - Regulator faulty	b - Renew regulator
Generator lamp continues to light with the ignition switched off	a - Regulator contact points sticking (burned)	a - Renew regulator

Type 4 Volkswagens are equipped with an alternator rather than a DC generator as used in other models. The alternator is an AC generator containing diodes, or rectifiers, which serve to limit current flow to one direction only.

With this charging system, certain cautions must be observed. Never run an alternator on an open circuit. Never short across alternator or alternator regulator terminals. Never try to polarize an alternator. Always maintain correct polarity when installing a battery, charging the battery or connecting booster cables. Also make sure that the ground strap between the body and transmission has tight connections.

OIL PRESSURE SWITCH

The oil pressure switch is installed in the oil pressure line between oil pump and oil cooler. With the engine stopped, a spring-loaded contact connected with a diaphragm, is closed, Fig. C-17. With the

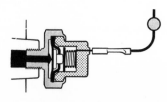

Fig. C-17. Diagram of oil pressure switch reveals makeup of assembly. Note diaphragm and contacts.

ignition switch on, the green oil pressure warning lamp in the speedometer dial lights up. The warning lamp on later "Beetle" models is red. Fastback and squareback models have a green-yellow lamp in the fuel gauge. Two oil pressure relief valves are used in "1600" engines, Fig. C-18, in 1970.

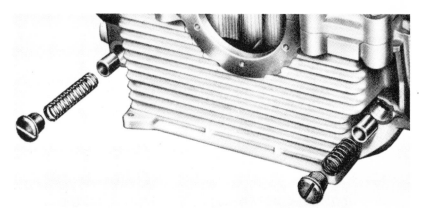

Fig. C-18. Late model VW cars with "1600" engine have larger oil passages, two oil pressure relief valves and oil pump housing was altered.

With engine operating, oil pressure actuates diaphragm, contact opens and control lamp goes out.

NOTE: If lamp lights up continuously when engine is running, oil circulation has been interrupted and lubrication of engine has ceased.

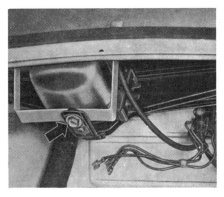

Fig. C-19. Windshield wiper motor is located at fire wall under front hood.

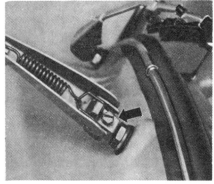

Fig. C-19A. To remove wiper arms, back off clamping screw on bracket.

Occasional lighting of the lamp with the engine warm and at low speed does not indicate trouble if it goes out again as the speed increases.

At low outside temperatures, the lamp lights up at idling speed, but at high outside temperatures, the lamp may light up at low speed in various gears, or when changing gears, if the engine oil has a very low viscosity. Check adjustment of the oil pressure switch before suspecting any other part.

WINDSHIELD WIPER

A one-speed wiper motor is used on all "Beetle" models through 1966. Fastback and Squareback models used a variable speed wiper in 1966. In 1967, with the introduction of the 12-volt electrical system, a two-speed wiper motor is used.

The windshield wiper motor is accessible after the hood is raised, Fig. C-19. All moving joints of the wiper gearing and linkage should be oiled at regular intervals, Fig. C-20. In case of improper action, refer to trouble shooting chart and Fig. C-21.

WINDSHIELD WIPER MOTOR TROUBLE SHOOTING

Complaint	Cause	Correction
Windshield wiper motor operates too slowly, cuts out or comes to a standstill	a - Brushes (1) worn b - Brush tension spring (2) too weak	a - Replace brushes b - Replace tension spring
	c - Brush levers (3) not free on their pivots	c - Free brush levers by working them backward or forward by hand and by applying a trace of thin machine oil
	d - Commutator (4) dirty	d - Clean commutator
	e - Moving joints of windshield wiper linkages devoid of grease	e - Thoroughly lubricate all moving joints with grease
Windshield wiper motor continues to run after manual switch is turned off	a - Brake band (5) effect not sufficient	a - Increase servo effect of brake band by lightly greasing brake band contact surface of armature
	b - Brake band broken	b - Replace brake band. Gap of ground contact points (a) .031 in.

Simplified Electrical Service

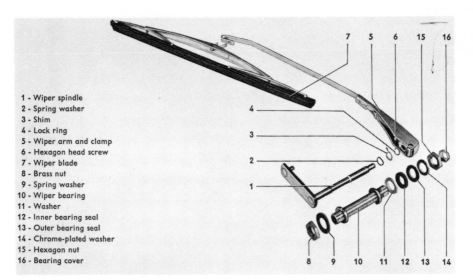

1 - Wiper spindle
2 - Spring washer
3 - Shim
4 - Lock ring
5 - Wiper arm and clamp
6 - Hexagon head screw
7 - Wiper blade
8 - Brass nut
9 - Spring washer
10 - Wiper bearing
11 - Washer
12 - Inner bearing seal
13 - Outer bearing seal
14 - Chrome-plated washer
15 - Hexagon nut
16 - Bearing cover

Fig. C-20. Details of windshield wiper spindle, arm and blade are shown in exploded view of Fastback and Squareback setup.

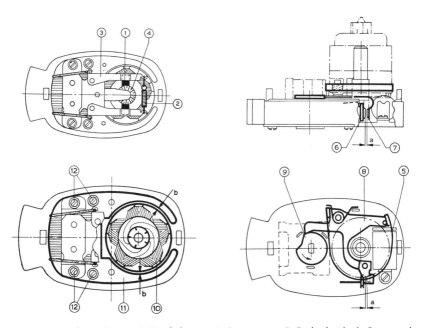

Fig. C-21. 1—Brush. 2—Spring. 3—Brush levers. 4—Commutator. 5—Brake band. 6—Contact plate 7—Contact spring. 8—Cam lever. 9—Cam. 10—Armature. 11—Pole shoe. 12—Four fixing screws.

a = 0.8 mm. (.031)
b = Free movement

Fix Your Volkswagen

Complaint	Cause	Correction
Windshield wiper motor does not return blades to parking position but stops at whatever point manual switch is turned off	a - Excessive gap of ground contact points (6 and 7) b - Cam (9) incorrectly reinstalled c - Windshield wiper motor for right-hand drive car installed in left-hand drive car	a - Check and adjust gap (a) to .031 in. b - Correctly install cam c - Install correct windshield wiper motor
Gabbling noise when switching on motor and in some cases delayed operation of motor	a - Gap of ground contact points (6 and 7) too small	a - Increase gap by bending ground contact to approx. .031 in.
Squeaking noise of windshield wiper motor and in some cases connected with slow operation or burned armature	a - Moving joints of windshield wiper linkages devoid of grease b - Armature (10) fouls pole shoe (11)	a - Thoroughly grease all moving joints b - Check armature for free movement. If necessary, loosen four fixing screws (12) and bend pole shoe (b) into proper position
Windshield wiper motor inoperative	a - Pole shoe (11) disarranged by blow on motor cap so that it makes contact with armature (10) b - Armature burned by short circuits, caused by disarranged pole shoe or overload due to brake band not clearing armature	a - Check armature for free movement (b). If necessary loosen four fixing screws (12) and bend pole shoe into proper position b - Replace motor

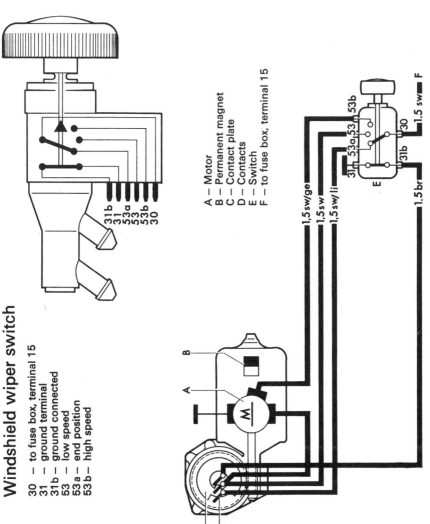

Windshield wiper switch

30 — to fuse box, terminal 15
31 — ground terminal
31b — ground connected
53 — low speed
53 a — end position
53 b— high speed

31b
31
53a
53
53b
30

A — Motor
B — Permanent magnet
C — Contact plate
D — Contacts
E — Switch
F — to fuse box, terminal 15

53b
53a,53
31
31b
30
E
1,5 sw ▬ F
1,5 br
1,5 sw/li
1,5 sw
1,5 sw/ge

Fig. C-21A. Windshield wiper switch wiring and typical wiring from switch to motor are shown.

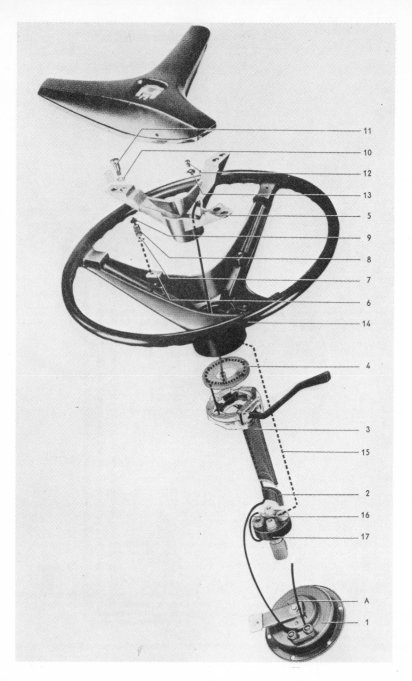

Fig. C-21B. Exploded view shows Type 4 horn controls and circuit: 1—Horn. 2—Socket. 3—Turn signal switch with contact. 4—Contact ring. 5—Horn lever. 6—Contact disc. 7—Spring washer. 8—Spring. 9—Insulating bushing. 10—Insulated disc. 11—Shoulder screw. 12—Cheese head screw. 13—Clamp. 14—Steering wheel. 15—Steering column. 16—Ground cable. 17—Steering coupling disc. A—To terminal 15.

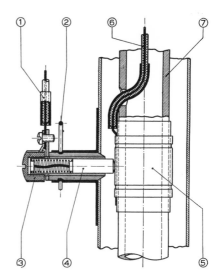

Fig. C-22. 1—Cable to horn. 2—Spring clip. 3—Tapped cap. 4—Brush and spring. 5—Contact ring. 6—Cable to horn button. 7—Steering column.

ELECTRICAL HORN

On older models electrical current for the horn is drawn through a brush in the steering column tube and a sliding contact ring on the steering column, Fig. C-22. The horn may fail to operate if the contact ring is worn or dirty. To clean the ring, remove the spring clip and pull out the brush holder. Place a narrow strip of fine emery cloth on a wooden stick and insert it in the opening. Turn the steering wheel back and forth while putting light pressure on the stick and emery cloth.

Later models utilize a ground wire which passes through the hollow steering column and connects to the steering gear by means of a terminal on a coupling disc, Fig. C-23. Trouble here may be due to poor connection at the coupling disc or at the contact ring in the steering wheel hub.

Fig. C-23. Ground wire for horn on late model cars connects to steering gear at coupling disc.

Fig. C-24. *Loosen front rim retaining screw and pull out complete headlight unit.*

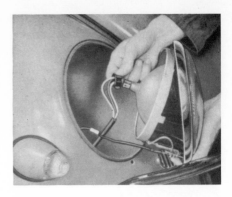

Fig. C-25. *Pull connector off sealed beam unit.*

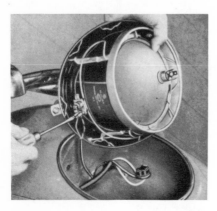

Fig. C-26. *Disconnect two wires from parking light bulb and screw off parking light socket.*

Fig. C-27. *Remove five spring clips from retaining ring.*

On all models, make sure that the fuse is good and that the horn does not touch the body of the car. Do not attempt to turn the adjusting screw on the horn. Check for defects in the wire from fuse box to horn.

SEALED BEAM HEADLAMPS

Replacement of a sealed beam unit in older models is shown in Figs. C-24 to C-27. Installation in later models is illustrated in Fig. C-28. A blue lamp in the instrument panel lights up when the high beam is in use. This bulb is accessible by raising the hood and turning down the protective cover in front of the instrument panel.

Because of the construction of the sealed beam headlight it is impossible to install the lamp incorrectly. Furthermore, these lights do not require focusing and the only adjustment required is to aim them correctly so that the light is directed along the road and will not blind the oncoming drivers.

TAILLIGHT AND STOPLIGHT

The taillight and stoplight are combined in a single housing. Later "Beetle" models also include the turn signal and back-up light bulbs, Fig. C-30. The stoplight switch is located in the brake master cylinder, Fig. C-29. Two switches are used in conjunction with the dual braking system on later models.

Separate dual back-up lights are featured on Fastback and Squareback models through 1969, part of stop/tail assembly in 1970.

TURN SIGNAL INDICATORS

The front direction indicator lamps are incorporated in the parking lamp assembly. At the rear, the taillight, stoplight and direction indicator lights are combined into one unit. The direction indicator switch is connected to the flasher unit which opens and closes the circuits to the front and rear direction indicator lights, and to the pilot light on the

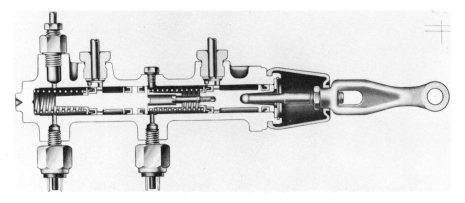

Fig. C-29. Dual braking system introduced on 1967 Volkswagen utilizes tandem type master cylinder with two stoplight switches. Later models incorporate a brake system warning device on dash.

Fix Your Volkswagen

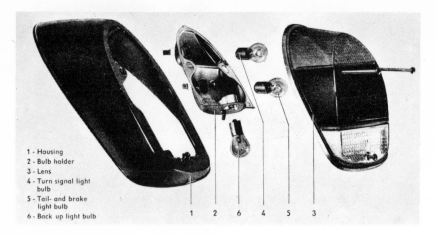

1 - Housing
2 - Bulb holder
3 - Lens
4 - Turn signal light bulb
5 - Tail- and brake light bulb
6 - Back up light bulb

Fig. C-30. Later "Beetle" models incorporate backup lights in taillights.

instrument panel. On 1966 and later models, an electronically operated device flashes both front and rear direction indicator lights as an emergency warning.

Access to front turn signal bulbs on later models is accomplished by removing one Phillips screw from the housing and lifting off housing and lens. Older models call for the following procedure:

1 - Pull rubber boot from bulb holder and disconnect cable.
2 - Loosen hex nut with a box wrench.
3 - Take off bezel and lens after removing two slotted screws.
4 - Replace bulb.
5 - Be sure rubber seal between bezel and fender is in perfect condition. Replace if necessary.
6 - When tightening nut, make sure bezel properly seats in channel provided in rubber seal.

DIRECTION INDICATOR REPLACEMENT

The direction indicator switch is mounted on the steering column below the steering wheel. The lever returns automatically to the neutral position when a turn is completed.

To avoid short circuits, disconnect ground cable from battery before carrying out the following operations:

REMOVAL

1 - Remove horn lever and contact pins.
2 - Loosen steering wheel nut and take off wheel.
3 - Remove instrument panel cover in front luggage compartment.

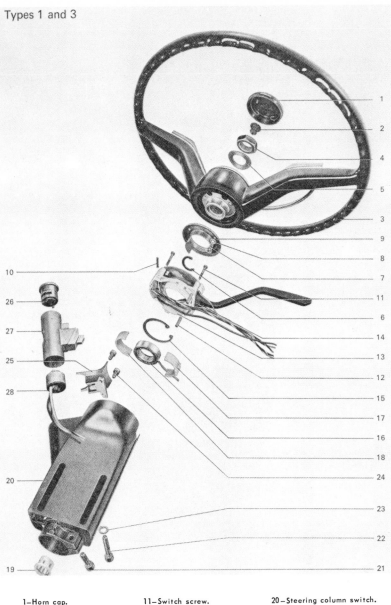

1–Horn cap.	11–Switch screw.	20–Steering column switch.
2–Rubber plug.	12–Spacer.	21–Clamping screw.
3–Steering wheel.	13–Turn signal switch.	22–Socket head cap screw.
4–Hex nut.	14–Contact for flasher.	23–Spring washer.
5–Spring washer.	15–Circlip.	24–Fillister screw.
6–Circlip.	16–Ball bearing.	25–Retainer.
7–Fillister screw.	17–Left insulating half ring.	26–Lock cylinder.
8–Toothed washer.	18–Right insulating half ring.	27–Steering lock.
9–Canceling ring.	19–Contact ring.	28–Ignition/starter switch.
10–Signal switch spring.		

Fig. C-30A. Exploded view shows details of steering column switch and turn signal.

Type 3 from August 1969

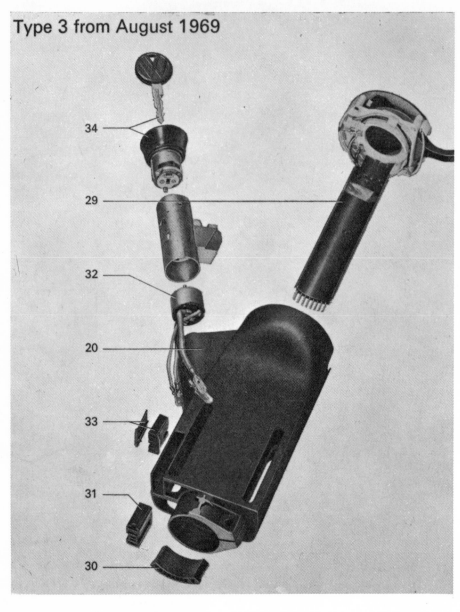

20—Steering column switch.
29—Turn signal switch.
30—Switch plug.
31—Starter switch plug.

32—Starter switch.
33—Cable guide.
34—Lock cylinder and key.

Fig. C-30B. Exploded view shows details of steering column switch and turn signal.

4 - Disconnect cables from flasher relay, warning light and cable connectors.

5 - Pull cable with protective sleeve out of partition.

6 - Loosen switch securing screw and remove switch from column.

ASSEMBLY

To install the switch, reverse the removal procedure and observe the following points:

1 - Make sure cables are properly connected.

2 - Note proper position of cables and protection strip.

3 - See that brass washer is located correctly with recess to right when wheels are straight ahead, Fig. C-31.

Fig. C-31. Brass washer that locates in steering wheel hub must have recess to right for correct installation.

4 - Tighten steering wheel nut 35 to 42 ft. lbs.

5 - Check direction indicator for proper function and automatic cancelling.

6 - Distance between upper edge of direction indicator switch and lower edge of steering column hub must be at least 0.08 in. on older models, at least 0.04 in. on 1960 and later models, Fig. C-32.

7 - If lever does not return to neutral position when turn is completed, correct position of switch by turning it slightly on steering column.

SPEEDOMETER AND DRIVE CABLE

Speedometer and mileage recorder are driven by a cable from the left-hand front wheel, Fig. C-33. The speedometer is of the eddy-current type operating on electromagnetic principles. The magnetic eddy-currents produced by induction when the armature revolves, cause the cup to rotate together with the speedometer hand shaft which is firmly attached to it. The speedometer unit also incorporates a mileage recorder.

The speedometer cable consists of several strands of wire and is protected by a flexible metal housing. Should a speedometer cable become defective, a new cable may be inserted in the old metal housing, if the housing has no sharp bends or fractures.

Fig. C-32. Clearance at steering wheel hub must be at least .04 in. on early Fastback and Squareback models.

REMOVING AND INSTALLING SPEEDOMETER CABLE

REMOVAL
1 - Loosen knurled nut at speedometer.
2 - Remove outer hub cap from left-hand front wheel.
3 - Remove cotter pin in square end of speedometer cable at hub cap.
4 - Pull cable out of steering knuckle.
5 - Pull cable out of its flexible metal housing.

INSTALLATION
This is a reversal of preceding operations, but the following points should be noted:
1 - Lubricate cable with special grease.
2 - Do not sharply bend or tear cable.
3 - Upper end of fixed conduit tube should be in line with connecting piece projecting from speedometer housing.
4 - Upper square end must correctly fit into square hole in connecting piece.
5 - Install new rubber sleeve in steering knuckle.
6 - Use new cotter pin for securing square end to hub cap.

Simplified Electrical Service

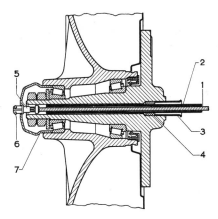

Fig. C-33. Drive assembly for speedometer includes: 1—Speedometer cable. 2—Metal hose. 3—Metal sleeve. 4—Rubber sleeve. 5—Square drive piece. 6—Cotter pin. 7—Hub cap with square hole.

IMPORTANT
Special care should be taken when laying the speedometer cable.

During operation, the cable must not be noisy. The bends of the cable should not be below a radius of 6 in. With the front wheels in the straight ahead position, the speedometer cable must run in a smooth curve and it should not kink or pull in any wheel position. Pressure on the flexible metal housing results in a run-out of the cable which is indicated by an unsteady speedometer hand. If there is a sharp bend, the free movement of the cable is restricted and the cable will break at this point after a short time of operation.

Make sure the rubber sleeve is properly seated in the steering knuckle. The function of this sleeve is to seal the unit against splash water, which may lead to bearing trouble and freezing of the cable in winter, Fig. C-33(4).

Only cold-resistant and water-repellent grease should be used as a cable lubricant.

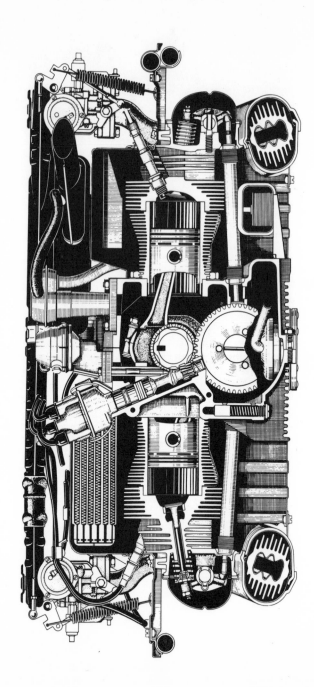

Sectional view of 1967 Fastback-Squareback engine with twin carburetors gives clear picture of oil cooler, oil pressure relief valve and crankcase breather.

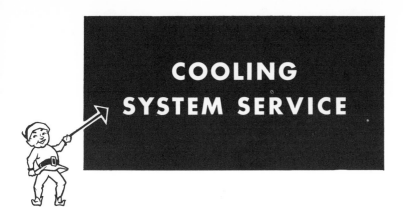

COOLING SYSTEM SERVICE

The cooling system used on the Volkswagen engine is one of the best examples of highly developed air cooling. Very little in the way of maintenance is required and provision has been made to accomplish the service quickly and easily. Important parts of the "Beetle" engine cooling system are shown in Fig. D-1.

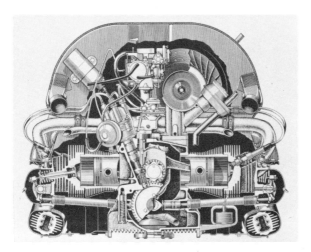

Fig. D-1. Cutaway end view of 1971 Beetle engine shows typical arrangement of air cooling components.

Air cooling is done by a fan on the extended generator shaft driven by a V-belt from the crankshaft at twice engine rpm, Fig. D-2. This fan draws air through an opening in the fan housing and forces it through fins of the cylinders and cylinder heads. Air flow is directed by deflector plates and is controlled by a thermostat connected to four flaps in the fan housing at the point where cooling air enters. Adjustment is made by

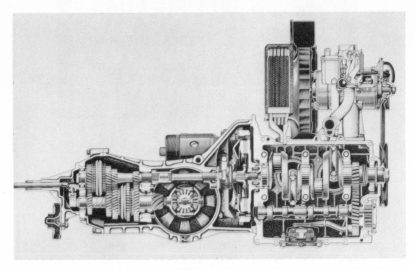

Fig. D-2. Sectional side view of 1971 Beetle engine illustrates how cooling fan attaches to generator shaft.

Fig. D-3. Adjust cooling air control flaps on late model "Beetle" engines by moving thermostat bracket up or down on lower air duct.

Fig. D-4. Thermostat adjustment on Fastback and Squareback engines calls for 1/16 in. preload at "b."

moving the thermostat bracket up or down, Fig. D-3. With the flaps in the open position on "Beetle" engines, move the thermostat bracket until the thermostat just touches the upper part of the bracket. Tighten the bracket screw, recheck the operation of the flaps, then tighten the thermostat securing screw. On Fastback and Squareback engines, Fig. D-4, valve must contact housing at "A," have preload of 1/16 in. at "b."

FAN RING ADJUSTMENT TIPS

On older models, the cooling fan draws air through an opening in the center of the fan housing fitted with a thermostatically controlled ring, Fig. D-5. The quantity of air flow is controlled by the amount the fan ring opens. It is obvious that proper adjustment of this throttle ring is

Fig. D-5. Thermostat adjustment on older "Beetle" models must result in approximately 1 in. opening at fan ring at normal operating temperature.

of utmost importance. If the ring opens too soon or stays open, the engine will be slow to warm up. If the ring opens too slowly the engine is likely to overheat. If the ring opens too far, it may foul the fan.

Factory instructions for adjustment are as follows:

1 - Release throttle ring operating lever.
2 - Allow engine to warm up until upper end of thermostat touches upper stop of support (at normal outside temperature).
3 - Adjust throttle ring so that it opens 1 in., Fig. D-5.
4 - Tighten operating lever.

Make sure that throttle ring and linkage move freely in each position.

EASY WAY TO ADJUST FAN

Because of the fact that engine cooling is entirely dependent upon the fan, it is essential to make sure that belt and pulleys are in good condition and fan belt tension is correct at all times. Frayed, cracked or oily belts must be renewed. The tension is correct when light thumb pressure, Fig. D-6, will deflect the belt about .6 in.

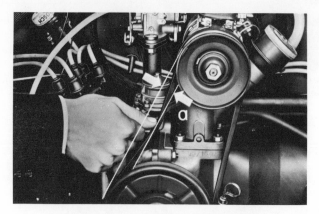

Fig. D-6. Method of checking fan belt tension.

Fig. D-7. Adjustment of fan belt tension is by means of fewer or more washers between pulley halves.

Fig. D-8. Fastback and Squareback engines require fan belt adjustment by fitting spacer washers between pulley halves. Note location of fan.

Cooling System Service

The tension of the fan belt is adjusted by fitting more or less spacer washers between the two pulley halves, Figs. D-7 and D-8. Removal of washers increases the diameter of the driven pulley. When all washers are removed, the belt must be replaced, Fig. D-9.

Fig. D-9. To adjust belt tension on Type 4 engine, remove insert from cover plate, loosen bolt and socket head cap screw, move alternator, tighten bolts.

To adjust, proceed as follows:

1 - Remove nut from generator shaft pulley: insert screwdriver in slot cut into inner half of pulley and support it against upper generator housing bolt.
2 - Remove outer pulley half, Fig. D-10.
3 - Arrange spacer washers as required.
4 - Install outer pulley half.
5 - Place surplus washers between outer pulley half and pulley nut.

NOTE: After chassis No. 1-0575415 on "Beetle" models, a finer adjustment is made possible by the use of 6 washers .06 in. thick and 8 washers .02 in. thick.

Fig. D-10. Inner pulley has slot to aid in removing and replacing fan pulley nut.

Fix Your Volkswagen

After chassis No. 1-0929746 the generator-blower unit is balanced dynamically and the inner half of the pulley is welded to the hub. The outer pulley half is held in place by lugs of different widths, allowing reinstallation in its original position only.

CAUTION: Do not attempt to remove or replace belt by stretching it over pulley flanges.

Fig. D-11. Spark plugs on all VW engines must be "sealed" in place as illustrated. A poor fit here will cause cooling system malfunctions.

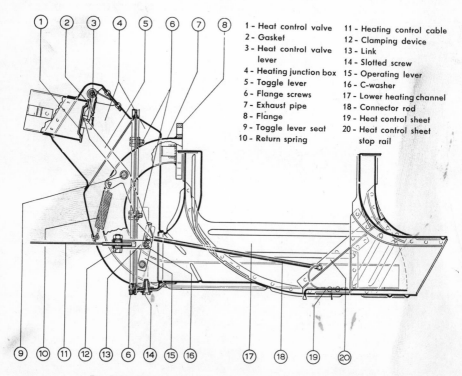

1 - Heat control valve
2 - Gasket
3 - Heat control valve lever
4 - Heating junction box
5 - Toggle lever
6 - Flange screws
7 - Exhaust pipe
8 - Flange
9 - Toggle lever seat
10 - Return spring
11 - Heating control cable
12 - Clamping device
13 - Link
14 - Slotted screw
15 - Operating lever
16 - C-washer
17 - Lower heating channel
18 - Connector rod
19 - Heat control sheet
20 - Heat control sheet stop rail

Fig. D-12. Typical "Beetle" engine heating junction box assembly.

Cooling System Service

COOLING SYSTEM INSPECTION

A thorough inspection of the cooling system should be made when cold or warm seasons begin. The enclosed cooling system cannot operate correctly if there are any air leaks. All panels of the outer housing should fit together closely and any bent or damaged sheet metal must be repaired, straightened or replaced.

Leakage is often found at the spark plugs where a rubber cap is used to seal the terminal caps, Fig. D-11. These should seal tightly and be replaced if defective.

It should be kept in mind that a premature opening or a permanent "open" position of the throttle ring, or flaps, are responsible for a slow "warm-up" of the engine. These conditions are likely to cause "popping" and "spitting" at the carburetor. If the throttle ring opens too far, it may contact the fan and result in noisy operation. A retarded opening of the ring, or flaps, in the warm season may cause overheating.

If the throttle ring, or flaps, remain open when the engine is cold, the thermostat may be defective. To avoid possible damage to the engine, the ring, or flaps, open automatically when the cooling system is out of order.

COOLING SYSTEM TROUBLE SHOOTING

Cause	Correction
Overheating	
a. Fan belt loose	a. Adjust
b. Fan belt oil soaked	b. Replace fan belt
c. Thermostat sticks closed	c. Replace thermostat
d. Cooling system clogged	d. Remove any obstructions
e. Air leaks in housing	e. Check all seals
f. Retarded ring opening	f. Adjust throttle ring
g. Excessively dirty cooling fins	g. Clean cooling fins
h. Clogged muffler	h. Replace muffler
i. Slipping clutch	i. Repair clutch
j. Incorrect ignition timing	j. Retime engine
k. Brakes dragging	k. Adjust brakes
Overcooling	
a. Thermostat remains open	a. Replace thermostat

NOTE: When searching for the cause of engine overheating, it should be kept in mind that the trouble is seldom any one specific thing. It is usually a combination of several minor defects. For example, a slightly loose fan belt plus a leaking seal at a spark plug plus slightly late ignition timing will equal a major fault.

CAR HEATING SYSTEM

Hot air to heat the car interior is obtained from the engine. A control valve opens and closes flaps in the heating boxes on each side of the engine but the heat does not enter the body in any great quantity unless the car is in motion with the vent window or windows opened slightly to establish circulation.

These heating boxes are built around the exhaust pipes as shown in Fig. D-12. Any leak in the exhaust pipe or gaskets may allow exhaust fumes to enter the car with danger to the occupants so these points should be checked carefully. Unwanted heat passes out through flap valves at the rear of the car called heat control sheets.

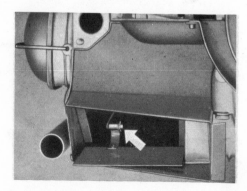

Fig. D-13. Heat control sheet connector rod attachment.

The heat control valves, heat control valve levers, toggle levers, links, operating levers, connector rods and control cables should have periodic lubrication at the pins and joints, D-12, in order to avoid sticking. Use a mixture of graphite and high melting point grease for this purpose.

If removal of either or both heating boxes becomes necessary, they are removed as a unit with the exhaust pipe. Detach the heating pipe and control cables, remove the screws from the exhaust flange. Take out the exhaust pipe clips and the screw on the bottom of the box. Remove the cotter pin from the connector rod, Fig. D-13, and the box and exhaust pipe will lift off.

Before replacement, make sure that the heat control valve closes fully and that the gasket is in good condition. Replace the complete valve if it is damaged in any way. Lubricate all pivot points. Make a final check for correct operation after the cables are reconnected.

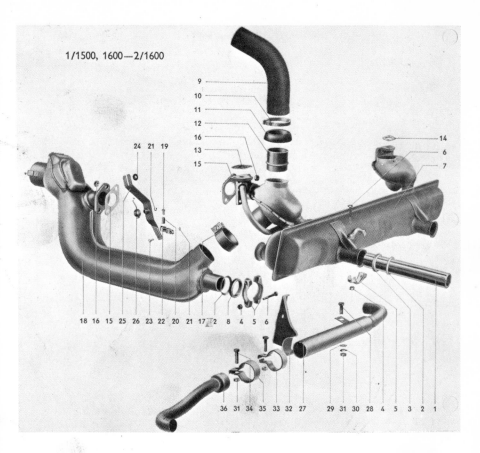

Fig. D-14. Exhaust system for Beetle models having 1500 or 1600 engine. 1—Tail pipe. 2—Retaining ring. 3—Seal. 4—Hex nut. 5—Clamp. 6—Hex bolt. 7—Muffler. 8—Seal. 9—Heater hose. 10—Hose clamp. 11—Grommet. 12—Connecting pipe. 13—Preheating pipe gasket (left). 14—Preheating pipe gasket (right). 15—Exhaust pipe flange gasket. 16—Hex nut. 17—Clamp. 18—Heat exchanger. 19—Hex bolt. 20—Pin. 21—C-washer. 22—Link. 23—Pin. 24—Clamp washer. 25—Heater flap lever. 26—Return spring. 27—Damper pipe. 28—Hex bolt. 29—Washer. 30—Lock washer. 31—Hex bolt. 32—Damper pipe bracket. 33—Clamp. 34—Hex bolt. 35—Clamp. 36—Tail pipe.

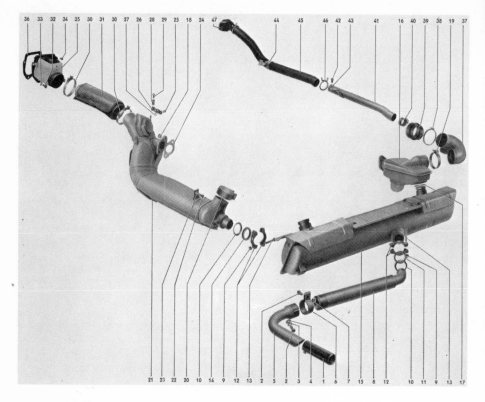

Fig. D-15. Exhaust system on Model 411, Type 4 Volkswagens incorporates: 1—Tail pipe. 2—Hex bolt. 3—Lock washer. 4—Washer. 5—Tail pipe. 6—Clamp. 7—Hex nut. 8—Damper pipe. 9—Hex nut, self-locking. 10—Retaining ring. 11—Seal. 12—Clamp. 13—Hex bolt. 14—Seal. 15—Muffler. 16—Heat exchanger, rear. 17—Seal. 18—Hex nut, self-locking. 19—Clamp for elbow. 20—Clamp for heat exchanger. 21—Heat exchanger. 22—Hex bolt. 23—Washer. 24—Flange gasket. 25—Pin for link. 26—Link. 27—C-washer. 28—Pin. 29—Hex bolt. 30—Clamp for metal hose. 31—Metal hose. 32—Hex bolt. 33—Lock washer. 34—Cheese head tapping screw. 35—Warm air mixer housing. 36—Seal. 37—Elbow. 38—Clamp. 39—Connecting hose. 40—Pipe clamp. 41—Pipe. 42—Cheese head screw. 43—Washer. 44—Hose support. 45—Fresh air hose. 46—Clamp. 47—Fresh air duct elbow.

SIMPLIFIED
VALVE CONDITIONING

Compared with conventional automobile practice, it seems strange to remove the engine to do a valve reconditioning job. Actually, however, the engine can be taken out of the Volkswagen in a few minutes.

The engine is not attached directly to the frame. It is attached to the transmission assembly by means of two studs and two bolts, Fig. E-1. The transmission is flexibly mounted on the frame. The engine, complete with clutch, slides backward and downward after being disconnected and is removed from under the rear of the car.

Fig. E-1. Key step in engine removal is unbolting of engine from transmission which, in turn, is mounted on frame.

TIPS ON ENGINE REMOVAL

There are several ways to remove the engine but the favorite way is for two men to work together with the aid of suitable jacks, Fig. E-2, and a hoist.

The procedure is: Disconnect the battery, generator wires, coil primary wire, oil pressure light wire, carburetor throttle and choke cables, heating control cables and pipes. Close fuel valve, disconnect fuel line, air cleaner and rear cover plate.

Fix Your Volkswagen

Place wheel type jack to support engine solidly. Raise rear end of car high enough to permit engine to be removed from underneath. Remove two bolts and two nuts from studs in crankcase. Roll engine back until transmission shaft is clear then lower and tilt so that it will come out under the rear of the car. In doing this be careful that the engine does not get out of alignment too soon as this might bend the transmission shaft or clutch.

Fig. E-2. With rear end of car raised about three feet by hoist or lift, engine is lowered carefully and tipped slightly to rear after transmission shaft is clear.

HINTS ON DISASSEMBLY

With the engine out of the car, swing the bail to one side and remove the valve cover on each cylinder head. This will permit access to the valve rocker arm shaft which is held in place by two nuts, Fig. E-3. Remove as a unit.

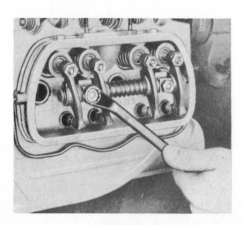

Fig. E-3. Rocker arm shaft assembly is held in place by two nuts.

Simplified Valve Conditioning

Fig. E-4. Cylinders should be held in place on crankcase when head is lifted off.

Next remove the cylinder head retaining nuts, screw off thermostat and remove the link rod. Lift off the cylinder heads while holding the cylinders in place in the crankcase, Fig. E-4. There is no gasket between the cylinder head and end of the cylinder, except for spacers which might be used on reconditioned cylinder heads. There is a sealing ring between the cylinder head and a shoulder on the cylinder, Fig. E-5.

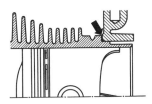

Fig. E-5. A sealing ring is used between cylinder head and a shoulder on cylinder.

With the cylinder heads off, depress the valve springs and remove the valve key or "cotter," Fig. E-6. Slide the valves out of the guides.

If valve seat and valve refacing euipment is not available, many shops take the cylinder heads to an automotive machine shop for the necessary reconditioning. After the machine shop has reconditioned the valves and reassembled them in the cylinder head, it is only necessary to place the assembly on the cylinders. Only conventional tools are required.

VALVE INSPECTION

After the valves are removed, clean and carefully inspect them for defects. Cleaning can be accomplished by using chemical cleaners or by holding the valve against a rotating wire brush. Valves with bent stems or with stems which are worn more than the wear limit specified should be replaced with new ones.

Exhaust stem diameter on older "Beetle" engines is .2738 - .2734 in. (new), replace if worn to .2724 in. Inlet stem diameter is .2742 - .2738 in. (new), replace if worn to .2724 in. On later engines, and on Fastback and Squareback engines, exhaust stem diameter is .3118 - .3114 in. (new), replace if worn to .3098 in. Inlet stem diameter is .3130 - .3126 in. (new), replace if worn to .3110 in.

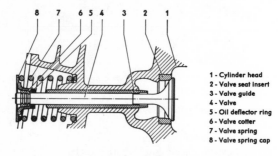

1 - Cylinder head
2 - Valve seat insert
3 - Valve guide
4 - Valve
5 - Oil deflector ring
6 - Valve cotter
7 - Valve spring
8 - Valve spring cap

Fig. E-6. Parts of individual valve assembly are called out. Spring must be depressed and "cotter" removed to free valve from spring.

Check the valve stems for wear with a micrometer to be sure the measurement is absolutely correct. Worn valve stems and guides will result in poorly seating valves which, in turn, will result in early failure. In addition, excessive clearance between the intake valve stem and its guide will permit air to be drawn into the combustion chamber and in that way the combustible mixture will be seriously diluted with loss in power and impossibility of correct carburetor adjustment.

Fig. E-7. Valve refacing machine is used to grind valves to specific angle and to a smooth finish.

If the valve stems are in good condition, the next step is to reface the valves on a valve refacer, Fig. E-7. If after refacing, the edge of the valve head is less than .043 in., Fig. E-8, the valve should be replaced. Valves with a narrow margin will operate at excessive temperatures and soon burn.

CLEANING CYLINDER HEAD

The next step is to clean the cylinder head. One advantage of having the complete assembly overhauled in an automotive machine shop is that the entire cylinder head is immersed in a cleaning solution which removes carbon from the combustion chamber and also cleans the cooling fins.

If machining is not required, an electric drill with a wire brush can be used for cleaning the combustion chamber. Then wash the entire cylinder head in solvent.

Particular attention should also be paid to the condition and cleanliness of the valve guides in the cylinder head. All accumulations of carbon and gum in the valve guides should be removed to prevent sticking valves after the job is reassembled. Special attachments for use with electric drills are available for cleaning the guides.

Fig. E-8. Valve margin or edge should not be less than .043 in. in width.

In addition to cleaning the cylinder head, clean carbon from the tops of the pistons and cylinder block. Particularly important are the mating surfaces of the cylinder and cylinder head. If all dirt, carbon and other accumulations are not removed from these surfaces, compression leaks will result after the engine is reassembled. This will result in loss of power and reduced economy of operation.

CUTTING NEW VALVE SEATS

The next step in the valve reconditioning program is to cut new valve seats in the cylinder head. Special valve seat grinders with the necessary pilots are available for doing this work accurately and quickly. Grinding equipment is necessary because the inserted valve seats are quite hard. If such equipment is not available, the cylinder head should be taken to a machine shop where the work can be done.

Before cutting new valve seats, the valve guides should be checked for wear with special gauges. If there is found to be more than .006 in.

clearance between the valve stem and its guide, it will be necessary to install new or reconditioned heads. The valve guides are shrunk into position by means of liquid air chilling, and any attempt to push or drill the worn guides will probably result in a ruined cylinder head.

It is important that the valve seats are cut to the proper width. If the valve seats are too narrow, excessive valve temperatures will result, and valve life will be materially reduced. Valve seats that are too wide will permit an accumulation of carbon and the seats will soon become pitted and reconditioning will again be required. The Volkswagen factory recommends that the intake valve seats should be narrowed to a width of .051 in. to .063 in. and the exhaust valve seat widths should range from .067 in. to .079 in, Fig. E-9. The correct width of the valve seat is secured by means of a grinder which will machine the valve port and then the top of the valve seat.

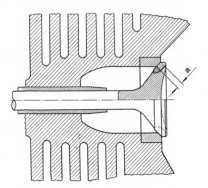

Fig. E-9. Point of measurement for valve seat width.

Damaged valve seat inserts can be reconditioned with suitable equipment as long as the specified width of the seat face is maintained, and the outer edge of the 15 deg. chamfer does not exceed the outer diameter of the valve seat insert. This procedure is illustrated in Figs. E-10, E-11 and E-12. All valve seats in Volkswagen's engines are ground to a 45 deg. angle, except intake seats on Type 2 and Type 4 "1700" engines (30 deg.).

This is a precision operation and the cutter must be firmly piloted in the guide which must be in good condition so that the cut will be concentric with the guide.

VALVE SPRING CHECK

After the valves and valve seats have been reconditioned, but before they are reinstalled in the heads, the valve springs should be checked.

The springs should all be approximately the same length when not compressed. They should be straight when checked as shown in Fig. E-13.

Simplified Valve Conditioning

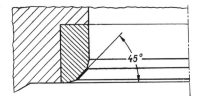

Fig. E-10. The 45 deg. angle is cut first.

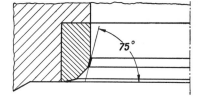

Fig. E-11. The second cut is the 75 deg. angle.

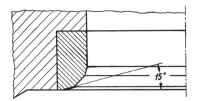

Fig. E-12. The 15 deg. cut is the final step.

If the springs are not square, an unwanted side thrust will be exerted on the valve stem and guides.

All springs should be measured for strength as shown in Fig. E-14. When compressed to a length of 1.10 in., valve springs from older "Beetle" engines should have a strength of 73.6 lbs. If below 66 lbs., they should be discarded. On later engines, springs compressed to 1.32 in. should have a strength of 96.7 lbs. Replace springs below 90 lbs. On "Beetle" engines after 1966, and on Fastback and Squareback engines, springs compressed to 1.22 in. should have a strength of 128 lbs.

VALVE ROCKER ARM INSPECTION

Rocker arms and shafts must also be serviced. All sludge and gum must be removed or normal flow of oil to the rocker arms and valves will be restricted.

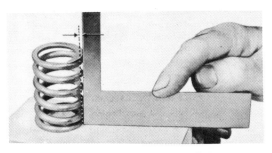
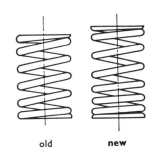

old   new

Fig. E-13. Left. Method of checking valve springs for squareness. Right. On later engines, close-ly coiled end of springs should be installed toward cylinder head.

To disassemble: First remove the hairpin locks, springs and rocker arms, Fig. E-15. Then clean all the sludge or gum formation from the inside and outside of the shafts. Also clean all oil holes and passages in the shafts and rocker arms.

After cleaning the separate parts, inspect the shafts for wear and check the fit of the rocker arms on the shafts. Check the adjusting screws for excessive wear. Replace all worn parts. If the valve contact surfaces of the rocker arms are worn, the machine shop can "touch them up" when the valves are refaced.

Fig. E-14. Valve spring pressure tester permits test of spring strength at a given compressed height.

Fig. E-15. Exploded view of rocker assembly shows correct sequence of rocker arms, spring washers, spacer blocks and hairpin clips.

CYLINDER HEAD INSTALLATION

Before installing cylinder heads, install new sealing rings between heads and cylinder flanges, Fig. E-5. Also make sure that the oil seals at the ends of the push rod tube are properly seated, Fig. E-16. The press seam of the oil seal must not bear on the seating surface.

Make sure that threads on cylinder head retaining studs and nuts are clean and coated lightly with graphite grease and then tighten down

Simplified Valve Conditioning

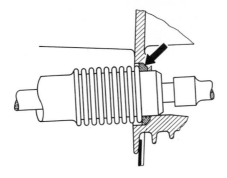

Fig. E-16. Proper placement of push rod tube seals.

lightly with a torque wrench to 7 ft. lbs. in the order shown in Fig. E-17. On older "Beetle" engines, retighten them to 26-27 ft. lbs. On later engines, and on Fastback and Squareback engines, retighten them to 22-23 ft. lbs. Follow the tightening sequence shown in Fig. E-18.

The next step is to reassemble the rocker arm units. Before reinstallation, loosen the valve adjusting screws.

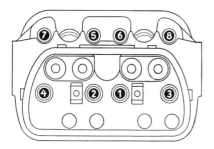

Fig. E-17. Sequence of preliminary cylinder head stud tightening.

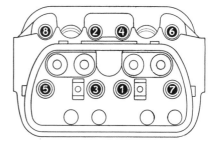

Fig. E-18. Sequence of final tightening of cylinder head.

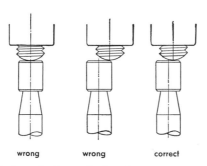

wrong   wrong   correct

Fig. E-19. Desired relation of valve adjusting screw to valve stem.

Before tightening the rocker arm shafts in place, the relation of the adjusting screws with the valve stem ends should be checked and adjusted if necessary. To make the valves rotate during operation, the rocker arm adjusting screws should contact the valve stem slightly off center, Fig. E-19.

Adjustment of this desired relation can be obtained by moving the rocker arm shaft in its clearance holes before it is tightened down. If necessary, further adjustment may be obtained by varying the length of the spacers or the thickness of the washers on each side of the rocker arms. Then tighten the rocker assembly mounting nuts and adjust the valves as described in the Chapter on Tune-Up.

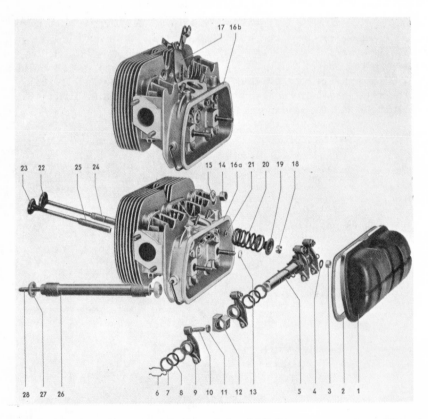

Fig E-20. Cylinder head assemblies for Types 1, 2 and 3 Volkswagen engines basically are the same: 1—Cylinder head cover. 2—Cover gasket. 3—Hex nut. 4—Spring washer. 5—Rocker shaft. 6—Clip. 7—Thrust washer. 8—Spring washer. 9—Rocker arm. 10—Adjusting screw. 11—Hex nut. 12—Support. 13—Seal for stud. 14—Nut. 15—Washer. 16a—Cylinder head. 16b—Cylinder head for Type 3, 1600 engine only. 17—Thermostat link. 18—Valve cotter. 19—Spring cap. 20—Valve spring. 21—Oil deflector ring. 22—Inlet valve. 23—Exhaust valve. 24—Inlet valve guide. 25—Exhaust valve guide. 26—Push rod tube. 27—Sealing ring. 28—Push rod.

QUICK SERVICE ON BRAKES

Hydraulic foot brakes and cable-operated hand brake are used on all export models of Volkswagen, Figs. F-1 and F-2.

The system on "Beetle" models consists of: A fluid reservoir for containing the supply of hydraulic fluid; a master cylinder in which the pressure on the fluid is generated by means of pedal pressure; a series of pipes and tubes for conducting the fluid under pressure from the master

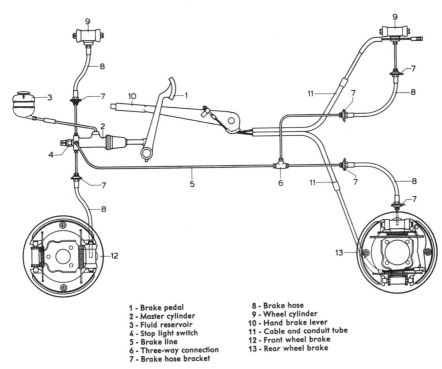

1 - Brake pedal
2 - Master cylinder
3 - Fluid reservoir
4 - Stop light switch
5 - Brake line
6 - Three-way connection
7 - Brake hose bracket
8 - Brake hose
9 - Wheel cylinder
10 - Hand brake lever
11 - Cable and conduit tube
12 - Front wheel brake
13 - Rear wheel brake

Fig. F-1. Diagram of models with direct cable operation of hand brake.

cylinder to the wheel cylinders; four wheel cylinders, each having two pistons, for forcing the brake shoes against the wheel drums to create friction to stop the vehicle; one brake drum attached to each wheel.

When the brake pedal is depressed, the piston is forced into the master cylinder, generating high pressure by means of the leverage built into the pedal linkage. This pressure is transmitted with equal and undiminished force to each of the wheel cylinders, forcing the two pistons in each wheel cylinder outward and expanding the brake shoes against the inside of the drums.

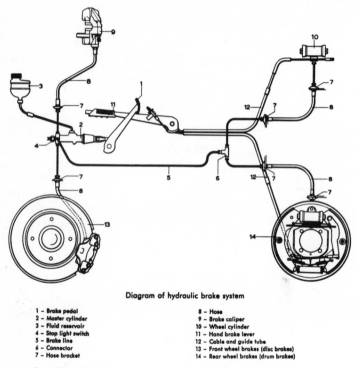

Diagram of hydraulic brake system

1 – Brake pedal	8 – Hose
2 – Master cylinder	9 – Brake caliper
3 – Fluid reservoir	10 – Wheel cylinder
4 – Stop light switch	11 – Hand brake lever
5 – Brake line	12 – Cable and guide tube
6 – Connector	13 – Front wheel brakes (disc brakes)
7 – Hose bracket	14 – Rear wheel brakes (drum brakes)

Fig. F-2. Diagram of brake system on Fastback and Squareback models. Note front wheel disc brakes.

When the brake pedal is released, master cylinder piston, wheel cylinder pistons and brake shoes return to their released positions by means of their respective return springs. This action also pushes the fluid back into the master cylinder.

On 1967 models, and later, a dual circuit system is used, featuring a tandem master cylinder. This assures that even if the front or rear half of the system becomes inoperative, the other half still functions. Disc brakes are standard on the front wheels of Fastback and Squareback models.

Brake Service

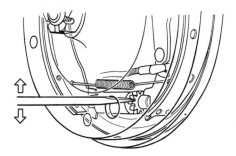

Fig. F-3. Method of using screwdriver through opening in wheel to adjust brake shoes.

ADJUSTMENT FOR WEAR

Normal wear of the brake linings on drum brakes will result in a need for periodic adjustment of the brake shoes. This need will be indicated when full application of the brakes brings the pedal within two inches of the floor board. Front wheel disc brakes do not require an adjustment.

If the brakes are operating satisfactorily, and it is known that the lining is not worn thin, adjustment of the shoes will compensate for lining wear. The procedure is as follows:

1 - Raise car and release hand brake.
2 - Check wheel bearings for looseness.
3 - Depress brake pedal several times in order to centralize shoes within drums.
4 - Remove hub cap.
5 - Turn wheel to be adjusted until hole in brake drum is in line with one of the adjusting nuts.
6 - Insert a screwdriver through hole and turn adjusting nut, using a screwdriver as a lever, until a light drag is felt when wheel is turned, Fig. F-3.
7 - Back off adjusting nut 3 or 4 teeth until wheel turns freely.
8 - Repeat procedure on other adjusting nut.

There are two adjusting nuts on each brake and both have normal right-hand threads. Since these nuts are opposite one another, it is necessary to turn them in opposite directions.

9 - Repeat procedure on other wheels.

ADJUSTING HAND BRAKE

Operations A and B apply to models with push bar. Later models have adjustment on hand brake lever, Fig. F-4.

A - Raise car.
B - Remove frame head cover.

123

Fig. F-4. Adjusting screws for hand brake cables are accessible through slots in boot on lever.

C - Loosen lock nuts on ends of each cable and tighten adjusting nuts to a degree which will still allow rear wheels to turn freely when hand brake is released.

D - Pull up hand brake lever two notches and make sure braking effect is equal on both rear wheels. At fourth notch it should be impossible to turn wheels by hand.

E - Tighten lock nuts securely.

SERVICING HYDRAULIC BRAKE SYSTEM

Safety and good operation of the brakes is dependent largely on the condition of the hydraulic system. Leakage, dirt, old fluid or fluid that does not meet the Society of Automotive Engineers' specifications will cause faulty operation and safety will be sacrificed. A high boiling point fluid is especially necessary on disc brake applications. Whenever the brake has a spongy feel or when steady pressure on the pedal causes the pedal to go closer to the floor board or if improved braking is secured by "pumping" the pedal, the hydraulic brake system needs attention.

The various troubles and their corresponding causes are listed under Brake Trouble Shooting at the end of this section. However, considerable trouble can be avoided by careful periodic inspection, particularly after new brake lining is installed.

Whenever the brake drums have been removed for any purpose, the rubber boots at the end of the wheel cylinders should be pulled aside for a leak check. If any brake fluid is found in the interior of the rubber boots, it indicates that the wheel cylinders are leaking and should be replaced, or rebuilt. In addition the boot at the rear end of the master cylinder should be inspected in a similar manner.

Due to heat, air and chemical action between the hydraulic fluid and the brake lines, the brake fluid will gradually deteriorate. It is advisable after 20,000 miles of operation to drain the hydraulic fluid and flush the system thoroughly with fresh brake fluid.

The hydraulic fluid level in the master cylinder should be maintained at 5/8 in. from the top of the reservoir. On dual circuit systems, the fluid level must be above the dividing wall of the reservoir. Whenever

Brake Service

additional fluid is needed, or when the system is flushed and refilled, only fluid meeting the Society of Automotive Engineers' specifications should be used. There are inferior makes of brake fluid on the market which do not meet these requirements. Such fluid will vaporize readily and may not mix with quality brake fluids. Its viscosity may change with temperature changes, with the result that brake operation will be erratic and safety sacrificed.

Before adding any fluid to the master cylinder, wipe all dirt and grease away from the master cylinder filler plug. Otherwise dirt may enter the reservoir, pass into the master cylinder and clog the inlet port or compensating port, and also prevent the master cylinder valve from seating properly. Also make sure that the vent hole in the cover is clear of obstruction to prevent a vacuum or pressure from forming in the fluid reservoir.

MASTER CYLINDER SERVICE TIPS

When the brake pedal feels spongy or gradually goes to the floor board as sustained pressure is applied to the pedal, or if the cylinder leaks, it should be replaced or rebuilt.

The master cylinder can be removed by disconnecting and plugging the hydraulic lines, disconnecting the wires from the stoplight switch, removing bolt that attaches piston push rod to brake pedal, loosening brake pedal stop, removing piston push rod and the two master cylinder retaining bolts, Fig. F-5.

Fig. F-5. Final step in removing master cylinder from car is unscrewing of attaching bolts at mounting frame.

Repair kits are available for repairing the master cylinder. Or if desired, commercially rebuilt units or new units can be secured to replace the worn one.

Disassembly of the master cylinder is obvious from the views of various cylinders shown in Figs. F-6 to F-9.

After disassembly the first step is a thorough cleaning with alcohol or clean brake fluid. It is important that mineral oil does not come in contact with any brake parts. The work should be done on a clean bench with clean tools.

Fix Your Volkswagen

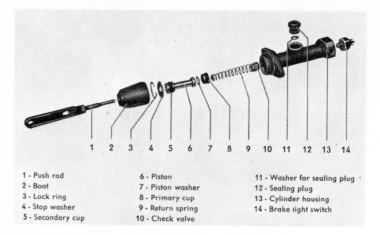

1 - Push rod
2 - Boot
3 - Lock ring
4 - Stop washer
5 - Secondary cup

6 - Piston
7 - Piston washer
8 - Primary cup
9 - Return spring
10 - Check valve

11 - Washer for sealing plug
12 - Sealing plug
13 - Cylinder housing
14 - Brake light switch

Fig. F-6. Exploded view gives correct sequence of parts that make up master cylinder in older "Beetle" models.

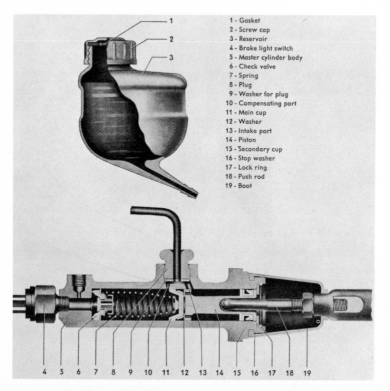

1 - Gasket
2 - Screw cap
3 - Reservoir
4 - Brake light switch
5 - Master cylinder body
6 - Check valve
7 - Spring
8 - Plug
9 - Washer for plug
10 - Compensating port
11 - Main cup
12 - Washer
13 - Intake port
14 - Piston
15 - Secondary cup
16 - Stop washer
17 - Lock ring
18 - Push rod
19 - Boot

Fig. F-7. Sectional view of master cylinder and reservoir reveals assembled positions of hydraulic components.

Brake Service

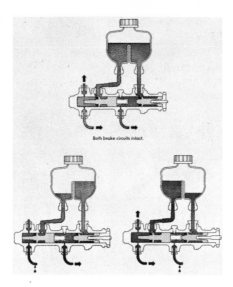

Both brake circuits intact.

Fig. F-8. Tandem master cylinder provides safe braking if brake fluid leak occurs in one side of system. Lower left shows failure in front circuit; lower right shows action of pistons when rear circuit fails.

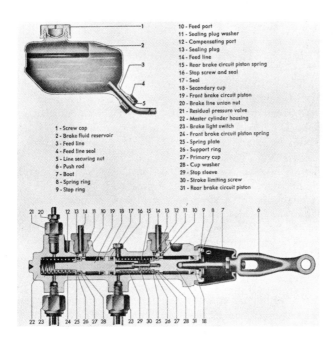

10 - Feed port
11 - Sealing plug washer
12 - Compensating port
13 - Sealing plug
14 - Feed line
15 - Rear brake circuit piston spring
16 - Stop screw and seal
17 - Seal
18 - Secondary cup
19 - Front brake circuit piston
20 - Brake line union nut
21 - Residual pressure valve
22 - Master cylinder housing
23 - Brake light switch
24 - Front brake circuit piston spring
25 - Spring plate
26 - Support ring
27 - Primary cup
28 - Cup washer
29 - Stop sleeve
30 - Stroke limiting screw
31 - Rear brake circuit piston

1 - Screw cap
2 - Brake fluid reservoir
3 - Feed line
4 - Feed line seal
5 - Line securing nut
6 - Push rod
7 - Boot
8 - Spring ring
9 - Stop ring

Fig. F-9. Sectional view of tandem master cylinder gives locations of two pistons and related parts which divide cylinder into two independent pressure chambers.

Examine all parts for wear and make sure the intake and by-pass ports are open and free from burrs. If the pistons are heavily scratched, scored or worn, they must be replaced. Check the piston fit in the cylinder bore. If the cylinders are lightly scratched, they can be honed with special equipment. If the cylinder walls are deeply scored or excessively worn, replace the entire assembly.

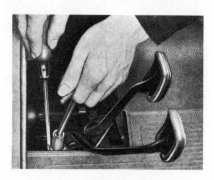

Fig. F-10. Do not change length of push rod to adjust pedal play. Clearance must be set by moving brake pedal stop as shown.

Examine the check valve and seat and replace them if any doubt exists as to their condition. It is always necessary to replace the two rubber cups when the master cylinder is disassembled. Since different size master cylinders have been used, make sure the new cups are the proper size.

When reassembling, dip all parts in clean brake fluid. Make sure that the lip of the main cup does not cover the by-pass port after the parts are all in place and that the lock wire is bedding correctly in its recess. When installing the fluid reservoir on older models, check before tightening that the bead at the bottom of the reservoir points to the stop light switch.

When installing the reconditioned unit on the car, replace spacer sleeves and check that the length of piston push rod has not been altered. Next adjust brake pedal clearance by shifting the stop plate, Fig. F-10, until there is clearance of .04 in. between push rod and piston, Fig. F-11.

Reconnect hydraulic lines and stoplight wires and fill reservoir with fluid. Bleed the system to remove any air.

BLEEDING HYDRAULIC BRAKES

Whenever a wheel or master cylinder is replaced, whenever a fluid line has been opened, or if the fluid has become too low in the master cylinder, it is necessary to bleed the hydraulic system so all air is removed. This is important, for instead of the brake pedal action moving the fluid through the lines to actuate the brake shoes, it will simply

Brake Service

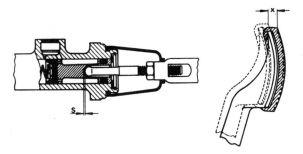

Fig. F-11. On reinstallation of master cylinder, adjust brake pedal free play to obtain approximately 1/4 in. play at "X" and .04 in. at "S."

compress the air. This condition is easily recognized by the spongy brake pedal when the brakes are applied. Bleeding of air from the system can best be carried out by two men. Proceed as follows:

1 - Remove bleeder valve dust cap of one wheel cylinder.
2 - Attach one end of the bleeder drain hose to valve.
3 - Allow free end of hose to be submerged in a clean glass container partially filled with hydraulic fluid. End of drain hose should, if possible, be above level of bleeder valve, Fig. F-12.
4 - Back off bleeder valve about one turn, using a 7 mm wrench.
5 - Depress brake pedal quickly, allow it to return slowly, and continue to pump in this manner until fluid runs out of bleeder hose in a continuous stream, without air bubbles. It is extremely important that master cylinder reservoir is full of fluid and that it is refilled before being completely exhausted.

Fig. F-12. Brake bleeding process is made more efficient by using jar-and-hose setup at each wheel cylinder in turn.

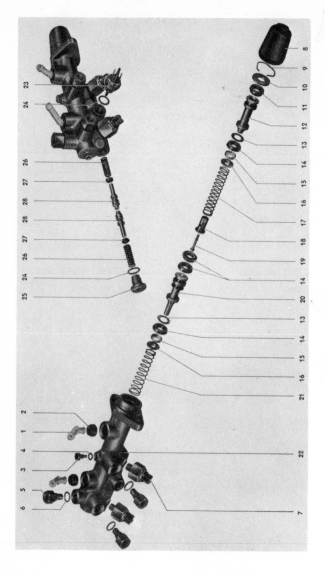

Fig. F-12A. Typical tandem brake master cylinder.

1—Elbow.
2—Sealing plug.
3—Stop screw.
4—Seal.
5—Residual pressure valve.
6—Sealing ring.
7—Brake light switch.
8—Boot.
9—Spring ring.
10—Stop ring.
11—Seal.
12—Rear brake circuit piston.
13—Cup washer.
14—Cup.
15—Support washer.
16—Spring plate.
17—Rear brake circuit spring.
18—Stop sleeve.
19—Stroke limiting screw.
20—Front brake circuit piston.
21—Front brake circuit spring.
22—Master cylinder housing.
23—Warning lamp switch.
24—Seal.
25—Plug.
26—Spring.
27—Cup.
28—Piston.

6 - Brake pedal should be kept in fully depressed position, until bleeder valve is closed.

7 - Tighten bleeder valve and replace dust cap.

8 - Repeat operation on each of remaining wheel cylinders. If necessary, fill master cylinder after complete system has been bled.

If the used fluid is discolored, it is advisable to flush the system. The flushing procedure is the same as bleeding and should be continued until the fluid is clear. Always be careful that the level of the fluid within the master cylinder does not reach the bottom of the reservoir, Fig. F-13. When that occurs, air will be introduced in the system and the bleeding operation will have to be repeated.

Fig. F-13. A translucent plastic brake fluid reservoir is found behind spare tire on most models.

On dual circuit brakes used on later models, bleed each circuit separately, making sure that the level of fluid is maintained in the reservoir designated for the circuit being bled, Fig. F-8. Start with the front circuit.

Fig. F-14. Rear wheel cylinder and anchor block bolt to backing plate. Replacement calls for disconnecting line and unscrewing attaching bolt.

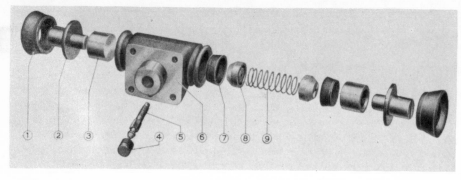

Fig. F-15. Wheel cylinder on early "Beetle" model: 1—Boot. 2—Push rod. 3—Piston. 4—Dust cap. 5—Bleeder valve. 6—Cylinder body. 7—Cup. 8—Cup filler. 9—Return spring.

SERVICING THE WHEEL CYLINDERS

Whenever the brake drums are removed, the wheel cylinders should be examined for leakage by pulling back the rubber boot at the ends of the cylinder and noting if any fluid is present. If so, the cylinder should be overhauled or a new unit installed. Repair kits of the necessary parts needed for overhauling are available.

To replace a wheel cylinder, first jack up the wheel and remove the brake drum and brake shoes. Disconnect the hydraulic brake line from the rear of the brake backing plate and plug it to prevent fluid loss. Remove the wheel cylinder by taking out the cap screw that holds it to the backing plate, Fig. F-14.

Disassemble the wheel cylinder by removing the rubber boots from each end of the assembly. Push the pistons, piston caps, and return spring from the cylinder, Figs. F-15 and F-16.

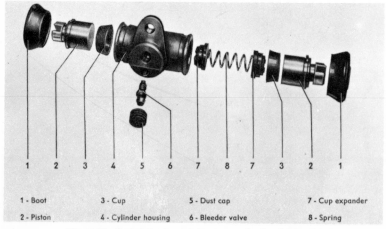

1 - Boot	3 - Cup	5 - Dust cap	7 - Cup expander
2 - Piston	4 - Cylinder housing	6 - Bleeder valve	8 - Spring

Fig. F-16. Exploded view of late type wheel cylinder shows relative locations of pistons, cups and cup expanders.

Brake Service

Before installing new parts, thoroughly clean the brake cylinder with alcohol or clean brake fluid. Then examine the bore of the cylinder carefully for scratches, pitting, ridges, gummed fluid, and other irregularities of the surface. If the surface is marred in any manner, the cylinder must be honed or replaced.

Except in cases of extreme mileage or when inferior brake fluid has been used, or when the system has not been flushed at regular intervals, it will be found that the wheel cylinder can be reconditioned. Therefore, many mechanics will thoroughly clean and examine the bore of the wheel cylinder before removing it from the backing plate. If the bore is found to be in serviceable condition, it can be honed and rebuilt on the backing plate.

New parts for wheel cylinders are available in kit form. Before installation, coat the bore of the cylinder with brake fluid. Dip the various parts in brake fluid before placing them in the cylinder. Study the accompanying illustrations, Figs. F-15 and F-16, be sure the parts are installed in their correct position.

When replacing wheel cylinders or parts, make sure the proper size is obtained as wheel cylinders of different size have been used in production. Position the brake shoes on the backing plate and install the mechanical linkage, Fig. F-17. The final step is to adjust the brakes and bleed the system.

Fig. F-17. Rear brake shoe disassembly includes disconnecting parking brake lever and connecting link.

BRAKE LINING SHORT CUTS

Relining the brakes is not difficult. Relined brake shoes, ready for installation, can be secured from any Volkswagen dealer. The removal of the worn brake shoes and installation of new shoes is easily accomplished, Figs. F-17 to F-19.

The first step in relining the brakes is to raise the car and remove the wheels. To remove the front drums, first remove the dust cover from the front wheel bearing. This has a press fit in the hub and can be removed by tapping on one side and then the other until it is free. Remove the spindle nut and pull the drum, by hand, from the spindle. Do not drop the wheel bearings.

To remove the rear wheels, a brake drum puller is required. If difficulty is encountered in pulling off the rear drum, make sure the hand brake is not applied. If difficulty is still encountered, increase the clearance between the brake shoes and the brake drum by means of the brake clearance adjustment.

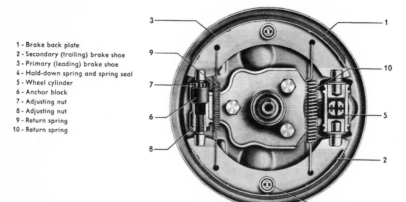

1 - Brake back plate
2 - Secondary (trailing) brake shoe
3 - Primary (leading) brake shoe
4 - Hold-down spring and spring seal
5 - Wheel cylinder
6 - Anchor block
7 - Adjusting nut
8 - Adjusting nut
9 - Return spring
10 - Return spring

Fig. F-18. Late model front wheel brake assembly.

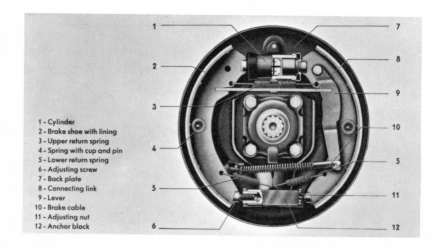

1 - Cylinder
2 - Brake shoe with lining
3 - Upper return spring
4 - Spring with cup and pin
5 - Lower return spring
6 - Adjusting screw
7 - Back plate
8 - Connecting link
9 - Lever
10 - Brake cable
11 - Adjusting nut
12 - Anchor block

Fig. F-19. Layout is shown for late type rear wheel brake with all parts assembled in correct order and free to operate.

Brake Service

To keep the wheel cylinder pistons in place and prevent leakage of brake fluid from the wheel cylinder, place a clamp over the wheel cylinder.

To service the rear wheel brakes, it is also necessary to disconnect the hand brake cables, Fig. F-17. When installing the relined shoes, make sure the oil seals on the front wheels are in good condition and that the oil deflector on the rear wheels is properly positioned, Fig. F-20.

WHAT TO DO ABOUT BRAKE DRUMS

Whenever the brake drums are removed, they should be carefully inspected to make sure that they are not scored, grooved or out-of-round.

Brake drums which are slightly scored should be trued or resurfaced on a brake drum lathe. Automotive machine shops are equipped to render

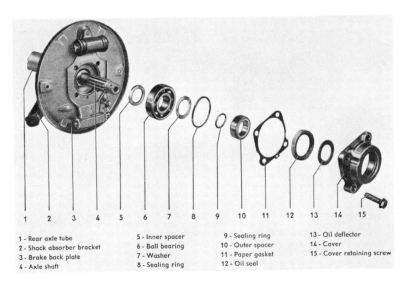

1 - Rear axle tube	5 - Inner spacer	9 - Sealing ring	13 - Oil deflector
2 - Shock absorber bracket	6 - Ball bearing	10 - Outer spacer	14 - Cover
3 - Brake back plate	7 - Washer	11 - Paper gasket	15 - Cover retaining screw
4 - Axle shaft	8 - Sealing ring	12 - Oil seal	

Fig. F-20. Installation sequence is indicated for parts making up rear axle outer support, including bearing, spacer, oil seal and cover.

such service. A rough check to determine whether a brake drum is out-of-round can be made before the brake drum is removed by rotating the drum on its spindle. The brake shoe clearance is then reduced and if the sound of the drum rubbing against the lining is intermittent, the drum is not round but oval. A perfectly true drum will remain in contact with the brake shoe at all times after the shoe-to-lining clearance has been reduced.

If the brake drum is resurfaced, it must never be reduced to a thickness of less than 0.16 in. It should not be tapered more than .004 in. and the permissible lateral and radial run-out should not be more than .010 in. If it cannot be kept within these specifications, new drums are required. When the drums are thus resurfaced, it will be necessary to use brake shoes fitted with oversize lining.

Whenever the brake drums are removed, remove the accumulated dust from the interior and exercise care that no grease reaches the braking surface of the drum. Do not touch the braking surface since this will tend to cause erratic braking. If new brake drums are installed, remove the rust-proofing oil from the braking surface. If this is not done, the brakes will grab severely and it may be necessary to completely reline the shoes. Either naphtha or carbon tetrachloride may be used to remove the rust-proofing oil.

After the relining procedure, it will be necessary to readjust both hand and foot brakes and bleed the hydraulic system as previously described.

DRUM BRAKE TROUBLE SHOOTING

Complaint	Cause	Correction
Pedal goes to floorboard	a - Normal lining wear	a - Adjust shoes
Spongy response at brake pedal	a - Air in system b - Lack of fluid in master cylinder reservoir	a - Bleed system b - Fill up to fluid level
Pedal goes to floorboard without brake action, even though system has been bled and adjusted	a - Check valve in master cylinder inoperative b - Check valve seat dirty	a - Renew check valve b - Clean or renew check valve seat
Brake action is obtained only by pumping pedal several times	a - Air in system b - Weak piston return spring	a - Bleed system b - Renew piston return spring
Brake action decreases and pedal goes to floorboard, even though brakes have been adjusted	a - Fluid leak in system b - Damaged or unserviceable cups in master or wheel cylinder	a - Locate point of leakage and repair b - Replace faulty cups

Brake Service

Complaint	Cause	Correction
Brakes drag	a - By-pass port in master cylinder clogged	a - Clean master cylinder
	b - Too little clearance between piston push rod and master cylinder piston	b - Adjust brake pedal
	c - Shoe return springs broken or weak	c - Replace springs and adjust shoes
	d - Improper brake fluid	d - Drain fluid, remove all rubber parts, and flush system with fresh brake fluid. Install new rubber parts, including check valve and seat
Brake pedal suddenly has excessive travel	a - Brake fluid leak in one circuit of dual system	a - Find and correct leakage in system at fault
Excessive pressure on pedal, poor stop	a - Oil on brake shoe lining	a - Replace lining. Locate point of leakage age and clean wheel brake
	b - Improper brake shoe lining	b - Replace lining
Brakes lock while driving	a - By-pass port in master cylinder not free (possibly caused by a deformed cup)	a - Clean by-pass port by means of a piece of suitable wire. Remove any burr. Replace cup
	b - Improper brake fluid	b - Drain fluid, flush system and refill with fresh brake fluid
	c - Incorrect position of brake pedal stop plate	c - Check position of brake pedal and adjust pedal play so as to ensure that by-pass port is not closed by piston cup

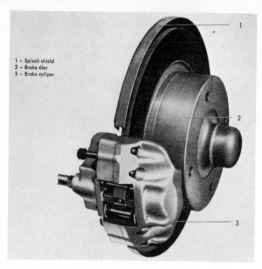

1 - Splash shield
2 - Brake disc
3 - Brake caliper

Fig. F-21. Major parts are called out for front disc brake assembly on Fastback and Squareback models.

Complaint	Cause	Correction
Brakes uneven	a - Brake drum eccentric	a - Replace brake drum or remachine it
	b - Tires not properly inflated or worn	b - Check tire pressure replace worn tires
	c - Oil on brake shoe lining	c - Replace lining. Only replace in axle sets (both front wheels or both rear wheels)
Brakes chatter and tend to tie up	a - Brake shoe lining not chamfered at ends	a - Chamfer lining ends
	b - Brake shoe lining worn, rivets make contact with drum	b - Replace lining or reset the rivets
	c - Brake drum eccentric	c - Replace brake drum or remachine it
Brakes noisy	a - Improper brake shoe lining. Lining not chamfered at ends	a - Reline shoes
	b - Lining loose on shoe	b - Reline shoes
	c - Brakes dirty	c - Clean wheel brakes

DISC BRAKE CONSTRUCTION

Front wheel disc brakes are used on Fastback and Squareback models, Fig. F-21. The major components are the disc, or rotor, and the caliper which contains hydraulically operated parts, Fig. F-22. The caliper

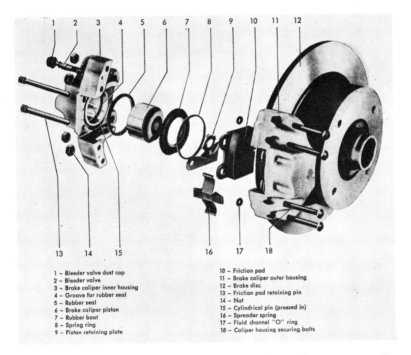

1 – Bleeder valve dust cap
2 – Bleeder valve
3 – Brake caliper inner housing
4 – Groove for rubber seal
5 – Rubber seal
6 – Brake caliper piston
7 – Rubber boot
8 – Spring ring
9 – Piston retaining plate
10 – Friction pad
11 – Brake caliper outer housing
12 – Brake disc
13 – Friction pad retaining pin
14 – Nut
15 – Cylindrical pin (pressed in)
16 – Spreader spring
17 – Fluid channel "O" ring
18 – Caliper housing securing bolts

Fig. F-22. Exploded view of front wheel disc brake shows relative positions of disc, caliper and hydraulic components.

Fig. F-23. Friction pads of disc brake consist of a metal plate with friction material bonded to one one side, plastic sound deadening layer to other.

consists of two housings, one on each side of the disc. A cylinder is machined into each caliper housing and a piston and rubber seal form the operating hydraulic parts.

Each piston is hollow and contains a brake disc deflection compensator. Friction pads, Fig. F-23, slide axially in grooves in the housing, between the pistons and the brake disc, Fig. F-24. The pads are held in place by two retaining pins which are held in the caliper by a split clamping bushing. A spreader spring presses the friction pad against the piston. The two cylinders in the brake caliper housings are connected by internal fluid channels.

Fig. F-24. Friction pad must be free to move in and out when installing it. Never replace one pad or one pair, do both wheels at same time.

DISC BRAKE OPERATION

When the brake pedal is depressed, hydraulic pressure in the caliper cylinders forces the pistons toward each other and the friction pads clamp against the machined surface of the disc with equal pressure. Rubber seals in grooves in the cylinder are deflected in the direction of piston movement.

When the brake pedal is released, the system is relieved of hydraulic pressure; and the pistons in the caliper cylinders are retracted by the action of the rubber seals, allowing the disc to rotate freely. The friction pads adjust automatically for wear and do not require a manual adjustment of any kind.

DISC BRAKE SERVICE

Disc brake friction pads must be replaced when they are heavily grooved, oily or worn to less than 3/32 in., Fig. F-25.

To remove and install friction pads: Remove front wheel. Use a punch to drive out friction pad upper retaining pin. Remove spreader spring. Drive out lower retaining spring. Pull friction pads out of brake

Brake Service

caliper (mark individual pad and corresponding caliper housing if pad is to be reused). Remove approximately one-half of brake fluid from master cylinder reservoir to provide space for fluid which will be forced back from cylinder of caliper being worked on. Push both pistons back to end position, using a piston retaining pliers. (If pads must be replaced, renew all friction pads for both front wheels.)

Remove retaining plates and clean seating and sliding surfaces of brake caliper. Blow out caliper with compressed air. Check rubber boot for damage; replace if brittle or cracked. Insert piston retaining plate with circular part pressed into piston crown to lie below relieved part of piston. Insert friction pads into caliper, Fig. F-24. Insert friction pad lower retaining pin, driving it in with a hammer only to avoid possibility of shearing off front shoulder. Install new spreader spring and hold down while pushing upper retaining pin into brake caliper.

Depress brake pedal several times while car is stationary, to position pistons and friction pads properly. Check level of fluid in brake system reservoir. Test brakes on road.

If the brake caliper needs to be serviced, allow it to cool down to room temperature before removing it. Then remove brake hose and seal open end of brake line. Bend up lock plate on both bolts and unscrew attaching bolts. Remove caliper. Reinstall caliper in reverse order, tightening attaching bolts to 43 ft. lbs.

Fig. F-25. Friction pads that have worn down to a thickness of 3/32 in. at ''a'' must be replaced with new ones.

If brake disc needs to be resurfaced: Detach brake caliper from steering knuckle and hang it to one side. Remove wheel bearing nut and remove brake disc. On reinstallation, lubricate bearings with lithium grease. Install disc on spindle and tighten inner bearing nut to 11 ft. lbs. while turning disc. Back off nut until axial play is between .001 and .005 in. Tighten clamp nut screw to 11 ft. lbs. Recheck adjustment to insure that bearings have end play specified.

DISC BRAKE TROUBLE SHOOTING

Complaint	Cause	Correction
Pedal goes to floorboard	a - Friction pads worn	a - Fit new pads
	b - Brake disc runout exceeds .008 in.	b - Rework disc or fit new part
	c - Disc too thin (less than .335 in.)	c - Fit new part
Pedal fades	a - Piston seal damaged	a - Recondition caliper
Brakes overheat as pads stay in contact with disc	a - Passage in check valve blocked	a - Clean master cylinder
	b - Slots in caliper dirty	b - Clean pad contact surface on caliper
	c - Piston seals damaged or cylinders corroded	c - Recondition caliper
	d - Weak spreader springs	d - Fit new springs
Hard brake pedal but poor braking action	a - Pads worn and plates contact spreader springs	a - Fit new pads
Brakes rattle	a - Inferior or incorrect pads	a - Fit new pads
	b - Loose wheel bearings	b - Adjust bearings
	c - Disc runout excessive	c - Rework disc or fit new part
	d - Disc too thin	d - Fit new part
	e - Slots in caliper dirty	e - Clean pad contact surface on caliper
	f - Loose caliper	f - Tighten caliper attaching bolts, and turn down lock plate on bolts
Brakes pulsate	a - Loose wheel bearings	a - Adjust bearings
	b - Disc runout excessive	b - Rework disc or fit new part

Brake Service

Complaint	Cause	Correction
	c - Disc too thin	c - Fit new part
	d - Disc not running parallel to caliper	d - Check caliper mounting on steering knuckle
	e - Loose caliper	e - Tighten caliper attaching bolts and turn down lock plate on bolts
Brakes squeak	a - Inferior or incorrect pads	a - Fit new pads
	b - Pistons have turned from prescribed 20 deg. position	b - Correct piston position; fit new retaining plates
	c - Disc not running parallel to caliper	c - Check caliper mounting on steering knuckle
Brakes pull	a - Slots in caliper dirty	a - Clean pad contact surface on caliper
	b - Rust in cylinders	b - Recondition caliper
	c - Pistons have turned from prescribed position	c - Correct piston position, fit new retaining plates
	d - Disc worn unevenly	d - Rework disc or fit new parts
Pads worn unevenly	a - Inferior or incorrect pads	a - Fit new pads
	b - Slots in caliper dirty	b - Clean pad contact surfaces on caliper
	c - Piston seal damaged	c - Recondition caliper
	d - Rust in cylinders	d - Recondition caliper
Pads worn wedge-shaped	a - Pistons have turned from prescribed position	a - Correct piston position; fit new retaining plates
	b - Disc not running parallel to caliper	b - Check caliper mounting on steering knuckle

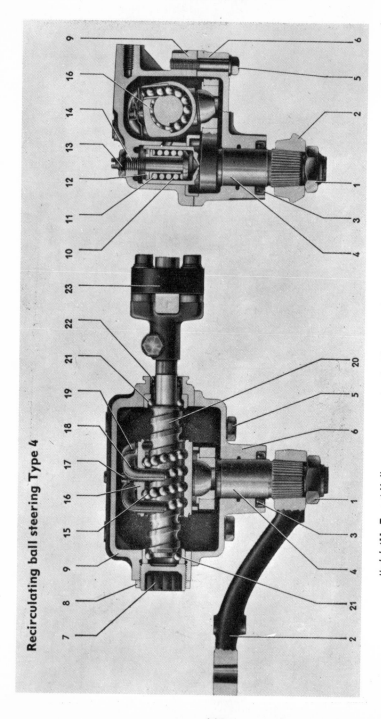

Recirculating ball steering Type 4

Model 411, Type 4 Volkswagens are equipped with a recirculating ball steering gear. 1—Lock nut. 2—Pitman arm. 3—Seal. 4—Pitman shaft. 5—Screw. 6—Gear case cover. 7—Worm adjuster. 8—Lock nut. 9—Steering gear case. 10—Spring. 11—Sleeve. 12—Thrust washer. 13—Lock nut. 14—Adjusting screw. 15—Ball (58). 16—Steering nut. 17—Screw. 18—Ball return guides. 19—Clamping plate. 20—Worm. 21—Ball bearing. 22—Seal. 23—Steering coupling.

SUSPENSION, WHEEL ALIGNMENT

The unique construction of the Volkswagen makes it necessary to consider the entire suspension system as well as front wheel alignment when making any adjustments. Front and rear wheels, steering gear, front and rear torsion bars and front and rear shock absorbers are all closely related and each has an effect on the whole.

Good handling of the car and satisfactory tire wear is dependent upon:

1 - Proper adjustment of all front axle and steering components.
2 - Proper tire inflation along with approximately equal wear of front tire treads.
3 - Proper adjustment of torsion bars.
4 - Proper wheel balance and bearing adjustment.
5 - Proper action of shock absorbers.
6 - Proper steering geometry angles.

In order to obtain maximum tire life and have good steering conditions, without shimmy or other steering difficulties, it is important that the caster, camber, toe-in, and king pin inclination be correct. Toe-in, as the name implies, is the amount the front wheels are closer together

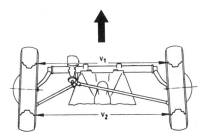

Fig. G-1. Difference between V1 and V2 is amount of toe-in.

at the front than at the rear. Caster is the amount in degrees that the king pin or steering axis (center line of ball joints) is tilted toward the rear of the car. Camber is the amount the wheels are tilted outward at the top of the wheel. King pin inclination is the amount the king pins, or ball joints, are tilted toward the center of the car. These terms will be clearly understood by studying Figs. G-1, G-2, and G-3. On 1966 and later models, ball joint suspension replaced the king pin setup. King pin inclination thus becomes an imaginary steering axis drawn through the centers of upper and lower ball joints, Fig. G-5.

The steering angles must be checked with special equipment designed for the purpose. Need for servicing the front suspension will be indicated by rapid tire wear, hard steering and the tendency for the car to wander on the road.

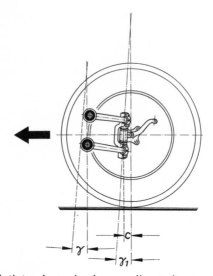

Fig. G-2. Caster is built into front axle tubes as well as inclination of king pins or ball joints.

Before attempting to correct the alignment of the front wheels, inflate the tires to specified pressure and inspect them for wear. Also inspect the front suspension system for evidence of wear. The car should be empty of all luggage or other weight except the spare tire. Place the car on a level surface, then settle the springs and shock absorbers into their normal positions by bouncing the front end of the car up and down several times.

WHEEL ALIGNMENT METHODS

The front axle consists of two rigidly joined tubes bolted to the frame. Within each of these tubes is a laminated square torsion bar made up of flat steel strips welded together at each end. These torsion bars reach across the car but are anchored in the center to counteract twisting, avoid lateral movement and segregate road shocks to one side or the other, Figs. G-4 and G-5.

Attached to the outer end of each bar is a lever or torsion arm. Between the ends of each pair of arms the wheel spindle is mounted on pivot pins or ball joints. Thus the wheel spindle trails behind the axle

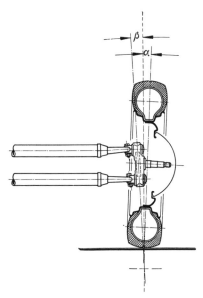

Fig. G-3. Camber angle is shown at "a" and king pin or ball joint inclination at "b."

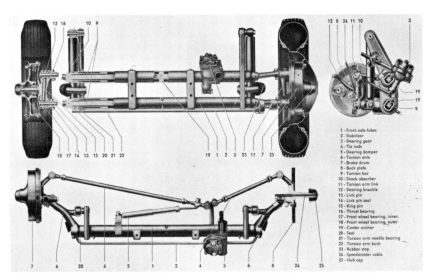

1 - Front axle tubes
2 - Stabilizer
3 - Steering gear
4 - Tie rods
5 - Steering damper
6 - Torsion arm
7 - Brake drum
8 - Back plate
9 - Torsion bar
10 - Shock absorber
11 - Torsion arm link
12 - Steering knuckle
13 - Link pin
14 - Link pin seal
15 - King pin
16 - Thrust bearing
17 - Front wheel bearing, inner.
18 - Front wheel bearing, outer
19 - Center anchor
20 - Seal
21 - Torsion arm needle bearing
22 - Torsion arm bush
23 - Rubber stop
24 - Speedometer cable
25 - Hub cap

Fig. G-4. "Beetle" front end before August, 1965, incorporates king pins and full length torsion bars anchored in middle.

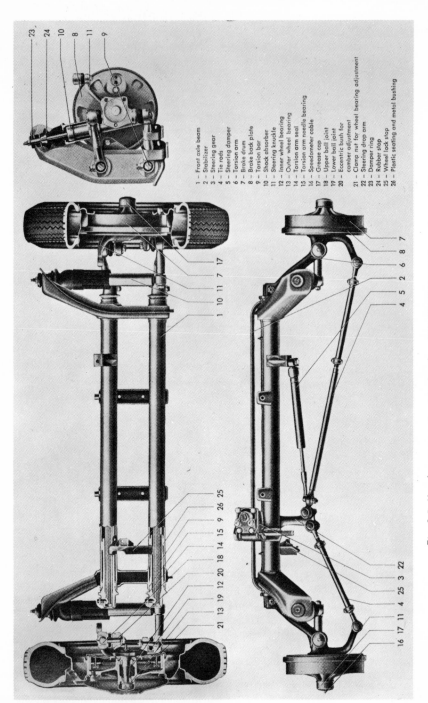

1 – Front axle beam
2 – Stabilizer
3 – Steering gear
4 – Tie rods
5 – Steering damper
6 – Torsion arm
7 – Brake drum
8 – Brake back plate
9 – Torsion bar
10 – Shock absorber
11 – Steering knuckle
12 – Inner wheel bearing
13 – Outer wheel bearing
14 – Torsion arm seal
15 – Torsion arm needle bearing
16 – Speedometer cable
17 – Grease cap
18 – Upper ball joint
19 – Lower ball joint
20 – Eccentric bush for camber adjustment
21 – Clamp nut for wheel bearing adjustment
22 – Steering drop arm
23 – Damper ring
24 – Rubber stop
25 – Wheel lock stop
26 – Plastic seating and metal bushing

Fig. G-5. New front suspension introduced on 1966 VW-1300 models continues trailing link arrangement but features ball joints (18 and 19).

and tends to swing in an arc when moved up and down by road irregularities. This lessens the degree of road shock transmitted to the car.

Following the front end inspection, all worn, loose or bent parts should be replaced. Camber is adjustable on cars built after August, 1965, since the upper ball joint is provided with an eccentric bushing. If adjustment is necessary, turn the eccentric bushing up to 90 deg. to the right or left of its basic position (notch in bushing facing normal driving position and aligned with notch in torsion arm eye), Fig. G-6. On Fastback and Squareback models, the upper ball joint has a square end which may be turned to obtain correct camber.

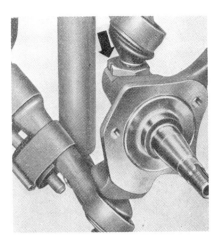 

Fig. G-6. *Eccentric bushing on upper ball joint provides camber adjustment on Beetle models, after 1965. Notch (arrow) aids in balancing settings between wheels.*

Fig. G-6A. *On Type 3 and Squareback models, both ball joints are notched. In basic position, deeper side of notch faces forward with 90 deg. adjustment in either direction.*

On VW-1200 models, the camber is given as zero deg. and 40 min., plus or minus 30 min. The caster angle should be 2 deg. and 30 min., plus or minus 30 min. Toe-in should be 0.04-0.12 in. and is adjustable at the tie rod on the right side. Clamping screws are loosened at both ends and the rod turned as desired. On VW-1300 models, the camber specification is also zero deg. and 40 min., plus or minus 30 min., but the caster angle calls for 2 deg., plus or minus 15 min., and toe-in is 0.08-0.16 in.

On later "Beetle" models, camber is 30 min., plus or minus 20 min. The toe-in specification is .07-.21 in. On the Super Beetle introduced in 1971, camber setting is 1 deg., 30 min.; toe-in should be .08-.26 in. Fastback and Squareback models call for camber of 1 deg., 20 min., plus or minus 20 min.; toe-in of 0.16 in. In any case, maximum variation of 20 min. is allowed on left and right camber settings.

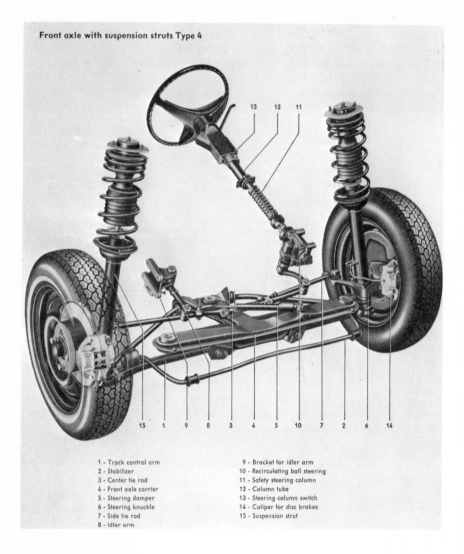

Front axle with suspension struts Type 4

13   12   11

15 1   9   8   3   4   5   10   7   2   6   14

1 - Track control arm	9 - Bracket for idler arm
2 - Stabilizer	10 - Recirculating ball steering
3 - Center tie rod	11 - Safety steering column
4 - Front axle carrier	12 - Column tube
5 - Steering damper	13 - Steering column switch
6 - Steering knuckle	14 - Caliper for disc brakes
7 - Side tie rod	15 - Suspension strut
8 - Idler arm	

Fig. G-7. Type 3 and Squareback Volkswagens feature front axle design based on sheet steel axle beam, adjustable torsion bars, stabilizer bar and other components listed here.

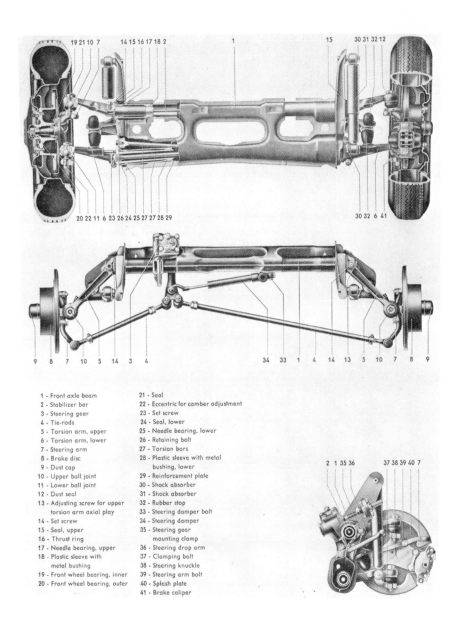

1 - Front axle beam	21 - Seal
2 - Stabilizer bar	22 - Eccentric for camber adjustment
3 - Steering gear	23 - Set screw
4 - Tie-rods	24 - Seal, lower
5 - Torsion arm, upper	25 - Needle bearing, lower
6 - Torsion arm, lower	26 - Retaining bolt
7 - Steering arm	27 - Torsion bars
8 - Brake disc	28 - Plastic sleeve with metal
9 - Dust cap	bushing, lower
10 - Upper ball joint	29 - Reinforcement plate
11 - Lower ball joint	30 - Shock absorber
12 - Dust seal	31 - Shock absorber
13 - Adjusting screw for upper	32 - Rubber stop
torsion arm axial play	33 - Steering damper bolt
14 - Set screw	34 - Steering damper
15 - Seal, upper	35 - Steering gear
16 - Thrust ring	mounting clamp
17 - Needle bearing, upper	36 - Steering drop arm
18 - Plastic sleeve with	37 - Clamping bolt
metal bushing	38 - Steering knuckle
19 - Front wheel bearing, inner	39 - Steering arm bolt
20 - Front wheel bearing, outer	40 - Splash plate
	41 - Brake caliper

Fig. G-7A. Type 4 Volkswagen models have front wheels suspended on suspension struts, connected to the body at top and on track control arm at bottom. Suspension struts serve as double-acting shock absorbers fitted with coil springs at top and bolted to steering knuckles at bottom.

Specifications for wheel alignment on 1971 and 1972 Volkswagen models are as follows: On Beetle models (111), camber is 30 min., plus or minus 20 min. The toe-in setting remains at .07-.21 in. The caster angle is 3 deg. 20 min., plus or minus 1 deg.

On Super Beetle models (113), camber is 1 deg., plus 20 min. to minus 40 min. On both Beetle lines, maximum permissible difference between sides is 30 min. Toe-in on the Super Beetle is .08-.26 in., while caster is 2 deg., plus or minus 35 min.

On Type 3 cars, the camber setting is 1 deg. 20 min., plus or minus 20 min.; toe-in is 0.16 in. Maximum permissible difference between sides remains at 20 min. Caster is 4 deg., plus or minus 40 min.

On Type 4 models (411), the camber angle is set at 30 min.; toe-in is .08 in.; caster is 1 deg. 10 min., plus or minus 35 min.

Independent suspension on torque bars is used for the rear wheels on "Beetle" models through 1968. In the rear, however, the bars are shorter with one on each side, and they are round instead of square and splined on each end, Fig. G-8. Here again the bars are anchored in one end of a lever and the axles at the other end so that wheels trail as in front.

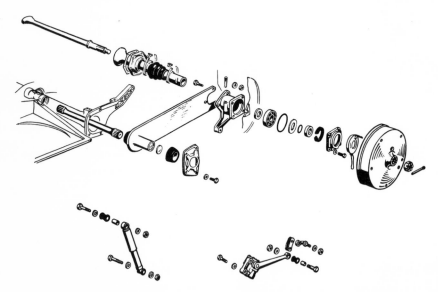

Fig. G-8. Typical trailing link type of rear suspension system used on Volkswagen through 1968 models.

Compensation for sagging or heavy loading can be made at the rear torsion bars by means of the splines on each end. To make a fine adjustment possible, the inner end of the bar has 40 splines while the outer end has 44 splines. Turning the bar one spline at the inner end will make a change of 9 deg. One spline at the outer end will make a change of 8 deg. and 10 min. This adjustment should result in the angle on both sides being the same. Bear in mind that excessive raising or lowering of the rear end will affect the caster angle of the front axle.

In 1969, a double-joint rear axle with new rear wheel suspension was introduced. This suspension setup features trailing and control arms, Figs. G-9 and G-10.

Because the rear wheels swing independently, it is important to check alignment insofar as camber and toe-in are concerned. With the car loaded until the spring plates are level with the car on a level floor,

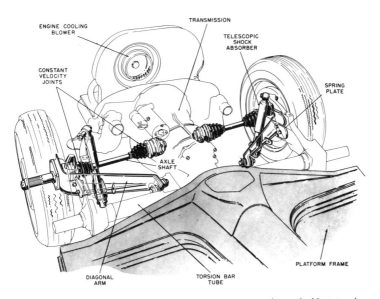

Fig. G-9. Large change in 1969 rear suspension introduces double-jointed axle shafts and diagonal trailing and control arms.

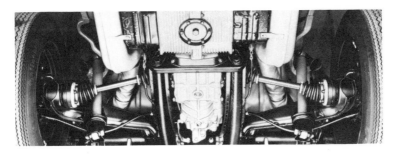

Fig. G-10. Diagonal arm rear axle has constant velocity joints at both ends of drive shafts, or half axles, which are covered by boots that require periodic visual inspections.

there should not be more than one degree difference in the camber of the rear wheels. If more than one degree, the correction should be made by turning the torsion bar as described.

A slight amount of toe-in or toe-out will be found in the rear wheels. In either case it is important that each wheel toes in or toes out to the same degree. The most desirable condition is a toe-out of 0.08 in.

Correction can be made by shifting the rear axle half in the slotted holes of the spring plate either to the rear or to the front.

EASY WAY TO REMOVE TORSION BARS

To remove either or both of the front torsion bars, raise the front end of the car and support it behind the frame head.

1 - Remove front wheels.
2 - Remove outer tie rod ends.
3 - Remove brake drums and brake backing plates (do not disconnect brake lines).
4 - Remove clamp bolts from torsion arm eyes, Fig. G-11.

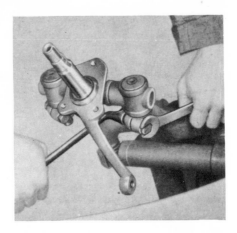

Fig. G-11. Loosening torsion arm eye clamp bolts.

5 - Remove torsion arm link and steering knuckle as a unit by bumping with a soft hammer.
6 - Remove shock absorbers.
7 - Remove torsion arms on one side.
8 - Release lock nut and setscrew at center anchor, and slide out torsion bars.

If the torsion arms are removed from both ends of the torsion bar it is not necessary to mark the bar for the direction of torsion application. Both arms should be removed and the laminated bar thoroughly cleaned in order to inspect for cracks. If the bar ends are loose, they must be welded together. A cracked or rusted torsion bar should be replaced.

To remove either of the rear torsion bars:

1 - Support car in a horizontal position and remove rear wheel.
2 - Remove screws at rear axle shaft bearing housing, Fig. G-8, and pull axle to rear until it clears spring plate.
3 - Remove cotter pin and take off torsion bar cap.
4 - Remove screws and take off spring plate hub cover.
5 - Remove spring plate and both rubber cushions.
6 - Remove about five of foremost fender screws.
7 - Pull torsion bar out while at same time pulling fender aside to allow torsion bar to clear it. Lubricate fittings, Fig. G-12.

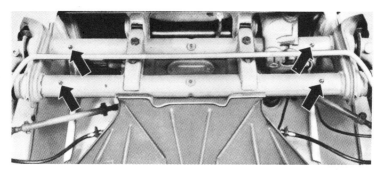

Fig. G-12. Late model "Beetle," Fastback and Squareback front suspension has four grease fittings on axle tubes which must be lubricated with lithium-based multipurpose grease. Service interval is 6,000 miles or once a year, except 1971 Super Beetle and 411, "Type 4," cars.

FRONT WHEEL BEARINGS

In the design construction of early Beetle models, each front wheel is supported on its spindle by two ball bearing assemblies pressed into the wheel hub. A special puller is needed to get the front brake drums off of the wheel spindle, Fig. G-13. If the bearings need to be replaced, the bearing races must be pressed out of the drum and pulled from the wheel spindle. Reinstallation is in reverse order with the assembly held in place on the spindle by a thrust washer, adjusting nut and lock nut.

To adjust front wheel bearings on earlier "Beetle" models: Tighten adjusting nut to 28 ft. lbs. while turning wheel. Back it off 72 deg., or distance between consecutive wheel bolt holes in drum, Fig. G-14. Tighten lock nut to 50 ft. lbs. while holding adjusting nut in place.

On later "Beetle," Fastback and Squareback models, each front wheel is supported on the spindle by two tapered roller bearings. The drum and bearing assembly is held in place on the spindle by a thrust washer and clamp nut (left spindle has left-hand thread). Wheel bearing replacement requires pressing old races out, new races in.

Fig. G-13. On early Beetle models, front brake drum removal necessitates "pulling" by means of a special tool. Ball bearings were used.

Fig. G-14. Front wheel bearing adjustment calls for tightening of spindle nut to a specific torque, then backing off distance shown.

To adjust front wheel bearings on later "Beetle," Fastback and Squareback models: Attach a dial gauge and bracket to one bolt hole in brake drum, Fig. G-15. Loosen screw in clamp nut. Tighten clamp nut on spindle while turning wheel to seat bearings. Back off clamp nut until dial gauge reading is from .001 to .005 in. when wheel is moved in and out on spindle. Tighten screw in clamp nut to 11 ft. lbs.

Note: Front wheel bearings should be lubricated with lithium grease. Press grease into cages and between balls or rollers, and lightly grease bearing races. Fill hub of drum with grease, but do not put any in hub cap.

BALL JOINTS

The front suspension ball joint setup on "Beetle" models differs from the ball joints used on Fastback and Squareback models. Ball joint replacement on "Beetle" models calls for the use of special removing tools and a torsion arm jack, Fig. G-16. On Fastback and Squareback front suspension, the ball joints are held in the steering knuckle by means of

Fig. G-15. Later "Beetle" front wheel end play tolerance is .001 to .005 in. Roller bearings are used.

Fig. G-16. On "Beetle" models, ball joints must be pressed out of steering knuckle as shown, then removed from torsion arm eye by means of a vertical shop press.

clamping screws. And, as mentioned, "Beetle" models utilize a hexagonal head eccentric bushing at the upper ball joint to adjust camber. Fastback and Squareback models have square-ended upper ball joints with built-in eccentric for this purpose.

To remove ball joints from a "Beetle" model: Remove front wheel, detach brake hose and remove brake drum and backing plate. Press out outer tie rod end. Unscrew hex nut on lower ball joint and press joint out of steering knuckle, Fig. G-16. Unscrew hex nut on upper ball joint and loosen eccentric bushing. Press joint out of steering knuckle. Raise upper torsion arm with special lifting tool to free steering knuckle from ball joints. Press upper ball joint from upper torsion arm eye, then remove eccentric bushing from upper joint. Press lower ball joint from lower torsion arm eye.

Fig. G-17. When new ball joints are installed on "Beetle" steering knuckle, self-locking nuts must be tightened to 36 ft. lbs.

Fig. G-18. Different ball joint arrangement on Fastback/Squareback models requires use of tensioning tool to draw torsion arms together.

To install new ball joints: Install upper ball joint in upper torsion arm eye. Install lower ball joint in lower torsion arm eye. Place eccentric in upper hole of steering knuckle with hex head up. Lift upper torsion arm enough to install steering knuckle on ball joints, then turn hex head on eccentric bushing until notch is pointed forward, Fig. G-7. Install self-locking nuts on ball joints and tighten them to 36 ft. lbs., Fig. G-17. Reinstall tie rod end, brake backing plate, drum, brake hose and wheel. Bleed brakes and adjust camber and toe-in.

To remove ball joints from a Fastback or Squareback: Remove front wheel and brake caliper. Tie caliper to suspension member. Place torsion arms under tension and remove ball joint clamping screws. Press torsion arms together and pull steering knuckle down and out, Fig. G-18. Remove ball joint nuts and spring washers. Then take ball joints from torsion arms.

To install new ball joints: Slide upper ball joint into upper torsion arm eye, Fig. G-19, keeping notch in ball joint pointing forward. Fit

Fig. G-19. Ball joints are held in torsion arm eye on Fastback/Squareback models by attaching nuts tightened to 80 ft. lbs.

spring washer and nut, tightening to 80 ft. lbs. Install lower ball joint in similar fashion. Position square end of ball joints downward and install steering knuckle on lower joint. Insert clamp screw and place tension on torsion arms until upper ball joint can be inserted in upper arm. Install upper clamp screw and tighten both clamp screws to 40 ft. lbs., Fig. G-20. Reinstall brake caliper and front wheel. Bleed brakes and adjust camber and toe-in.

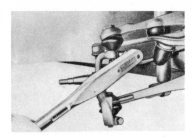

Fig. G-20. Clamp screws tightened to 40 ft. lbs. retain ball joints in steering knuckle on Fastback/Squareback cars.

STEERING GEAR HINTS

Looseness or free movement of the steering wheel may indicate the need for adjustment. However, the adjustments must never be so tight as to cause any appreciable stiffness or resistance in the gear itself. The gear used on "Beetle" models (prior to August, 1961) is of the worm and sector type, Fig. G-21. Two adjustments are provided; one for the worm shaft and another for the sector shaft.

    1 - Loosen lock nut and sector shaft adjusting screw, Fig. G-21, No. 18.

2 - Loosen adjusting sleeve clamping screw and tighten adjusting sleeve clockwise until worm shaft end play is taken up, Fig. G-21, No. 16.

3 - Tighten adjusting sleeve clamp screw.

4 - Bring sector shaft arm at a right angle with steering worm. Tighten adjusting screw, Fig. G-21, No. 18, as far as it will go and loosen 1/8 turn.

5 - Hold adjusting screw and tighten lock nut.

With the front wheels off the floor, check the steering gear for any binding or tightness at all positions from extreme right to extreme left turns.

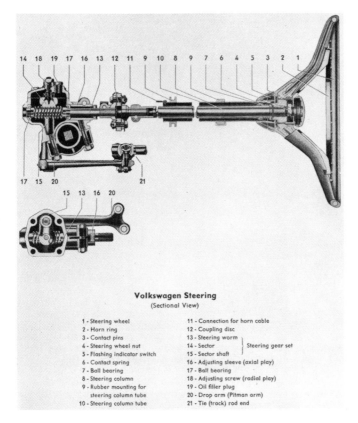

Volkswagen Steering
(Sectional View)

1 - Steering wheel	11 - Connection for horn cable
2 - Horn ring	12 - Coupling disc
3 - Contact pins	13 - Steering worm
4 - Steering wheel nut	14 - Sector Steering gear set
5 - Flashing indicator switch	15 - Sector shaft
6 - Contact spring	16 - Adjusting sleeve (axial play)
7 - Ball bearing	17 - Ball bearing
8 - Steering column	18 - Adjusting screw (radial play)
9 - Rubber mounting for	19 - Oil filler plug
steering column tube	20 - Drop arm (Pitman arm)
10 - Steering column tube	21 - Tie (track) rod end

Fig. G-21. Pictured is Volkswagen worm-and-sector type steering gear used in "Beetle" models before August, 1961. Details are called out.

The roller type steering gear, used on later "Beetle" models and on Fastback and Squareback models, consists of an adjustable steering worm which meshes with the steering roller shaft by means of a needle bearing mounted roller, Fig. G-22. The worm is mounted in two ball bearings in the steering gear case. The steering roller shaft is supported in the steering gear case and cover by bronze bushings.

The steering worm is adjusted by a shim which is situated under the upper ball bearing. The meshing depth of the roller shaft and the resulting lack of play in the steering lock is adjusted by an adjusting screw in the steering gear case cover, Fig. G-22.

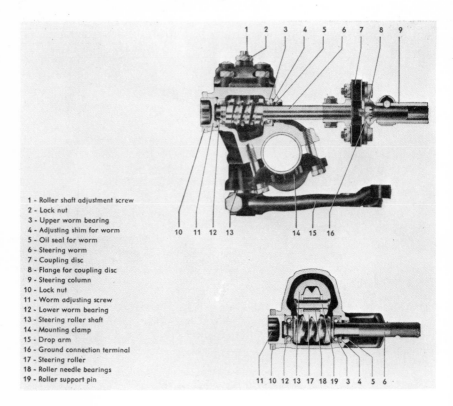

1 - Roller shaft adjustment screw
2 - Lock nut
3 - Upper worm bearing
4 - Adjusting shim for worm
5 - Oil seal for worm
6 - Steering worm
7 - Coupling disc
8 - Flange for coupling disc
9 - Steering column
10 - Lock nut
11 - Worm adjusting screw
12 - Lower worm bearing
13 - Steering roller shaft
14 - Mounting clamp
15 - Drop arm
16 - Ground connection terminal
17 - Steering roller
18 - Roller needle bearings
19 - Roller support pin

Fig. G-22. Roller type steering gear is used on all Beetle models (after August, 1961) and on Type 3 and Squareback models.

This steering gear must only be lubricated with Hypoid oil SAE 90 and not with grease or other oils. The oil capacity is 0.32 pts., or at a level with the lower edge of the oil filler plug hole.

ROLLER STEERING ADJUSTMENT

Three adjustments are required on roller steering gears for proper operation, Fig. G-23.

To adjust axial play of worm:

1 - If there is play at steering coupling, turn steering wheel to full stop left or right position.
2 - Loosen lock nut of steering worm adjusting screw, Fig. G-22, No. 11.
3 - Turn steering worm at coupling and tighten adjusting screw until play is taken up.
4 - Hold adjusting screw and tighten lock nut.

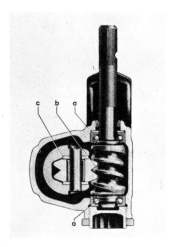

Fig. G-23. Maximum clearances: a—.00 in. b—1 in. measured at steering wheel turned 90 deg. to each side. c—Not more than .0016 in.

To adjust roller-to-worm clearance:

1 - If there is more than 1 in. of play at steering wheel when it is turned 90 deg. to left or right, loosen roller shaft adjusting screw lock nut, Fig. G-22, No. 11.
2 - Loosen adjusting screw about one turn, then tighten it until roller just contacts steering worm.
3 - Hold adjusting screw and tighten lock nut to 14 ft. lbs.
4 - Road test. If steering wheel does not return to within 45 deg. of straight ahead position after a turn at 20 mph, roller is too tight and must be readjusted.

To correct roller axial play:

1 - If first two adjustments fail to correct steering play problem, steering gear must be disassembled.

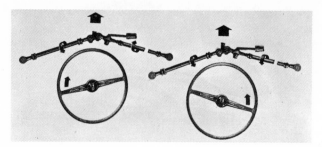

Fig. G-24. To center steering wheel, lengthen one tie rod and shorten other by same amount, by turning tie rod sleeves in direction shown. Toe-in will not be altered.

2 - With gear disassembled, axial play of roller, Fig. G-23, must not exceed .0016 in. If an .02 in. feeler gauge can be inserted between roller and washer, replace steering roller shaft.

3 - Assemble, adjust and reinstall steering gear. Center steering wheel, Fig. G-24.

WHEEL BALANCING IS IMPORTANT

In order to have a smooth riding car and keep tire wear at a minimum, it is essential that the wheel and tire assemblies are in balance. On-car and off-car wheel balancers are available, however, a reasonably accurate job can be done by mounting each of the tire and wheel assemblies on one of the front wheel spindles. Care must be taken that there is no brake drag and that the wheel bearings are not adjusted too tight.

Then allow the wheel to spin slowly until it comes to rest. Mark the tire to indicate the heavy side, which will be at the bottom. Select a wheel balance weight and attach it to the wheel rim at the top of the wheel. Again allow the wheel to spin. If the weight is too light, the wheel will stop at the same position as it did originally. If the weight is too heavy, the wheel will stop with the weight at the bottom.

Try different weights until there is no tendency for the wheel to stop in the same position.

SHOCK ABSORBERS

The shock absorbers are double-acting, hydraulic, telescopic type. They are not adjustable, and it is impractical to add fluid to them. If they are not working properly or have lost a large amount of fluid, it will be necessary to replace them with new units. Heavy-duty shock absorbers are available for installation on cars subjected to severe driving conditions.

When installing new units, replace rubber bushings if necessary. Check securing screw and pin in torsion arm for wear. Tighten shock absorber attaching nuts to 25 ft. lbs.

STEERING TROUBLE SHOOTING

Symptom	Cause	Remedy
Hard steering from lock to lock and front wheels do not automatically resume straight-ahead position after a turn	a - Front axle inadequately lubricated	a - Jack up front end of car and thoroughly lubricate front axle
	b - King pins or ball joints stiff or seized	b - Jack up car and disconnect tie rods. Try to free pivot points by thoroughly lubricating them (if necessary with thin oil). If seized, remove king pin or ball joints and replace damaged components
	c - Steering gear maladjusted	c - Check steering gear adjustments. Adjust sector shaft and worm shaft end play as prescribed. If necessary, fit new parts
	d - Low oil level	d - Check oil level
Hard steering and squeaking noise	a - Steering wheel binding in steering column top bushing	a - Check position of steering column; if necessary, check and correct position of steering gear (check toe-in). Lubricate or replace top bushing
	b - Steering wheel hub chafing on steering column top bushing face	b - Bushing projecting from steering column tube or steering column tube positioned too high. Lower tube
Hard steering, unequal resistance and chafing noise	a - Steering column fouling steering column tube	a - Alter position of steering gear so that the steering column is correctly centered in steering column tube (check toe-in)

Fix Your Volkswagen

Complaint	Cause	Correction
Front wheels do not resume straight-ahead position after a turn, although there is no binding in the steering system	a - Front wheels improperly adjusted b - Steering arms bent or twisted	a - Check and adjust caster, camber and toe-in b - Remove steering knuckles and check them for bends and twisting. Replace if necessary
Play in steering system caused by excessive clearance between steering wheel and steering column top bushing	a - Bushing worn	a - Replace bushing
Excessive play in steering gear	a - Steering gear improperly adjusted b - Steering set worn	a - Check steering gear adjustments. Adjust sector shaft and worm shaft end play as prescribed b - Replace sector shaft, sector, and worm
Excessive play in tie rod joints	a - Ball studs worn	a - Replace tie rod ends
Excessive play in front wheel suspension	a - Worn torsion arms, torsion arm links, front wheel bearings	a - Check adjustments of torsion arm link pins and front wheel bearings. Fit new parts

Also keep in mind that defective shock absorbers may cause the car to wander, bounce and provide an improper ride. Underinflated tires will cause hard steering, front wheel shimmy and road wander in addition to rapid tire wear. Tire wear is always aggravated by out-of-balance wheels or tires. Shimmy can be caused by an out-of-balance condition.

ENGINE LUBRICATION SERVICE

The service life and efficiency of Volkswagen engines is dependent upon a reasonable amount of care for the engine lubrication system. This system is simple and efficient but must have clean oil at all times. For the oil to remain in good condition, the oil cooler and crankcase ventilation system must have proper care.

The removable parts of the lubrication system are shown in Fig. H-1. All connecting passages are within the engine crankcase and crankshaft.

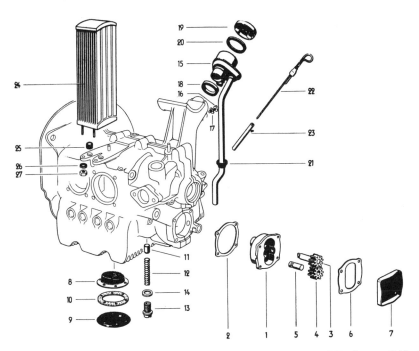

Fig. H-1. All parts shown can be serviced or repaired with engine in car. 1-7 oil pump; 8-10 oil strainer; 11-14 oil pressure regulator; 15-21 crankcase breather; 24 oil cooler.

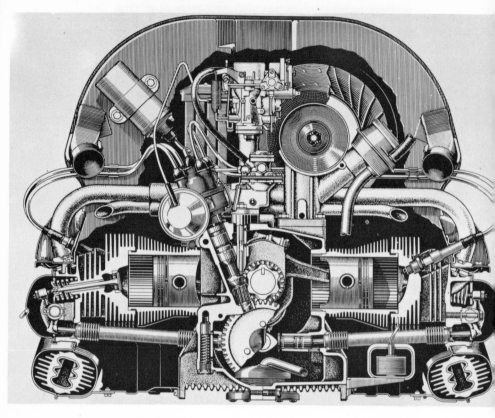

Fig. H-2. Valve operating rod tubes have a seal at each end.

These drilled passages conduct the oil from the oil pump to the oil cooler to the crankshaft, camshaft, valve action, etc. The tubes surrounding the valve operating rods are also used to conduct oil from the valve operating parts back to the oil pan, Figs. H-2 and H-3.

CRANKCASE VENTILATION

On early "Beetle" engines, a breather at the oil filler provides for crankcase ventilation, and a road draft tube to allow oil fumes to escape from the crankcase. If this breather becomes clogged with dust, it will hasten deterioration of the engine oil and lead to excess pressure in the crankcase resulting in oil leakage at the fan pulley. Some filler caps are equipped with filters, others are not. In either case the cap should be thoroughly cleaned with solvent at regular intervals.

Beginning with late 1961 models, a crankcase ventilation device was installed between the oil filler tube and the carburetor air cleaner. It consists of a special outlet fitting on the front side of the oil filler tube and a flexible tube extending from this fitting to a metal sleeve protruding from the side of the oil bath air cleaner.

Engine Lubrication Service

On later models, this connection is made to the air cleaner intake tube. The metal sleeve projects about 1/16 in. inside the air cleaner housing to prevent oil from entering the connecting hose. No ventilation valve is used; the road draft tube is eliminated. In operation, the crankcase fumes are carried from the oil filler pipe to the carburetor air cleaner and then into the engine to be burned in the regular combustion process.

On 1964-1968 models, and on Fastback and Squareback models, a condensed water drain pipe is fitted to the oil breather pipe much like the road draft tube, but with the lower end sealed by a rubber valve. The valve is held in place by an internal button that snaps into a hole in the drain pipe.

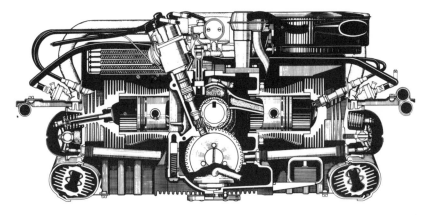

Fig. H-3. Engine for VW's 1968 Fastback and Squareback is first large-scale production power plant to use electronic fuel injection. System includes electric fuel pump and eliminates twin carburetors.

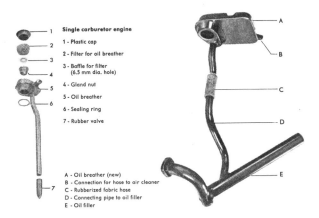

Single carburetor engine

1 - Plastic cap

2 - Filter for oil breather

3 - Baffle for filter (6.5 mm dia. hole)

4 - Gland nut

5 - Oil breather

6 - Sealing ring

7 - Rubber valve

A - Oil breather (new)
B - Connection for hose to air cleaner
C - Rubberized fabric hose
D - Connecting pipe to oil filler
E - Oil filler

Fig. H-4. Typical crankcase breather setup from 1964–1968, left, rubber valve was used to release condensation. In 1969, right, condensation drains into oil fill tube.

167

Fig. H-5. 1—Gasket. 2—Oil strainer. 3—Gasket. 4—Bottom plate.
5—Gasket. 6—Drain plug. 7—Nuts and lock washers.

In operation, condensed water collects in the pipe. When a certain amount of water has collected, its weight will open a slot in the valve and the water will drain off. The valve and the crankcase ventilation device should be inspected at regular maintenance service intervals (every 3,000 miles-through 1965; every 6,000 miles-after August 1965). If the valve is damaged or if the slot does not close properly, the valve must be replaced.

For 1969, all Volkswagens are fitted with a crankcase breather that routes condensation back to the crankcase by way of the oil fill tube, Fig. H-4. The rubber valve has been eliminated.

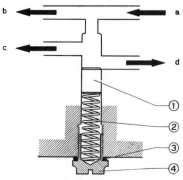

Oil Pressure Relief Valve [Schematic View]

Fig. H-6. 1—Plunger. 2—Spring. 3—Gasket. 4—Plug. a—From oil pump.
b—To oil cooler. c—Directly to lubrication points. d—To oil sump.

168

OIL STRAINER SERVICE

The engine oil pump draws oil from within a strainer located in the bottom of the crankcase, Fig. H-5. The oil suction pipe must fit snugly within the opening in the screen, otherwise the screen cannot function. Remove the screen and clean it. Also scrape and clean all mating surfaces. Reinstall the screen assembly, using new gaskets. Excess tightening of the retaining nuts may warp the metal bottom plate and result in oil leakage. It is not necessary to remove the filter to drain the crankcase oil as a separate plug is provided for that purpose.

OIL PRESSURE RELIEF VALVE HINTS

If any oil flow difficulty becomes apparent, check the oil pressure relief valve. This is particularly true if the oil cooler develops a leak. The function of the valve is shown in Fig. H-6. The plunger must be a free fit in the bore and the spring in good condition. If the plunger should stick in the bore, it can be pulled out by screwing a tap having a 10 mm. thread into the threaded hole provided in the plunger.

OIL COOLER SERVICE

The oil cooler is located in the cooling air stream and, therefore, the rear hood and bracket, as well as the fan housing, must be removed if service is required, Fig. H-7. The oil cooling unit is held in place by three studs. If the oil cooler is removed for cleaning, it should be

Fig. H-7. New oil cooler on 1971 Beetle engine is made of aluminum. It is relocated farther forward on engine and is mounted by means of an offset intermediate flange (arrow). Fan housing now has a separate duct to supply cooling air to oil cooler.

examined for mechanical condition. The tubes must be clean on the outside and straight. The tubes must not touch each other and the sheet metal partition must not be loose.

If a leak is evident or suspected, the unit can be tested at a pressure of 85 lb. per sq. in. In case of leakage, also check oil pressure relief valve to see that the plunger is free. When replacing unit, be sure to use new rubber seals.

The oil cooler used in Fastback and Squareback engines is mounted horizontally, Fig. H-3. On these engines, spacer rings are used between the crankcase and cooler at each securing screw, Fig. H-8. These rings prevent over-tightening of the cooler, which would flatten the seals and cut off the flow of oil. The three spacer rings must be in place when the oil cooler is installed.

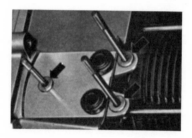

Fig. H-8. Spacer rings (arrows) must be in place on crankcase before oil cooler is installed or rubber seals will flatten out and stop oil flow.

Fig. H-9. Type of puller needed for oil pump removal.

HOW TO REPAIR OIL PUMP

The oil pump can be removed with the engine in place, but a special puller is desired since the pump housing fits tightly in the crankcase, Fig. H-9. It is necessary to remove the engine rear cover plate, fan pulley, pulley cover, oil pump cover and oil pump gears, Fig. H-10.

Fig. H-10. Oil pump as disassembled.

Fig. H-11. Measurement is made without gasket in place.

Excessive wear in the pump parts will result in low oil pressure. The clearance specifications are rather close:

Backlash between gears - 0.0012 - 0.0031 in.

End play with cover removed - 0.0026 - 0.0072 in.

Wear limit - 0.0079 in.

Any visible wear in housing or inside cover plate indicates replacement of parts is needed. The idler gear pin must be tight, no looseness is permissible. The clearance between the pump gears and cover, Fig. H-11, should never be in excess of 0.004 in.

FAN PULLEY OIL LEAK REMEDIES

Excessive wear in the crankshaft bearing, sticking oil pressure valve plunger, a bent pulley or stopped-up oil thread on pulley hub are the principal reasons for oil leakage at the fan pulley. As mentioned, a stopped-up crankcase breather will also cause or aggravate oil leakage.

Fig. H-12. Application of puller to fan pulley.

In order to remove the pulley, the fan belt and engine rear cover plate must be removed. A puller is then used to remove the fan pulley, Fig. H-12.

The fan pulley must not be bent and the oil return thread must be clean. If the thread is worn a pulley with oversize thread is available. When reassembling make sure the oil thrower is turned with the curved outer rim facing toward the pulley as shown in Fig. H-13.

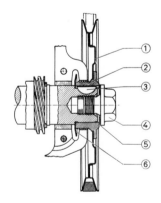

Fig. H-13.

1—Crankshaft pulley
2—Oil return thread
3—Woodruff key
4—Mounting bolt
5—Spring washer
6—Crankshaft oil thrower

ENGINE REPAIR METHODS

As previously mentioned, the engine should be removed from the Volkswagen if any extensive repairs are required. Cylinder head removal was covered in the Chapter on Valve Service.

Once you have removed the cylinder heads, lift off the tubes which enclose the valve rods and take off the sheet metal shield from between each pair of cylinders. Then slide off the cylinder barrels from the head bolts and piston, Fig. K-1.

Before removing the pistons, mark them to indicate which cylinder they came from and which side of the piston faces forward, Fig. K-2. The cylinders are arranged as follows: No. 1 - right front; No. 2 - right rear; No. 3 - left front; No. 4 - left rear, Fig. C-2, when viewed from the rear of the Volkswagen.

Mark the cylinder barrels in a similar manner as they are removed. Take the snap ring fron one side of each piston pin and remove the pin. Do not force the pins out or the pistons may be distorted. If you heat the piston to about 175 deg. F., pin removal is easy.

FLYWHEEL REMOVAL

The next step in disassembly is to remove the flywheel in order to get at two bolts near the camshaft bearing which go through both halves of the crankcase on older "Beetle" engines. The flywheel is held to the crankshaft by dowel pins and a large gland nut, Fig. K-3. This gland nut is accessible after removal of the clutch pressure plate and driven plate.

CRANKCASE DISASSEMBLY

Pull off the flywheel and remove two bolts from each side of the camshaft bearing. Then remove the oil strainer and oil pump housing before removing the balance of the bolts that hold the two halves of the crankcase together.

Separate the crankcase halves by using a rubber mallet to loosen and remove one half from the other. NEVER try to insert any tool

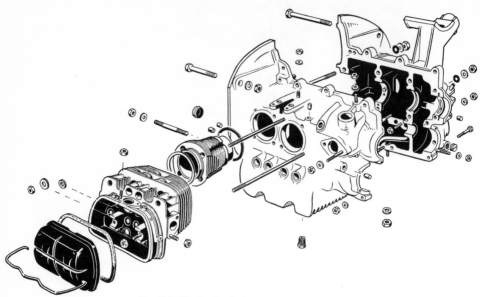

Fig. K-1. Each cylinder head serves two individual cylinder barrels, and crankcase is split in two vertically.

between the crankcase halves to separate them, or oil leaks will surely result. Lift out the crankshaft and camshaft. The connecting rods are still attached to the crankshaft and are removed as a unit, Fig. K-4.

The crankshaft rear main bearing and both front main bearings are of the sleeve type on older "Beetle" engines, Fig. K-5. The main bearing in the middle is split in half in the usual manner. Also the flange on the rear main (next to the flywheel) bearing takes the end thrust of the crank-shaft. The camshaft runs in three bearings machined in the crankcase. Beginning with 1966 engines, three aluminum alloy split shells are used.

Fig. K-2. One method of marking position and location of pistons.

Engine Repair Methods

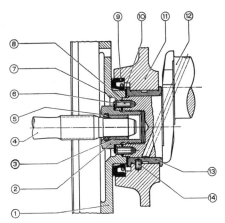

Fig. K-3. Flywheel-to-engine assembly: 1—Flywheel. 2—Gland nut. 3—Pilot bushing. 4—Main drive shaft. 5—Gasket. 6—Lock washer. 7—Dowel pin. 8—Gasket. 9—Oil seal. 10—Shims. 11—Crankcase. 12—Crankshaft. 13—Crankshaft main bearing. 14—Dowel pin.

Fig. K-4. Remove and reinstall crankshaft and connecting rods as a unit.

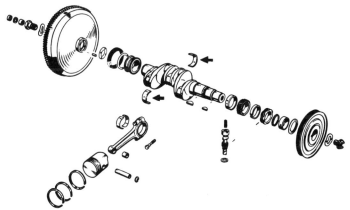

Fig. K-5. Note that center main bearing, indicated by arrows, is split in half, while other main bearings are sleeve type.

BEARING REMOVAL

The connecting rods are not held together by bolts in the usual manner. The caps are held to the rods with special cap screws which are locked in place, Fig. K-6. Before removing the rod caps, make sure that each rod and cap is marked on the same side so that they can be assembled correctly. The bearing inserts and rods must be reinstalled precisely as removed since they are not interchangeable once they have been in operation.

Further reference to Fig. K-5 will indicate that all the main bearings except the one behind the timing gear will slip out readily. To remove this one bearing it is necessary to remove both gears and spacers. The distributor drive gear is held in place by a snap ring, but the timing gear is a press fit and must be pulled. Heat the gears to approximately 175 deg. F. before removal to avoid damage to the crankshaft.

Fig. K-6. Cap screws instead of bolts are used on connecting rods on most VW engines.

INSPECTION AND REPLACEMENT HINTS

After complete disassembly of the engine, the next step is a thorough and complete cleaning of all parts before any inspection is attempted. Cleaning should be done inside and outside, including the oil passages in the crankcase, the cooling fins on cylinders and cylinder heads, carbon accumulation on pistons and in cylinder heads, etc. Use a solvent and/or manual scraping where needed.

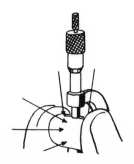

Fig. K-7. Method of using micrometer to check out-of-round.

Examine the crankcase for damage or cracks and remove all traces of gaskets or compound on joining faces. Remove any scratches or burrs. Check stud threads for wear. If any studs are loose, a special oversize tap can be used and new studs with oversize threads installed. Also examine the valve push rods and guide plates for wear. There should be no appreciable looseness. If wear is noticeable, oversize parts should be installed.

Care must be used when installing the push rod guide plates so that they do not turn out of position when being tightened. If these plates are twisted, the push rod ends will not bear squarely on the cams, resulting in noise and rapid wear.

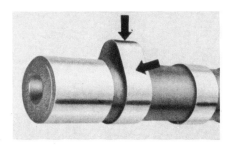

Fig. K-8. Points at which cam lobes should be checked.

CRANKSHAFT TIPS

Before attempting any measurements of the crankshaft, make sure that the oil passages inside the shaft as well as the bearing journals are completely clean. If there are any visible cracks or damage, it must be replaced. It is advisable to have the crankshaft checked by a specialist who has a magnetic crack detector since cracks are not always visible.

If the crankshaft is sound it must be measured for wear, out-of-round and taper on each of the journals. To check for out-of-round, a micrometer is used at several points around the circumference of each journal, Fig. K-7. If main or connecting rod journals are out-of-round more than .0012 in. the crankshaft should be replaced or reconditioned.

Measurement for taper is made with the same instrument and each journal is checked at each end of the journal surface. Any appreciable taper on any one journal is cause for rejection of the shaft.

Also check the dowel holes in the end of the crankshaft flange where the flywheel is attached. If these holes are damaged or worn, it will be necessary to drill and ream new holes in the flange.

As the crankshaft is hardened and balanced, any machine work requires skillful work on specialized equipment. For this reason a crankshaft unsuited for use should be exchanged for a new or reconditioned one complete with a set of bearings to fit.

CAMSHAFT CHECKS

Check the camshaft gear for cracks or looseness where it is riveted to the camshaft hub. Check the cams for wear, pitting or diagonal wear on cam face, Fig. K-8. Use a dial gauge mounted as shown in Fig. K-9 to check for straightness or run-out. If run-out exceeds .0016 in., a new shaft is needed. The clearance in the bearings should not be more than .005 in. and the end clearance should not exceed .0055 in.

The teeth on the camshaft gear should not be damaged in any way and the backlash between the gear teeth should not exceed .002 in. If backlash is excessive, gears are available in different sizes as needed.

Fig. K-9. Method of checking cam shaft for straightness.

CONNECTING ROD EXAMINATION

All rotating and reciprocating parts of a Volkswagen engine are carefully balanced and it is essential to maintain this condition in any repair operation. For example a difference of .18 oz. in the weight of the connecting rods in one engine should not be exceeded. This weight is checked on the rod alone with the piston pin and piston removed.

It is also essential that the bearing bore in the big end of the con-

Fig. K-10. Type of inside micrometer used for checking bearing bore.

Fig. K-11. Special tool for removing and replacing piston rings.

necting rod be round and true. This may be checked with an inside micrometer, Fig. K-10. This check is made with the bearing removed and the cap drawn down to 36 ft. lbs. with a torque wrench. If the bore is distorted or out-of-round, the rod should be replaced rather than attempt to remachine it.

Check the piston pin bushing in the small end of the connecting rod for visible wear or damage. The correct clearance for the piston pin in the bushing is indicated by a light finger push fit of the pin at room temperature. If the fit is too loose, the bushing should be replaced rather than fit oversize pins. The installation and fitting of these bushings is an exacting machine operation and special skill and equipment is required.

WHAT TO DO ABOUT PISTONS

In working with pistons, remember that they are fragile and easily distorted; the metal is soft and easily scratched. The same care should be exercised in handling the rings. Therefore, remove and replace piston rings with a special tool, Fig. K-11.

Next remove the accumulated carbon from the ring grooves. Here again a special tool is desirable to avoid damage to the ring grooves.

If after a thorough cleaning the piston does not appear to be damaged, it should be measured for wear. The nominal diameter is stamped on the piston top, Fig. K-12. Take the measurement at the bottom end of the skirt, Fig. K-13. If similar equipment is not available, a micrometer caliper can be used. If, on measuring the piston and corresponding cylinder, it is found that the clearance is near 0.008 in., replace piston and cylinder by another pair of the same size and weight grading.

Since Volkswagen cylinders can be obtained separately, a new piston must not be fitted in a worn cylinder. A damaged piston can be replaced by a new one in a cylinder that is not worn. The pistons--like the connecting rods--are carefully matched for weight and should all weigh the same within .35 oz. in any one engine.

The piston pin fit in the piston must also be checked. The clearance should be 0.0004 to 0.0008 in. If the pin can be pushed in with the piston cold, use an oversize pin and adjust the bushing in the connecting rod accordingly. With the piston heated to 175 deg. F., the pin should be a light finger push into the piston with the piston pin oiled.

Fig. K-12. Marking of pistons: A—Arrow must point toward flywheel on installation. B—Piston pin bore size. C—Grade of size marked by paint spot. D—Letter near arrow corresponds to index of part number. E—Details of weight grading (+ or −). F—Grade of weight marked by paint spot. G—Grade of size. H—Details of piston size in mm.

Fig. K-13. If pin appears to be reserviceable, measure for wear at longest point of piston skirt.

ARE NEW RINGS NEEDED?

Piston rings become seated in the cylinders during operation and once the cylinders are removed, this mating of surfaces is destroyed and a new seating must occur. A new ring will seat more satisfactorily than a used one.

The end clearance of the ring is measured with the ring seated squarely in the bottom of the cylinder barrel, Fig. K-14. If the gap

Fig. K-14. Method of measuring piston ring gap.

Fig. K-15. Checking piston rings for side clearance.

measured by a feeler gauge exceeds 0.037 in., the ring should be replaced. The gap for a new ring should be 0.012 - 0.017 in.

It is also necessary to check the clearance of the ring in the piston groove, Fig. K-15. The side clearance of the compression rings should be 0.002 to 0.0035 in. and should not exceed 0.005 in. The oil ring clearance should be 0.001 - 0.002 in. and should not exceed 0.004 in.

When installing rings, make sure the upper compression ring is installed with the marking "top" or "Oben" on the ring toward the top of the piston, Fig. K-16.

ENGINE CYLINDER HINTS

Since the Volkswagen engine has individual cylinder barrels, a damaged cylinder can be replaced. Volkswagen dealers have a large assortment of sizes in stock at all times.

The fitting clearance between piston and cylinder should be 0.0014 - 0.0022 in. The wear limit is given as 0.008 in. and out-of-round at 0.004 in. The clearance is determined by measurement of the piston and cylinder rather than by a feeler gauge inserted between piston and cylinder as is common practice.

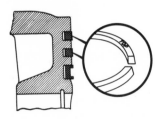

Fig. K-16. Compression rings should be installed as marked.

Measurement of the cylinder is made just below the top edge of the bore, using a suitable dial gauge for this purpose, Fig. K-17. Cylinders which are worn to the specified limit should be replaced with corresponding pistons. Cylinders and pistons in any one engine must be the same size; sets are all marked for size.

ENGINE BEARING TIPS

All crankshaft bearings are of the precision slip-in type and no filing, reaming or fitting is permissible. Bearings are available in a wide variety of sizes to fit any needs of either main or connecting rod journals. The clearance for the main bearing next to the flywheel is .002 to .004 in. If more than .007 in., replacement is needed. The other three main bearings should have a clearance of .0010 - .004 in. and should be replaced if more than .007 in. clearance exists. The connecting rod bearings are to have a clearance of .0008 - .003 in. and should be replaced if more than .006 in. exists, or if the side clearance is more than .03 in. This side clearance should be .004 to .016 in.

In addition to proper fit of the bearings they should be given a careful visual inspection. Discoloration or dull appearance does not affect the good quality or usefulness of the bearing insert. Look for excessive grooving, scoring or too much foreign material embedded in the insert. Shiny spots, indicating wiping action, are a sign of too little clearance brought about by crankshaft journal taper or out-of-round, damage to back of insert or dirt behind the insert.

If the bearing clearance is correct, all other factors, such as dull or varnished appearance, dark gray color, lack of brightness and similar minor irregularities can be disregarded.

It is of the utmost importance when installing new bearings that hands, tools and equipment are kept perfectly clean. Any dirt present on the crankshaft journal, on the face or back of the bearing insert, or on the bearing cap, will cause a false indication of bearing clearance and result in early bearing failure.

Fig. K-17. Measure for cylinder wear just below top edge of bore.

THINGS TO WATCH IN REASSEMBLY

After all repair or replacement operations are completed, reassembly starts with installation of the main bearing between the crankshaft timing gear and crankshaft throw. After the bearing is slipped on the shaft, the shaft is mounted in a press, Fig. K-18. Install timing gear key and heat timing gear to 175 deg. F. before pressing in place. The spacer and

Fig. K-18. Crankshaft is placed in a press for reinstallation of gears.

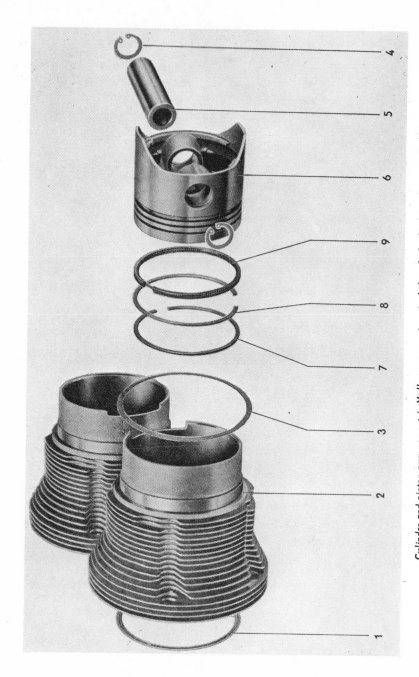

Cylinder and piston arrangement in Volkswagen engines includes: 1—Sealing ring (between cylinder and cylinder head). 2—Cylinder. 3—Sealing ring (between cylinder and crankcase). 4—Circlip. 5—Piston pin. 6—Piston. 7—Upper ring. 8—Lower ring (narrow face). 9—Oil scraper ring (with coil spring).

Fig. K-19. Distributor drive gear should be heated to 175 deg. F. before it is pressed in place.

distributor gear are then installed, Fig. K-19, and the distributor gear lock ring reinstalled.

Before the connecting rods are assembled on the crankshaft, they should be checked for correct alignment. Special equipment is available for this purpose, Fig. K-20. Oil the connecting rod bearing surface

Fig. K-20. One type of equipment used for connecting rod alignment.

and assemble the rod on the crankshaft, making sure that each rod is replaced as marked before removal. Torque the cap screws to 36 ft. lbs., and stake the heads to lock them in place. The rod should turn on the shaft of its own weight.

Fig. K-21. Note that oil thrower is cupped toward fan pulley.

The crankshaft main bearings are held in place by dowels. Check each dowel to make sure it is not loose. Place one-half of split main bearing in the crankcase. Install rear main bearing on crankshaft with dowel hole offset toward the flywheel. Install sleeve bearing in front of gears and oil thrower on crankshaft, making sure it is turned the proper way, Fig. K-21. Before lowering crankshaft in place, make certain that all bearings are properly dowel located. Also install other half of one split main bearing.

Fig. K-22. Left. Camshaft in place in older engine. Sealing compound should be used on outside of end cap. Right. Starting with 1966 engines, split bearings are used on camshaft.

Install the camshaft along with end plug and thrust washer, Fig. K-22. Be sure that timing marks on crankshaft gear and camshaft gear coincide, Fig. K-23.

Install the new oil seal. It must seat squarely on the bottom of its recess in the crankcase. Also coat outside with sealing compound, Fig. K-24.

Engine Repair Methods

Before replacing the other half of the crankcase, spread a thin coat of sealing compound on the crankcase joining faces. Sealing compound must not enter the oil passages of crankshaft and camshaft bearings.

When the crankcase is assembled, a torque wrench must be used to tighten the nuts. The 8 mm. nuts should be tightened to 14 ft. lbs.; 12 mm. nuts to 25 ft. lbs.

Fig. K-23. When installing camshaft, see that timing marks on crankshaft gear align with timing mark on camshaft gear.

Fig. K-24. Crankshaft oil seal replacement.

Before the flywheel is finally installed, the end play of the crankshaft must be checked. Endwise movement should be .0023 to .0047 in. If more than .006 in., make an adjustment by adding or subtracting shims at the outer end of the main bearing, Fig. K-25. These shims are available in several thicknesses, marked on the shim.

A dial gauge can be mounted to bear on either end of the crankshaft or on the fan pulley. The crankshaft is then pushed back and forth to get the dial readings.

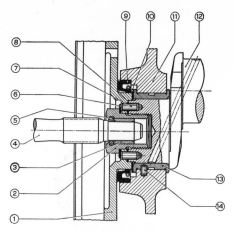

Fig. K-25. End play of crankshaft is adjusted by adding or subtracting shims at point 10.

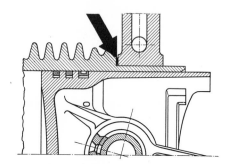

Fig. K-26. New gaskets must be used under cylinders.

Fig. K-27. One type of piston ring compressor which was designed for use on this engine. Other types can be used.

Engine Repair Methods

Install the flywheel to obtain a proper reading each time the shims are changed. After final adjustment, tighten the gland nut with a long handle torque wrench to a reading of 217 ft. lbs.

Oil the piston rings and pistons and space the ring gaps around the piston before reinstalling the cylinders. Oil ring gaps should be on the top side of the engine. Always use new gaskets between the cylinder barrels and crankcase, Fig. K-26.

Use a piston ring compressor to avoid damage to the piston rings when installing the cylinders, Fig. K-27. After the cylinders are in place, be sure to install the metal deflectors on each pair before replacing the cylinder heads.

Replacement of cylinder heads, valves, etc., and engine tune-up has been previously described.

SPECIAL SERVICE - FASTBACK AND SQUAREBACK

Basically, engine service on "Beetle" models and on Fastback and Squareback cars is very similar. However, the cooling fan is mounted directly on the crankshaft on Fastback/Squareback engines, Fig. K-28, as opposed to above the engine block on "Beetle" engines. Therefore any service to the cooling fan or crankshaft pulley necessitates pulling the engine from the car.

Engine with Manual Transmission

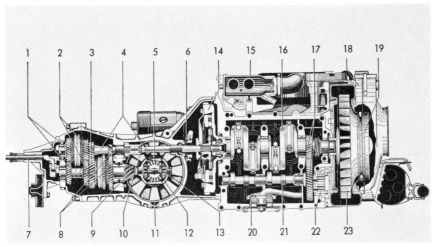

Fig. K-28. Details of 1971 Type 3/Squareback engine include: 1—Fourth gear train. 2—Third gear train. 3—Second gear train. 4—Main drive shaft. 5—Differential side gear. 6—Clutch release bearing. 7—Transmission shift lever. 8—First gear train. 9—Drive pinion. 10—Reverse gear. 11—Oil drain plug. 12—Differential housing. 13—Differential pinion. 14—Flywheel. 15—Intake air distributor. 16—Crankshaft. 17—Camshaft drive gears. 18—Fan housing. 19—Crankshaft pulley. 20—Oil strainer. 21—Camshaft. 22—Oil pump. 23—Fan.

To install a new crankshaft pulley: Remove muffler, generator and cooling air intake housing, Fig. K-29. Pry off plastic cap on crankshaft pulley and unscrew pulley bolt. Remove crankshaft pulley. On installation: Use new paper gasket between pulley and fan. Reinstall shim, if one was

Fig. K-29. Engine must be removed from Fastback or Squareback cars to service fan or crankshaft pulley.

Fig. K-30. Tighten crankshaft pulley 94 to 108 ft. lbs.

used (do not use more than two). Insert pulley with pin engaged in hole in fan. Tighten pulley nut 94 to 108 ft. lbs., Fig. K-30. See that generator pulley aligns with crankshaft pulley and that belt clearance at air intake housing is at least 3/16 in.

A special tool is required to pull the fan from the crankshaft. Likewise, on reinstallation, the fan must be pressed in place.

In other areas of difference, the generator on "Beetle" engines drives the cooling fan, while the generator on Fastback/Squareback engines does not include an extended generator shaft. As mentioned, the cooling fan on these engines is mounted on the crankshaft.

Except for piston displacement, internal engine construction is much the same on "Beetle" and Fastback/Squareback engines. One noticeable difference is that the Fastback/Squareback engine (and "Beetle" after Jan., 1966) uses fitted bolts and nuts on the connecting rods, Fig. K-31, whereas cap screws are used on earlier "Beetle" engine connecting rods, Fig. K-6.

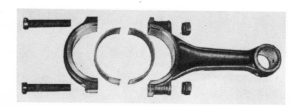

Fig. K-31. Connecting rods on later "Beetle" and Fastback/Squareback engines use fitted bolts and hex nuts.

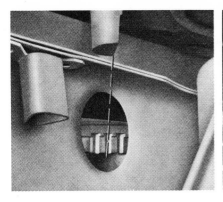

Fig. K-32. Ignition timing on Fastback/Squareback engines is set by aligning mark on crankshaft pulley with setting surface on fan housing and rotor arm points to No. 1 mark on edge of distributor housing.

Finally, installation of the distributor drive pinion differs in positioning. To "time" either engine, the piston in No. 1 cylinder must be on top dead center and the rotor arm must point to the mark on the rim of the distributor housing, Fig. K-32. Then, on "Beetle" engines, the distributor drive pinion must be positioned with the offset slot at right angles to the

Fig. K-33. When installing distributor drive pinion in Fastback/Squareback engines, offset slot in pinion must be at approximately 60 deg. angle to crankcase joint with smaller segment toward oil cooler.

engine center line with the smaller segment toward the crankshaft pulley. On Fastback/Squareback engines, the pinion must be positioned with the offset slot at approximately 60 deg. angle to crankcase joint with smaller segment toward the oil cooler, Fig. K-33.

ENGINE TROUBLE SHOOTING

Causes of Poor Performance
    Poor compression
    Worn piston rings
    Excessive piston clearance
    Stuck piston rings
    Stuck valves
    Valves not seating
    Improper valve adjustment
    Burned valves
    Weak valve springs
    Clogged exhaust system
    Leaking manifold gasket
    Incorrect ignition timing
    Burned distributor points
    Wrong automatic advance
    Incorrect carburetor adjustment
    Defective fuel pump
    Sticking fuel injector
    Loose connections
    Dirty trigger contacts
    Open pressure switch
    Poor ground at injectors
    Disconnected air hose
    Incorrect valve timing
    Clogged air cleaner
    Excessive engine friction
    Slipping clutch
    Dragging brakes
    Defective spark plugs
Causes of High Oil Consumption
    Oil leaks from engine
    Leaks at rear main bearing
    Leaks at front end of crankshaft
    Leaks at oil pump
    Leaks at valve covers
    Worn piston rings
    Worn pistons
    Worn cylinders
    Piston rings stuck in grooves
    Worn valve stems and guides
    Excessive rod bearing clearance
    Excessive main bearing clearance
    Wavy cylinder bores
    Excessive clearance of rings in grooves
    Insufficient ring end gap clearance

Engine Repair Methods

Rings installed in wrong grooves
Rings fitted too tight in grooves
Causes of Engine Overheating
 Obstructed air flow
 Thermostat installed incorrectly
 Defective thermostat
 Bent or loose air control plates
 Slipping fan belt
 Excessive engine friction (rings, bearings, pistons)
 Lean carburetor mixture
 Retarded ignition timing
 Incorrect automatic spark advance
 Insufficient engine oil
 Restricted exhaust system
 Excessive carbon accumulation
 Dirty cooling fins
 Dragging brakes
 Slipping clutch
Causes of Engine Misfiring
 Defective ignition breaker points
 Breaker points not correctly adjusted
 Weak breaker arm spring
 Leaking high tension wiring
 Defective distributor cap
 Corroded terminals in distributor cap
 Defective rotor
 Sticking valves
 Worn valve stem or guide
 Poor compression
 Insufficient tappet clearance
 Sticking valve tappet
 Weak valve spring
 Cracked valve seat
 Broken piston
 Warped cylinder head
 Cracked cylinder head
 Defective spark plugs
 Spark plug gap too wide
 Defective condenser
 Defective ignition coil
 Breaker arm sticking on pin
 Loose connections in primary circuit
 Defective ignition switch
 Worn distributor shaft or bushings
 Dirt or water in fuel system
 Defective intake manifold gasket
 Valves warped, burned or leaking

Causes of Engine Noise
      Worn connecting rod bearings
      Worn main bearings
      Worn piston rings
      Excessive crankshaft end play
      Worn timing gears
      Excessive piston clearance
      Rings striking ridge in cylinder
      Bent connecting rod
      Broken piston pin retainer rings
      Cracked piston
      Worn camshaft bearings
      Loose flywheel
      Loose engine mounts
      Worn valve tappets
      Excessive valve tappet clearance
      Worn fan belt
      Loose fan pulley
      Loose engine accessories

CLUTCH
SERVICING KINKS

A single-plate, dry disc type clutch is used between the Volkswagen engine and manual transmission. It is splined to the main drive shaft of the transmission and is held in place against the flywheel by a spring-loaded clutch pressure plate.

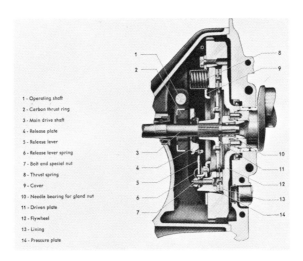

1 - Operating shaft
2 - Carbon thrust ring
3 - Main drive shaft
4 - Release plate
5 - Release lever
6 - Release lever spring
7 - Bolt and special nut
8 - Thrust spring
9 - Cover
10 - Needle bearing for gland nut
11 - Driven plate
12 - Flywheel
13 - Lining
14 - Pressure plate

Fig. L-1. Cross section of older "Beetle" clutch assembly with thrust springs, carbon thrust ring and needle roller pilot bearing.

Beetle models through 1972 utilize a clutch cover having three release levers, Figs. L-1 and L-2. All 1973 models are equipped with a diaphragm-spring cover assembly similar to the one used on all Fastback, Squareback and Type 3 models, Figs. L-3 and L-4.

In all clutch equipped Volkswagen cars, the clutch operating shaft and release bearing are mounted in the transmission housing. On older

"Beetle" models, the release bearing is fitted with a carbon thrust ring; Fastback/Squareback and later "Beetle" release bearings are ball thrust type with a small plastic ring. In all models, the release bearing operates by engaging a release plate, or ring, fitted to the pressure plate release levers.

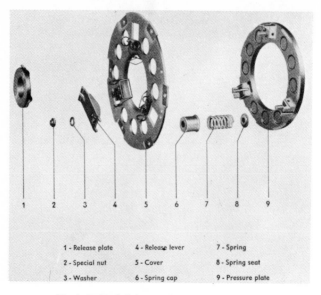

1 - Release plate	4 - Release lever	7 - Spring
2 - Special nut	5 - Cover	8 - Spring seat
3 - Washer	6 - Spring cap	9 - Pressure plate

Fig. L-2. Exploded view of "Beetle" clutch.

In normal usage, the clutch used on the Volkswagen will give in excess of 50,000 miles of good service. There is only one simple adjustment to provide the correct amount of free clutch pedal travel before the throwout bearing contacts the clutch fingers. As the clutch facings wear, the amount of pedal travel reduces and in time the clutch pedal will be forced against the floor pan. The effect will be the same as if the clutch pedal were partly depressed: there will be slippage between the facings and the surface of the flywheel. This will not only result in loss of power, but also extremely rapid clutch facing wear.

HOW TO REMOVE CLUTCH

The clutch is completely enclosed in a housing bolted to the engine crankcase. Clutch replacement requires removal of the engine from the car. When the engine is removed, the clutch slides off the main drive shaft of the transmission and remains bolted to the engine flywheel.

To remove the clutch from the flywheel, first mark the clutch pressure plate, clutch cover and flywheel with a prick punch so they can be reas-

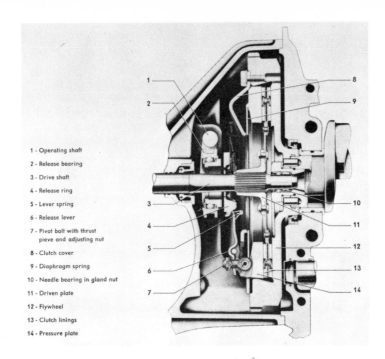

1 - Operating shaft

2 - Release bearing

3 - Drive shaft

4 - Release ring

5 - Lever spring

6 - Release lever

7 - Pivot bolt with thrust
pieve and adjusting nut

8 - Clutch cover

9 - Diaphragm spring

10 - Needle bearing in gland nut

11 - Driven plate

12 - Flywheel

13 - Clutch linings

14 - Pressure plate

Fig. L-3. Sectional view of Fastback/Squareback clutch assembly reveals how driven plate is engaged between flywheel and pressure plate.

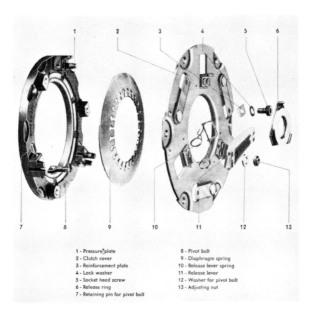

1 - Pressure plate
2 - Clutch cover
3 - Reinforcement plate
4 - Lock washer
5 - Socket head screw
6 - Release ring
7 - Retaining pin for pivot bolt

8 - Pivot bolt
9 - Diaphragm spring
10 - Release lever spring
11 - Release lever
12 - Washer for pivot bolt
13 - Adjusting nut

Fig. L-4. Exploded view of diaphragm spring clutch gives positioning information. Nuts are adjusted with clutch in place against flywheel.

sembled in their original positions. They are carefully and accurately balanced as an assembled unit. If they are not reassembled in their original position, severe vibration will result.

Loosen each of the cap screws holding the clutch cover to the flywheel a turn or two at a time, until the clutch spring pressure has been relieved. Remove the screws completely and the clutch can be removed from the flywheel.

Some mechanics will insert wooden wedges between the clutch cover and the clutch release levers. This takes the spring pressure from the cover and prevents distortion of this steel stamping.

To disassemble the clutch further, an arbor press is necessary. If one is not available, install a completely rebuilt or new unit. Note too that when assembling a clutch, special fixtures are necessary to properly adjust the clutch release fingers. If this equipment is not available, it is not advisable to attempt to rebuild a clutch.

If the clutch facing is oil soaked or the friction facing is loose or worn, the disc should be relined or replaced. Also carefully examine the surface of the clutch pressure plate to see if there are any fine cracks, ridges or

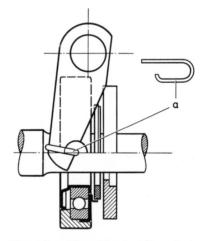

Fig. L-5. Later "Beetle" models and Fastback/Squareback cars use ball-type clutch release bearing with retaining springs.

score marks. If such defects are found, replace the complete pressure plate assembly. Also replace the assembly if the surface of the pressure plate shows signs of having been hot. This is characterized by a blue or burned appearance.

Also examine the clutch release bearing. If any roughness is felt, or if the hub is scored, replace the bearing assembly. If the bearing is still serviceable, do not clean it with a solvent. Remove any dirt with a clean cloth, Fig. L-5.

Clutch Servicing Kinks

The pilot bearing in the flywheel is a bushing on older "Beetle" models, and it is good practice to replace it whenever the clutch has been removed. The bushing can be driven out by means of an impact hammer.

Later "Beetle" and Fastback/Squareback cars have a needle roller pilot bearing which seldom requires replacement, Fig. L-6.

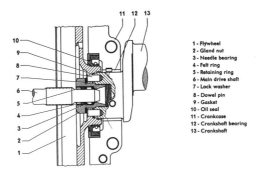

1 - Flywheel
2 - Gland nut
3 - Needle bearing
4 - Felt ring
5 - Retaining ring
6 - Main drive shaft
7 - Lock washer
8 - Dowel pin
9 - Gasket
10 - Oil seal
11 - Crankcase
12 - Crankshaft bearing
13 - Crankshaft

Fig. L-6. Later "Beetle" models have a needle roller pilot bearing fitted into gland nut which, in turn, is fitted into flywheel.

CLUTCH OVERHAUL

If for some reason a new or rebuilt clutch is not available, it is possible to replace damaged parts in an emergency. Exploded views, Figs. L-2 and L-4, show the structure of the two basic assemblies. Each part must be marked before disassembly in order to maintain balance when reassembling. In some cases, it will be necessary to use a saw to remove the metal peened into the adjusting screws.

Check the disassembled parts for wear. The pressure plate contact surface should be smooth and runout should not exceed .004 in.

All thrust springs should be straight and of the same length and strength. Pressure specifications vary with model year but, generally, when thrust springs are compressed to a length of 1.15 in., they should exert a pressure of 112 to 130 lbs. New thrust springs should show a pressure of from 10 to 20 lbs. higher. On diaphragm spring clutches (by two different manufacturers), the diaphragm, placed concave side down, should measure: LuK .335 in., F & S .358 in.

Generally, the clutch driven plate has twelve cushion segments which are set alternatively concave and convex, Fig. L-7. This structure provides smooth action.

See that the splines in the hub are free from rust or burrs so that the plate will slide freely on the splined shaft without appreciable looseness. Also check rivets holding plate to hub to make sure they are not loose. If the plate is the least bit warped, replace it.

Fix Your Volkswagen

REASSEMBLY AND REINSTALLATION HINTS

When reassembling the clutch, lubricate all moving joints with a small amount of grease. Make sure that all marks made on the release levers, clutch cover and pressure plate are in line. Draw the cover bolts down evenly a turn or two at a time on opposite sides. Install the release plate.

Make the release lever adjustment with the clutch assembly, including a new disc, firmly mounted in place on the flywheel.

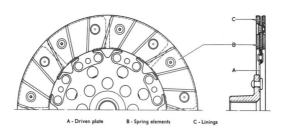

A - Driven plate   B - Spring elements   C - Linings

Fig. L-7. Sketch shows construction of clutch driven plate, or disc, with lining segments riveted to plate and cushioned by spring elements.

Before installing the clutch assembly, apply a small amount of short fibre grease in the clutch shaft pilot bushing or bearing in the flywheel. Also clean the surfaces of the flywheel and pressure plate thoroughly. Then hold the clutch cover plate and disc in place, making sure that the

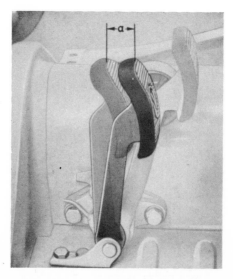

Fig. L-8. Pedal free movement should be 0.4–0.8 in at "a."

200

Clutch Servicing Kinks

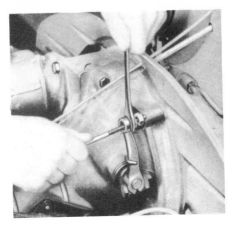

Fig. L-9. Method of adjusting pedal clearance.

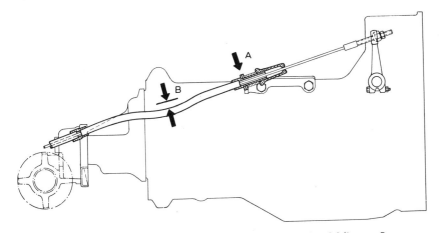

Fig. L-10. Clutch cable guide tube should bend down or sag 1 to 1 1/8 in. at B. This preload is obtained by insertion of washers at A.

disc is installed with the long part of the hub on the side away from the flywheel. A transmission drive shaft can be used as a pilot tool.

Line up the punch marks on the cover and flywheel. Bolt the cover plate loosely on the flywheel so that these parts are lined up in their original positions. To avoid distortion of clutch cover, tighten each bolt a few turns in progression until they are all tight.

Then measure the distance from the face of the release plate to the contact surface of the flywheel. Tighten or loosen the release lever adjusting nuts to obtain the following typical settings:

Release plate to flywheel - 1.054 to 1.070 in.

Release plate runout (max.) - .012 in.

Lock the release lever nuts in place.

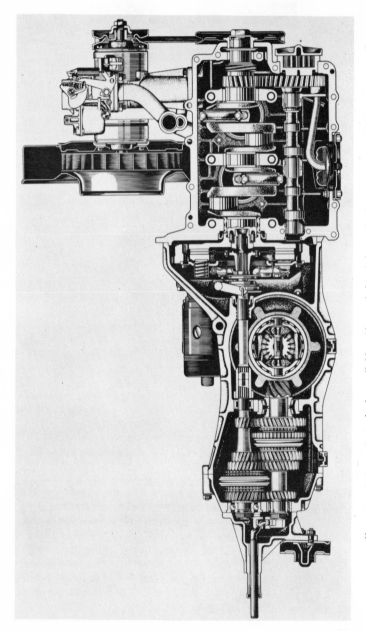

New transmission ratio in third gear (1.26 to 1), coupled with larger displacement engine (1493 or 1584 cc) give late model Volkswagens added performance.

Clutch Servicing Kinks

When installing the transmission, care must be taken not to bend the clutch disc. Be sure to support the transmission so the drive pinion can be guided through the hub of the disc. After installation, adjust the clutch pedal free travel.

PEDAL ADJUSTMENT TIPS

The clutch must be adjusted so that there is a clearance of .04-.08 in. between the release bearing and the release plate with the clutch engaged. Measure at the clutch pedal. This should be 0.4-0.8 in., Fig. L-8. The adjustment is made at the lock nut on the threaded cable end, Fig. L-9.

This adjustment must be maintained because of the wear on the clutch lining. As wear increases, the clearance between the release bearing and the release plate is decreased. If these parts stay in contact, rapid wear will result, as well as clutch slippage and burning of the clutch facings.

The clutch operating cable, Fig. L-10, is lubricated when installed and should slide freely. Avoid sharp bends in the cable and lubricate the ball end of the adjusting nut frequently to prevent bending of the cable at the exposed end.

CLUTCH TROUBLE SHOOTING

Complaint	Cause	Correction
Noise	a - Pilot bushing or bearing flywheel in gland nut worn	a - Renew bushing or bearing and fill it with grease
	b - Clutch release bearing dry or excessively worn	b - Renew release bearing. See to it that release plate and clutch clearance are correctly adjusted. Tell driver not to use clutch pedal as a foot rest
	c - Driven plate fouling pressure plate	c - Renew or straighten driven plate
	d - Weak release lever springs or unequal tension	d - Renew springs
Chatter or grabbing	a - Transmission case not tightly mounted	a - Tighten mounting bolts and nuts
	b - Insufficient pre-load on clutch cable guide tube	b - Increase sag

Complaint	Cause	Correction
	c - Grease or oil on driven plate, flywheel or pressure plate	c - Renew oil seal. Clean all parts and replace driven plate
	d - Uneven contact of pressure plate	d - Renew or resurface pressure plate
	e - Release plate not running true	e - Eliminate run-out. Max. permissible run-out; 0.012 in.
	f - Unequal tension of thrust springs	f - Renew thrust springs
Dragging or incomplete release	a - Excessive pedal free play	a - Adjust clutch clearance: 0.4 to 0.8 in. at clutch pedal
	b - Distorted driven plate or bent main drive shaft	b - Straighten or renew driven plate or main drive shaft
	c - Cushion segments excessively set or plate linings broken	c - Replace driven plate
Slippage	a - Lack of pedal free play due to wear of linings	a - Adjust clutch clearance
	b - Grease or oil on clutch linings	b - Replace driven plate. Replace engine or transmission oil seal if necessary

TRANSMISSION SERVICING

Volkswagen combines the transmission, rear axle, and engine in the rear of the car. The rear axle is of the swing half axle type, or on later models, the double-jointed axle shaft type. The rubber-cushioned transmission case is secured to the frame at three points. It incorporates the transmission and the differential.

TRANSMISSION CASE CONSTRUCTION

The transmission case is cast of light alloy. Prior to 1961 models, the transmission had synchromesh gears on 2nd, 3rd and 4th gears. On 1961 and later models, the transmission is synchronized in all forward speeds. On earlier models, the tranmission case is split lengthwise, while 1961 and later models have a case divided transversely, Figs. M-1 and M-2. When case replacement is necessary on the longitudinally split case, it is not permissible to fit a single half of the transmission case. They are machined in pairs to very close limits, so replacements must be made in pairs. When making repairs, use soft metal plates in the jaws of the vise to avoid damage to the mating surfaces of the case.

GEAR CONTROL

The shifting rod in the frame tunnel links the transmission to the gear-shift lever, which is located on the tunnel besides the driver's seat. The synchro-system consists of clutch gear, synchronizer shifting plates, synchronizer stop ring and operating sleeve.

The synchronizer stop rings are provided with internally female coned surfaces designed to engage with similarly shaped male coned surfaces on the gears. When the operating sleeve is moved toward the gear to be engaged, shifting plates bring the coned surface of the synchronizer stop ring into contact with the coned face of the gear. The faster moving gear carries the synchronizer stop ring around until the ring is stopped by the shifting plates. This brings the stop ring teeth out of line with the internally cut splines in the operating sleeve. The braking effect produces synchronization between the two cone surfaces. When exact synchronization

TRANSMISSION PRIOR TO 1961 MODELS

Fig. M-1. 1—Main drive shaft. 2—Drive pinion. 3—Ring gear (crown wheel). 4—Differential side gear. 5—Differential pinion. 6—Fulcrum plate. 7—Rear axle shaft. 8—1st gear train. 9—2nd gear train. 10—Synchronizer stop ring (2nd gear). 11—3rd gear train. 12—Synchronizer stop ring (3rd gear). 13—4th gear train. 14—Synchronizer stop ring (4th gear). 15—Transmission shift rod. 16—Selector shaft. 17—Selector fork. 18—Detent spring and ball. 19—Front rubber cushion. 20—Gearshift housing. 21—Ground connection. 22—Oil filler plug. 23—Oil drain plug. 24—Clutch operating shaft. 25—Clutch release bearing.

of speed is reached, the splines of the operating sleeve engage with the teeth of the synchronizer stop ring and then with the clutch teeth of the gear. This engagement is facilitated by the teeth being chamfered.

To insure a correct operation of the synchro-system, the clutch must release completely. Clutch pedal free play should be periodically checked. Insufficient declutching or a dragging clutch plate (damaged lining or distorted plate) leads to rapid wear of the synchronizer stop rings. With the clutch plate completely locked, it is not possible to shift gears because they will not synchronize. Only accredited clutch linings should be used.

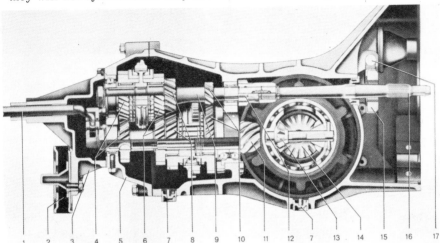

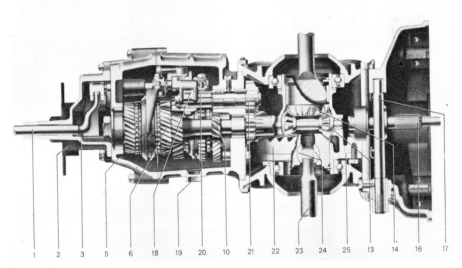

TRANSMISSION USED ON 1961 AND LATER MODELS

Fig. M-2. 1—Transmission shift lever. 2—Bonded rubber mounting. 3—Gearshift housing. 4—4th speed. 5—Gear carrier. 6—3rd speed. 7—Oil drain plugs. 8—2nd speed. 9—Main drive shaft, front. 10—1st speed. 11—Drive pinion. 12—Reverse gear. 13—Differential pinion. 14—Differential side gear. 15—Clutch release bearing. 16—Main drive shaft, rear. 17—Clutch operating shaft. 18—Reverse sliding gear. 19—Oil filler plug. 20—Reverse shaft. 21—Reverse drive gear. 22—Ring gear. 23—Rear axle shaft. 24—Fulcrum plate. 25—Differential housing.

REMOVAL OF TRANSMISSION

It is obvious that service work on the transmission will involve removal of the entire assembly consisting of engine, clutch, transmission, differential and rear axle.

If disassembly of the rear axle or transmission is intended, loosen the axle shaft nuts before lifting the vehicle.

With engine out of car, proceed with following steps:

1 - Remove rear wheels.

2 - Disconnect and plug hydraulic lines at rear.

3 - Unhook brake cables from push bar at frame head on models prior to 1961, or at hand brake lever on later models, and pull them out of conduit tubes.

4 - Remove bolts at rear axle shaft bearing housing.

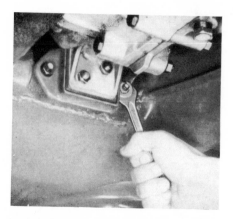

Fig. M-3. Removal of front transmission mounting.

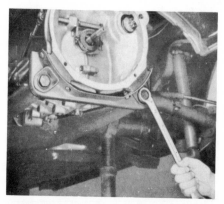

Fig. M-4. Removal of transmission carrier bolts.

5 - Disconnect clutch cable from clutch operating shaft lever and withdraw it from guide plate.
6 - Remove lower shock absorber mounting bolts.
7 - Unhook accelerator cable from retainer on gear carrier.
8 - Disconnect cables from starter motor.
9 - Remove cover plate under rear seat and disconnect shift rod in back of coupling.
10 - Remove nuts at transmission front mounting, Fig. M-3.
11 - Remove transmission carrier bolts, Fig. M-4.
12 - Remove assembly, being careful that drive shaft does not fall on floor and that dust sleeves on axles are not damaged.

DISASSEMBLY OF TRANSMISSION

At this point consider what is needed in the transmission. If gears and bearings are damaged or if the case must be replaced, it is advisable to take the assembly to a Volkswagen shop for rebuilding. Assembly and adjustment of bearing preload requirements are exacting and require special equipment and skill.

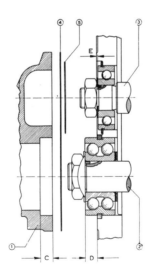

Fig. M-5. 1—Gearshift housing. 2—Drive pinion. 3—Main drive shaft. 4—Gasket. 5—Paper ring.

Refer to Figs. M-1 and M-2 to determine whether or not to disassemble the transmission unit. Note that shims of assorted thickness and gaskets of precise thickness are used in the adjustment of the bearing, Fig. M-5. If minor parts replacement or adjustment is needed, it may be accomplished by careful handling.

Note: For removal of axle tubes, see Chapter on Rear Axles.

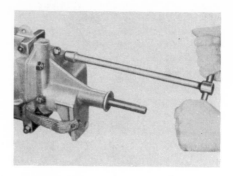

Fig. M-6. Support bracket is removed from transmission case.

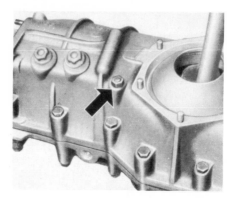

Fig. M-7. In addition to removal of bolts, this nut must be removed.

Fig. M-8. Use a rubber mallet to separate case halves.

PRIOR TO 1961 MODELS

Remove gearshift housing on early models as shown in Fig. M-6; remove transmission carrier, clutch release bearing and disconnect clutch operating lever return spring.

Remove bolts holding transmission housing halves together and also nut on stud near axle tube retainer, Fig. M-7. Right half of case can be lifted off after careful separation of housing, using care to avoid any scratching or damage to mating surfaces, Fig. M-8. Lift out main drive shaft and pinion shaft assemblies, Fig. M-9.

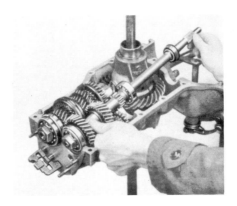

Fig. M-9. Both shaft assemblies can now be lifted out.

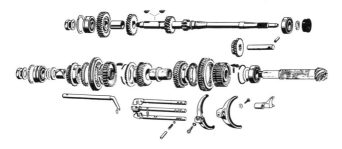

Fig. M-10. Details of transmission gears, bearings, shafts, etc.

Disassembly of gear shaft assemblies should not be attempted in absence of special equipment. An exploded view of these assemblies is shown in Fig. M-10 for reference.

This completes disassembly except for removal of reverse gear or shifting rods. Note location and grouping of shims and washers so that they may be correctly installed upon reassembly.

Reassembly is accomplished by reversing the preceding operations. If in doubt regarding the relationship of the various parts, study the exploded view Fig. M-10.

HINTS ON REASSEMBLY

When turning transmission case, do not let lock pin for reverse sliding gear shaft fall out. See that ball bearing retaining rings are seating correctly in provided ring grooves.

Install clutch operating shaft before two halves of case are reassembled.

Apply a light coat of sealing compound to mating surfaces of transmission housing before final assembly.

Torque transmission case screws to 14.5 ft. lbs., Fig. M-11.

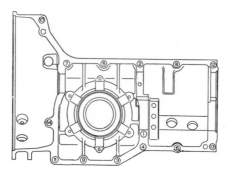

Fig. M-11. Sequence of tightening transmission bolts.

Always install a new seal on transmission drive shaft. Apply a light coat of sealing compound to outside of seal and oil inner lip of seal and shaft before installing. Install carefully to avoid spring around lip coming out of place.

When installing transmission carrier, do not tighten nuts until after front rubber cushion is tightened. Also make certain that carrier is installed as shown in Fig. M-12.

When connecting shifting shaft coupling, make sure points of coupling screws are seating in their recesses. Wire screws in place.

SPECIAL INSTRUCTIONS - ALL MODELS

Care must be taken when removing snap rings to avoid damaging shafts, gears and bearings. Discard old snap rings and replace with new ones. Special snap ring pliers will simplify removal of rings.

Clean main shaft bearings in clean solvent, then dry them by applying compressed air directly through bearing. Never spin a bearing with com-

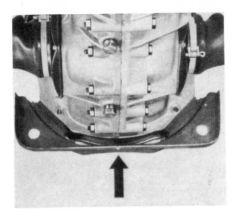

Fig. M-12. Proper position of installed transmission carrier.

pressed air as this may damage balls and races. Instead, apply a little oil and spin bearing several times by hand. Install a new bearing if old one is excessively loose or noisy. Inspect fit of bearing in case bores. If loose, inspect bearings, shaft and case for wear. If installation of new bearings does not correct condition, install a new shaft or case as required.

Inspect main shaft splines for wear, galling, or scoring on bearing mounting surfaces, and for damaged snap ring grooves. Slight nicks or burrs can be stoned off. Do not attempt to repair damage which would affect fit of gears, bearings or snap rings to shaft.

Examine all parts carefully. Some mechanics use a magnifying glass to study condition of gear teeth. If there are gall marks or other signs of wear, parts should be replaced. Bearings should be thoroughly cleaned in cleaning fluid and rotated to see if there is any binding present. When in doubt, install new bearings.

Fig. M-13. Transmission gears are locked for this operation.

Fig. M-14. Removal of final drive cover.

Fig. M-15. Removal of rear half of main shaft.

Fig. M-16. Drive pinion ball bearing retainer removal.

Transmission Servicing

Keep in mind at all times that Volkswagen transmission housings are made of light metal. Prying and pounding, or careless use of a press, is likely to distort the case and destroy alignment of bearings. Also, this metal is easily scratched by steel tools and a scratch on mating surfaces may cause a lubricant leak. Whenever it is necessary to hold the case in a vise, soft metal jaws must be used.

Excessive or uneven tightening of studs or nuts is also a frequent cause of distortion in housings. On mating parts of housings, make a light scratch mark on outside surface of each before disassembly so that parts can be reassembled in same relative position.

1961 AND LATER MODELS
(Also see preceding SPECIAL INSTRUCTIONS.)

Remove gearshift housing. After prying off lock plates for drive pinion and main shaft nuts, lock transmission by engaging reverse and third speed gears. Remove both shaft nuts and discard lock plates, Fig. M-13 (use new lock plates on reassembly).

Remove gear carrier stud nuts, ground strap and accelerator cable retainer. Remove retaining nuts on final drive covers, Fig. M-14. When removing covers, be sure to note thickness and arrangement of differential shims to facilitate reassembly.

Loosen retaining ring for reverse gear on main drive shaft. Slide reverse gear rearward and screw main drive shaft apart. Take off reverse gear and withdraw rear main shaft toward rear, taking care not to damage oil seal, Fig. M-15.

Pry up lock plates of screws attaching drive pinion ball bearing retainer and remove screws, Fig. M-16. Push transmission out of case.

To remove reverse gear shaft, remove a lock ring from gear, Fig. M-17, and a Woodruff key from the shaft.

Fig. M-17. Removal of reverse gear lock ring.

215

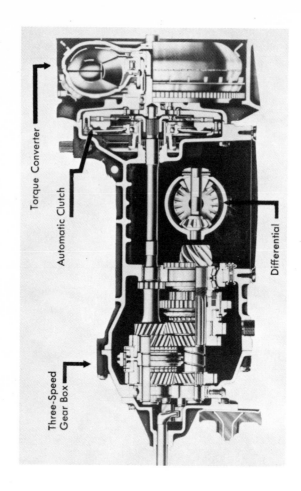

Volkswagen *Automatic Stick Shift* transmission couples 3–speed synchronized gearbox with vacuum-operated clutch and torque converter, which permits car to be brought to a stop in any gear range without shifting.

Torque Converter

Automatic Clutch

Differential

Three-Speed Gear Box

Transmission Servicing

Further disassembly of gear carrier is accomplished as follows:

1 - Remove reverse selector fork, including reverse sliding gear from reverse lever.

2 - Remove shims from drive pinion ball bearing, being sure to note thickness of shim pack.

3 - Place gear carrier in vise equipped with soft metal plates on jaws. Loosen locking screws of first-and-second and third-and-fourth selector forks, and remove selector fork for first and second gears.

4 - Fully withdraw selector shaft for third and fourth gears out of selector fork.

5 - Place rubber band around operating sleeve of first and second gear, and main drive shaft, Fig. M-18.

Fig. M-18. Note use of rubber band in disassembly and reassembly.

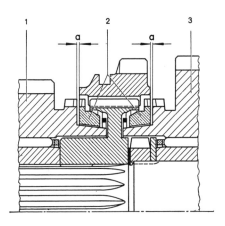

Fig. M-19. 1—Second gear. 2—Synchronizer stop rings. 3—First gear.

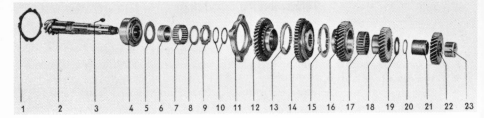

PINION SHAFT ASSEMBLY

Fig. M-20. 1—Shim. 2—Drive pinion. 3—Woodruff key for 4th gear. 4—Ball bearing. 5—Thrust washer for 1st gear. 6—Needle bearing inner race (1st gear). 7—Needle cage (1st gear). 8—Thrust washer for needle bearing (1st gear). 9—Round nut. 10—Shims, end play 1st gear. 11—Ball bearing retainer. 12—1st gear. 13—Synchronizer stop ring (1st gear). 14—Clutch gear for 1st and 2nd gears, and reverse gear. 15—Synchronizer stop ring (2nd gear). 16—2nd gear. 17—Needle cage (2nd gear). 18—3rd gear. 19—Concave washer. 20—Shims for concave washer. 21—Spacer sleeve. 22—4th gear. 23—Inner race, needle bearing in gear carrier.

6 - Remove gear assembly from gear carrier. Guide drive pinion to avoid tilting, which could lead to damage of gear or needle bearing in gear carrier.

In addition to cleaning and examining all gears and bearings, check synchronizer stop rings for wear. Clearances are indicated at "a" in Fig. M-19. This clearance is normal at 0.043 in. and stop ring should be replaced when clearance reaches 0.024 in.

For reference, parts of pinion shaft and main drive shaft assemblies are shown in Figs. M-20 and M-21.

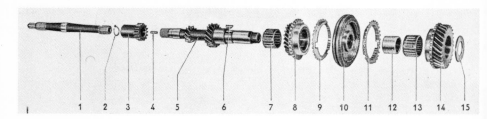

DRIVE SHAFT ASSEMBLY

Fig. M-21. 1—Main drive shaft rear half. 2—Snap ring for reverse gear. 3—Reverse gear on drive shaft. 4—Stud. 5—Main drive shaft front half. 6—Woodruff key for clutch gear. 7—Needle cage (3rd gear). 8—3rd gear. 9—Synchronizer stop ring (3rd gear). 10—Clutch gear (3rd and 4th speeds). 11—Synchronizer stop ring (4th gear). 12—Needle bearing inner race (4th gear). 13—Needle cage (4th gear). 14—4th gear. 15—Thrust washer (4th gear).

REASSEMBLY HINTS

Reassembly procedure is reverse of disassembly. When reinstalling gear assemblies, rubber band should again be used, Fig. M-18. Selector fork for 3rd and 4th gears should be positioned in operating sleeve beforehand. Take care that selector fork does not become jammed on selector shaft during installation.

Transmission Servicing

Detent springs should be inserted through holes for selector shafts. Detent springs for 1st, 2nd and reverse gears can be more easily installed by inserting them into top halves first.

After installation of selector shafts and interlock plungers, check for proper interlocking by engaging a gear. Selector shaft next to one used must be locked.

Before assembly of carrier to case, install a new gasket. Place drive pinion shims over ball bearing and temporarily screw two studs about 4 in. long into ball retainer to prevent retaining ring from turning during installation.

Use a rubber hammer to position pinion correctly in bearing seat. Tighten ball bearing retainer screws to 36 ft. lbs. Use new lock plates.

Apply oil to lip of oil seal before installing rear half of main drive shaft. Screw both halves of drive shaft together and then back off until splines for reverse gear are in line. Both halves of main drive shaft must not be screwed tightly together.

Torque gear carrier stud nuts to 14 ft. lbs.

Torque drive pinion nut to 22 ft. lbs.

Torque main drive shaft nut to 87 ft. lbs., then back off and retighten to 36 ft. lbs.

AUTOMATIC STICK SHIFT TRANSMISSION

Volkswagen's Automatic Stick Shift transmission, Fig. M-22, eliminates the clutch pedal and provides much wider driving ranges than corresponding gears of a conventional synchromesh transmission. The

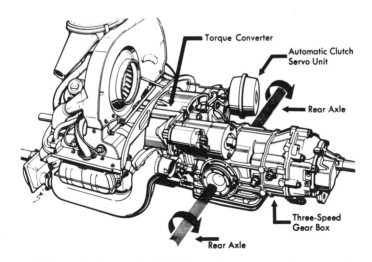

Fig. M-22. Volkswagen's Automatic Stick Shift locates torque converter between engine and transmission. Vacuum servo operates clutch automatically when selector lever is moved.

Automatic Stick Shift utilizes a normal 3-speed gearbox, a vacuum-operated clutch and a torque converter furnished with an independent oil supply by an engine-driven pump and reservoir.

The converter multiplies engine torque as dictated by driving conditions, and it permits the vehicle to be stopped while the engine is running. The clutch is actuated by movement of the selector lever, which interrupts the flow of power from the engine and torque converter while the transmission gears are being shifted.

The whole process of de-clutching takes only about 1/10 of a second after the selector lever is moved to a gear-engaged position. Two contacts in the inner transmission shift lever, Fig. M-23, close the circuit and the clutch is disengaged via its linkage.

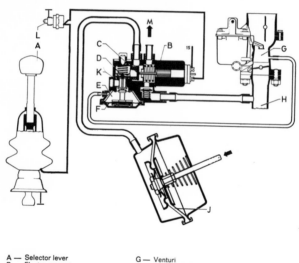

A — Selector lever
B — Electro-magnet
C — Main valve
D — Reducing valve
E — Diaphragm chamber
F — Diaphragm in control valve

G — Venturi
H — Intake manifold
J — Diaphragm in clutch servo
K — Compensating drilling
L — Starter locking switch with bridging switch
M — Connection to vacuum container

Fig. M-23. Schematic shows basic controls of Automatic Stick Shift. Note that contacts in lever connect to switch which controls electromagnet and, indirectly, main valve C.

When the driver releases the selector lever after changing the driving range, the switch (L) interrupts current flow to the electromagnet (B), which drops back to rest position and closes the main valve (C). Vacuum falls off as reducing valve (D) is energized and the clutch engages.

RANGE OF OPERATION

The shift pattern of the VW Automatic Stick Shift is the conventional "H" used with 3-speed manual transmissions. Neutral is the crossbar of "H" and is the only range in which the engine may be started. Since Drive

Transmission Servicing

1 and Drive 2 positions are the only two forward gears used in normal driving (Low is for heavy loads on steep hills), the selector lever remains at the right side of the pattern in Neutral, Fig. M-24.

Driving Range 1 is for starting and accelerating up to 35 mph. Normally, the car is started in this range before shifting to Drive 2, which is

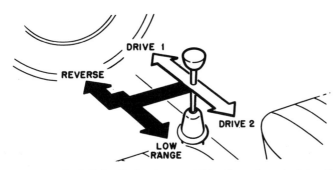

Fig. M-24. Automatic Stick Shift affords minimum shifting (leave lever in Drive 2) or maximum conventional Low to Drive 1 to Drive 2 shift.

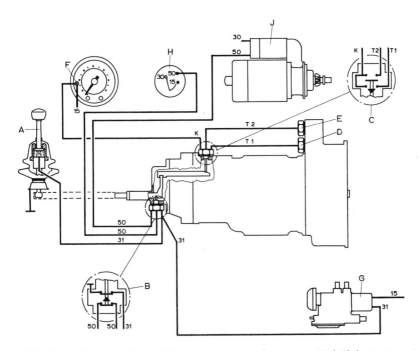

Fig. M-25. Wiring diagram calls out following components of Automatic Stick Shift circuitry: A— Selector lever with switch. B—Starter locking switch with bridging switch. C—Selector switch. D—Temperature switch—Drive 2. E—Temperature switch—Drive 1. F—Warning light. G—Electro- magnet for control valve. H—Ignition switch. J—Starter.

used for highway driving. Drive 2 can be used at any speed. It can be downshifted to Drive 1 at any speed under 55 mph. Reverse shift calls for the lever to be depressed to get by a safety stop, and it should be engaged only when the car is standing still.

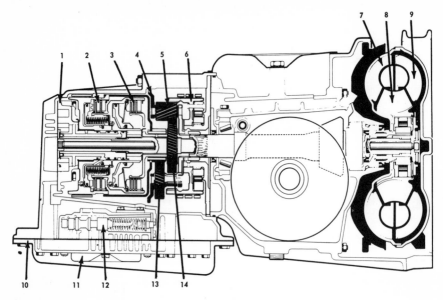

Fig. M-26. Major components of VW Automatic Transmission include: 1—Oil pump. 2—Direct-and-reverse gear clutch. 3—Forward clutch. 4—Planet carrier. 5—Small planet gear. 6—Ring gear. 7—Impeller. 8—Stator. 9—Turbine. 10—Oil pan. 11—Oil strainer. 12—Main pressure valve. 13—Large planet gear. 14—Large sun gear.

Fig. M-27. Planetary gear system features: 1—Small sun gear. 2—Planet carrier. 3—Large planet gear. 4—Large sun gear. 5—Small planet gear. 6—Ring gear.

Transmission Servicing

WARNING LIGHT AND FUSE

Cars with Automatic Stick Shift have a red warning light on the right side of the speedometer dial. If the light goes on, the automatic transmission fluid may be too hot. Either the car has been operating under too heavy a load or the fluid level is low, Fig. M-25. Two temperature switches are used, one each for 1st and 2nd Driving Ranges (D and E).

An 8-amp fuse protects the Automatic Stick Shift control valve. It is located in a fuse holder above the ignition coil. If the transmission cannot be shifted, check this fuse first. If it is burned out, test the circuit for a "short." Correct the problem and replace the fuse.

A Volkswagen with Automatic Stick Shift can be pushed to start, if necessary, but the selector lever must be left in Low Range and speed should not exceed 15 mph.

AUTOMATIC TRANSMISSION

Volkswagen's Automatic Transmission, Fig. M-26, also eliminates the clutch pedal and gives a broad range of speeds in each of three forward driving gears. The transmission utilizes an automatic shift 3-speed planetary gearbox and a hydrodynamic torque converter.

The converter permits easy stops and starts, and it also multiplies torque generated by the engine. The three elements of the converter - impeller, turbine and stator - are fitted in tandem in a housing composed of two dished steel shells welded together. An oil pump keeps the converter filled with oil.

PLANETARY GEARS

The gearbox incorporates a planetary gear set and two hydraulically operated multi-plate clutches. The planetary system consists of both a large and small sun gear, three large and three small planet gears, a planet carrier and a ring gear, Fig. M-27.

In operation, the small planet gears mesh with the large sun gear while the large planet gears mesh with the small sun gear, Fig. M-28. All gears are in constant mesh with a sun gear in the center, orbited by three planet gears and a common carrier. A ring gear with internal teeth rotates around the group. By locking the sun gear, planet carrier or ring gear, different ratios between driving and driven gears may be obtained, Fig. M-29.

MULTI-PLATE CLUTCHES

Members of the Automatic Transmission which perform the locking, releasing or driving action are two hydraulically operated multi-plate clutches. The clutches connect either sun gear to the torque converter output shaft. Aiding in the operation are two brake bands, one fitted on

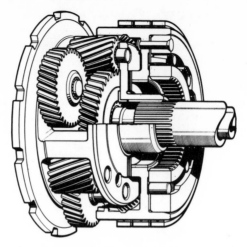

Fig. M-28. All gears in planetary system are in constant mesh. Change in gear ratios can take place under load by changing driving member and locking another part of planet cluster.

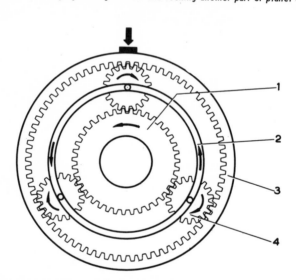

Fig. M-29. In this simplified planetary setup, sun gear (1) is driving, and power flow is through planet carrier (2), with ring gear (3) locked, and planet gears (4) revolving around inner teeth of stationary ring gear.

the ring gear and the other on the clutch drum connected to the small sun gear, Fig. M-30. The forward clutch is engaged in all forward gear settings while the direct-and-reverse gear clutch is engaged only when the transmission is shifted to Reverse or Drive 3.

The VW Automatic Transmission has three forward driving ranges and one reverse. The selector lever operates in a slotted housing marked:

P-Park; R-Reverse; N-Neutral; 3-Drive 3 Forward; 2-Drive 2 Forward; 1-Drive 1 Forward. Gear changing is automatic and Drive 3 is the "regular position." When in Drive 3, the transmission automatically shifts through all three gears as road and load conditions require. In Drive 2, third gear is blocked out and gears change only from first to second. Drive 1 will block out both second and third gears for use in climbing or descending steep hills.

Neutral position is required for starting the engine since a cut-out switch prevents closing of the ignition circuit in any other position. Re-

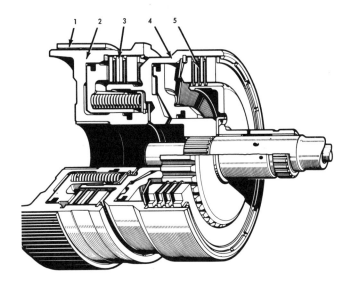

Fig. M-30. Two multi-plate clutches are applied as needed to connect sun gears to turbine output shaft: 1—Brake band, 2nd gear. 2—Direct-and-reverse clutch drum. 3—Direct-and-reverse clutch plates. 4—Forward clutch drum. 5—Forward clutch plates.

Fig. M-31. Symbols indicate various positions of selector lever on VW Automatic Transmission: P—Park. R—Reverse. N—Neutral. 3, 2, 1—Driving ranges.

verse gear must be engaged only when the car is stationary, and the selector lever must be lifted into "R" position. Park position mechanically locks the transmission. Again, the selector lever must be lifted into "P" position, Fig. M-31.

A special "kickdown" feature permits a downshift for greater acceleration at speeds below 50 mph. By "flooring" the accelerator pedal, a switch on the throttle linkage changes the transmission to the next lower gear.

AUTOMATIC TRANSMISSION CHECKS

The automatic transmission fluid level must be checked with the engine idling and the selector lever in Neutral. Checks are recommended every 6,000 miles; fluid change at 18,000 miles. At that time, clean the oil pan, oil strainer, replace the oil pan gasket and check for leaks. Torque oil pan screws to 7.25 ft. lbs.

Periodically test operation of the kickdown switch. If it fails to kick down, inspect the position of the switch on the throttle linkage. Reposition the switch or replace it, if necessary.

Starting the engine by towing or pushing the car will not work because the transmission oil pump is operative only when the engine is running. If the engine is stopped, there is no oil pressure in the hydraulic circuits so no power is transmitted.

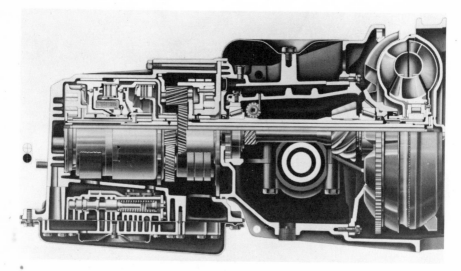

Fig. M-32. Optional fully automatic transmission utilizes 3-element torque converter, planetary gears, multi-plate clutches and two brake bands to provide three forward driving ranges and one reverse.

REAR AXLE SERVICE

The rear axle arrangement on "Beetle", Fastback and Squareback cars is basically the same through 1967 models. Power flow is through a spiral bevel drive pinion and ring gear to two swing axles to the rear wheels. On 1968 "Beetle" models equipped with Automatic Stick Shift transmission, and on all models starting in 1969, drive is through two double-jointed axles to the rear wheels.

Service work on the rear axle is preceded by removal of the engine and transmission, and disassembly is accomplished after removing the brake drums and backing plates. Construction and relationship of parts on older "Beetle" models is shown in Fig. N-1.

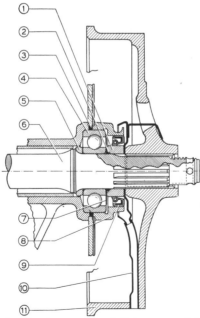

Fig. N-1. Rear wheel bearing assembly: 1—Outer spacer. 2—Gasket. 3—Gasket. 4—Ball bearing. 5—Inner spacer. 6—Axle shaft. 7—Washer. 8—Bearing cover. 9—Oil seal. 10—Oil deflector. 11—Brake drum.

Fig. N-2. Removal of rear axle tube.

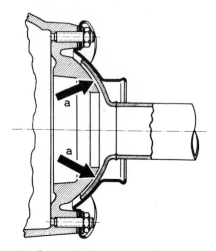

Fig. N-3. Construction of rear axle tube inner end. Dimension a, is 0.027 in. maximum.

Then remove the axle tube from each side of the housing, Fig. N-2. Construction of the axle tube inner joint is shown in Fig. N-3.

After separating the transmission-differential housing and lifting out the transmission shaft assemblies, remove the differential assembly with axle shafts. Then unscrew the cap screws from around the differential, Fig. N-4. Parts appear in an exploded view in Fig. N-5.

INSPECTION OF PARTS

After a thorough cleaning, inspect all parts carefully for wear or damage. The main points to check in the differential housing are shown in Fig. N-6.

If the differential gears are worn, they must be replaced in sets since different cutting methods are used in manufacture and they are not interchangeable.

Fig. N-4. Ring gear is held to differential housing with cap screws.

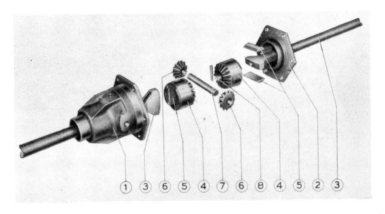

Fig. N-5. 1—Housing. 2—Cover. 3—Rear axle shaft. 4—Differential side gear. 5—Fulcrum plates. 6—Differential pinion. 7—Differential pinion shaft. 8—Lock pin.

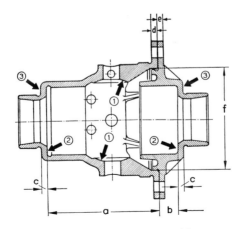

Fig. N-6. Points of measuring differential housing wear.

The flattened inner end of the axle shaft should have a clearance of 0.0012-0.004 in. when measured as shown in Fig. N-7. The clearance between flat of axle and fulcrum plates should be .0014 to .004 in., Fig. N-8. Oversize fulcrum plates are available to obtain proper clearance.

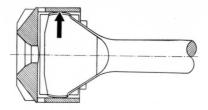

Fig. N-7. Point at which measurement is made.

Check the ring gear and drive pinion for wear and scoring. A magnifying glass is useful for this purpose, particularly in checking for surface pitting. If either pinion or ring gear is worn or scored, both must be replaced because they are mated in pairs.

Fig. N-8. Method of measuring fulcrum plates.

Since the pinion is a part of the transmission shaft assembly, Fig. N-9, disassembly of the unit requires special equipment, skill and meticulous care. If the pinion and ring gear must be replaced, the endwise location of the pinion and the sidewise location of the ring gear determine the contact of the gear faces. Extremely accurate measurements are required and Volkswagen dealers have the proper equipment for this purpose, Fig. N-10.

Furthermore, the gears have different tooth design and proper contact for gears made by one method is different from the contact pattern of gears made by another method.

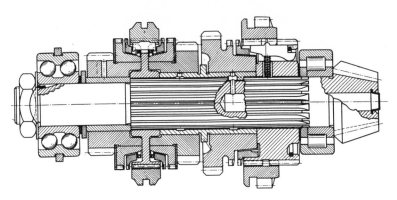

Fig. N-9. The pinion gear is a part of the transmission gear assembly.

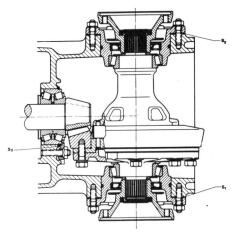

Fig. N-10. Shims are located at S1, S2, and S3, to provide means of adjustment for amount of preload on tapered roller bearings and to obtain correct amount of backlash between ring gear and pinion teeth.

HINTS ON REASSEMBLY

When reassembling the differential, thread the wire through the cap screw holes in a way which insures a righ-hand tension on all screws, Fig. N-11.

Reassembly of the transmission-differential housing was covered in a previous chapter.

Before installing axle tubes, loosen dust sleeve retaining bands to avoid damage to sleeves. Tighten clips only after axle is in car and resting on wheels.

Tighten nuts on axle tube retainer to 14 ft. lbs.

When reassembling rear wheel bearings, examine the condition of the bearings and replace if damaged, Fig. N-12.

Check bearing housing for cracks or damage.

Tighten brake backing plates 40 to 47 ft. lbs.

Make sure that oil seal rests squarely in housing.

Renew both gaskets in each assembly.

Check outer surface of spacer and make sure it is smooth to avoid damage to oil seal.

Be certain correct amount of proper lubricant is installed in the transmission-differential case.

Tighten axle nut to 216 ft. lbs. and secure it with a cotter pin.

Tighten lower shock absorber mounting nut to 43 ft. lbs.

Fig. N-11. Method of wiring lock on differential housing cap screws.

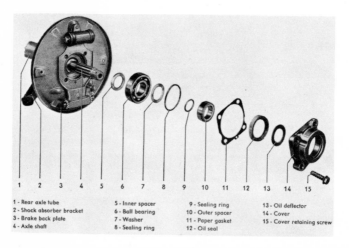

Fig. N-12. Exploded view of rear axle assembly shows correct sequence of parts installation and reveals that gasket and cover must be installed one way only.

FASTBACK AND SQUAREBACK FEATURES

All Fastback and Squareback models have a differential assembly similar to the "Beetle" unit. However, since September, 1965, new hex bolts and special spring washers have been used to attach the ring gear

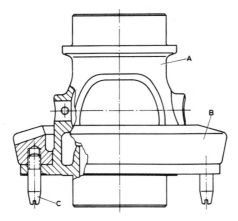

Fig. N-13. Modified Fastback/Squareback differential housing eliminates need for lock wire on attaching bolts. Housing (A), ring gear (B) and centering pin (C) identify later design, along with recesses for attaching bolts and larger holes.

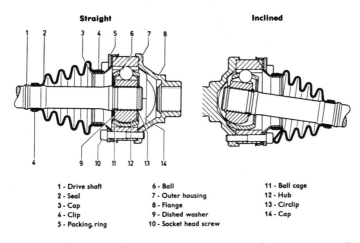

1 - Drive shaft	6 - Ball	11 - Ball cage
2 - Seal	7 - Outer housing	12 - Hub
3 - Cap	8 - Flange	13 - Circlip
4 - Clip	9 - Dished washer	14 - Cap
5 - Packing ring	10 - Socket head screw	

Fig. N-14. Action of constant velocity joints in new VW rear axle arrangement is illustrated in straight line drive and when axle shaft is inclined.

to the differential housing. The new attaching bolts must be used on the modified differential housing only, Fig. N-13. Correct torque for the new attaching bolts is 43 ft. lbs.

A change in rear axle and suspension design in all 1969 models, including "Beetle," affects rear axle service to some extent. Each axle shaft has two identical constant velocity joints, one at the transmission housing and the other at the wheel, Fig. N-14. All changes in relative position and distance between the wheels and transmission are compensated for by these rolling and sliding joints.

REAR AXLE TROUBLE SHOOTING

Complaint   Correction

EXCESSIVE BACKLASH
  a. Loose wheel bolts

                                     a. Tighten nuts securely. Make sure tapered end of nut is toward wheel

  b. Loose ring gear and pinion adjustment

                                     b. Adjust ring gear and pinion

  c. Worn differential gears or case

                                     c. Replace worn parts

  d. Worn axle shaft

                                     d. Replace worn parts

AXLE NOISY ON DRIVE
  a. Ring gear and pinion adjustment too tight

                                     a. Readjust ring gear and pinion

  b. Pinion bearings rough

                                     b. Replace bearing and readjust ring gear and pinion

  c. Rough or uneven tire tread

                                     c. Replace tires

AXLE NOISY ON COAST
  a. Ring gear and pinion adjustment too loose

                                     a. Readjust ring gear and pinion

  b. Pinion bearings rough

                                     b. Replace bearing and readjust ring gear and pinion

  c. Excessive end play in pinion

                                   c. Tighten pinion bearing retaining screws or replace bearing

  d. End play in double row bearing

                                   d. Replace pinion bearing

AXLE NOISY ON BOTH DRIVE
AND COAST
  a. Pinion bearings rough

                                     a. Replace bearings and adjust ring gear and pinion

  b. Loose or damaged differential side bearings

                                   b. Replace or adjust differential side bearings

  c. Damaged axle shaft bearing

                                   c. Replace bearing

  d. Badly worn ring gear or pinion teeth

                                   d. Replace ring gear and pinion

  e. Loose or worn wheel bearings

                                   e. Replace bearings

  f. Rough or uneven tire tread

                                   f. Replace tires

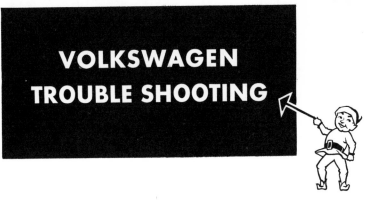

VOLKSWAGEN TROUBLE SHOOTING

This general trouble shooting guide is supplemented by additional specific charts at the end of several chapters of this book. After the trouble is located here also check the chapter charts.

ENGINE

ENGINE DIFFICULT TO START OR FAILS TO START

1. Hard Starting - Mechanical Causes
(a) Fuel System
Determine if fuel is reaching carburetor. Disconnect fuel line at carburetor and crank engine. If no fuel flows, line is clogged or fuel pump is at fault.

At fuel pump, disconnect line which leads to fuel tank and apply compressed air carefully at reduced pressure. Reconnect line and crank engine. Fuel pump is at fault if no fuel flows from cleaned out line. Inspect pump and recondition as necessary.

Inspect for clogging by disconnecting fuel lines at carburetor and fuel pump and blowing out line carefully with compressed air at reduced pressure. Check lines for possible air leaks on vacuum side of pump, especially at connections or in areas where line contacts sheet metal.

Choke - Inspect choke for proper adjustment.

Intake Manifold Leaks - Inspect for loose manifold or defective intake manifold gasket. Inspect carburetor gasket for air leaks.

(b) Electrical
Inspect for weak or discharged battery. Inspect cables for looseness and battery terminals for corrosion.

Check spark plugs for fouling, cracked porcelain or improper gap.

Inspect wiring for breaks, frayed or worn insulation. Inspect connections for looseness and corrosion.

Inspect distributor for wet or cracked cap, poor connections or corroded terminals in cap towers. Also check for worn, dirty, corroded, burned or improperly adjusted contact points, or for a defective condenser.

Inspect for a weak coil.

Set ignition timing as recommended.

If solenoid switch fails to "click" when ignition key is turned to starting position, connect a jumper wire from positive battery post to small terminal on solenoid. If this causes solenoid to "click", check for loose connections on small terminal on solenoid switch, ignition-starter switch or charge indicator. If solenoid switch fails to "click" when energized with jumper wire, install a new solenoid.

Starting Motor - Test starter for adequate cranking speed.

(c) Compression

Perform compression test to determine if compression is being lost due to worn or leaking valves or worn piston rings.

2. Hard Starting - Nonmechanical Causes

Moisture may collect in distributor cap, on spark plugs and plug wires and connectors.

Use of excessively heavy oil may cause a heavy drag on engine, preventing proper cranking speed.

ENGINE LACKS POWER

1. Fuel System - Inspect fuel lines for obstructions or leaks. Inspect carburetor for presence of dirt or water. Test fuel pump for pressure. Check carburetor float level.

2. Inspect spark plugs for fouling, improper gap or cracked porcelains. Check ignition timing and inspect distributor.

3. Perform a compression test to determine mechanical condition of engine.

4. Check for dragging brakes, tight wheel bearings or under-inflated tires.

ENGINE MISSES ON ACCELERATION

1. Ignition System - Inspect spark plugs for fouling, improper gap or cracked insulator. Check distributor for a cracked cap, loose or corroded terminals in cap towers, pitted or improperly adjusted contact points, or a worn rotor. Check vacuum advance, condenser and coil with testing equipment. Inspect high tension wires for frayed or worn insulation.

2. Weak valve springs may cause engine to miss on acceleration or at high speeds.

ENGINE WILL NOT IDLE SMOOTHLY

1. Fuel System - Turn idle mixture screw out (counterclockwise) to obtain an over-rich mixture. This should cause engine to roll. Also try to make engine stall by turning idle mixture screw in to too lean a mixture.

2. Ignition System - Inspect spark plugs for fouling, cracked insulators or improper gap. Check high tension wires for frayed or worn insulation or loose connections.

Check distributor shaft for wear. Inspect for a cracked distributor cap, loose or corroded terminals in cap towers, burned, pitted or improperly adjusted contact points, corroded or worn rotor. Also test coil and condenser with testing equipment.

OVERHEATING

Common causes of overheating directly traceable to cooling system, are clogging or improper circulation of cooling air.

Another cause of overheating is operation or excessive engine idling under extreme conditions of heat or altitude.

IMPORTANT - Thermostat is seldom responsible for overheating. If damaged, bellows expands and valve stays in wide-open position.

1. Fan Belt - If fan belt is loose, or slipping, fan will not circulate cooling air at proper rate to cool engine.

ENGINE WARMUP--SLOW

If cooling system is dirty, sediment may collect in folds of thermostat bellows and prevent valve from seating fully.

ENGINE NOISES

Noises described here are only those which could originate inside engine. No attempt has been made to describe other noises.

1. A main bearing noise (usually a deep-toned knock) is more noticeable when engine is under load. Check by driving up steep hill or ramp. Also check for this noise by shorting out spark plugs, one at a time, when engine is under load; approximately 35 mph. If noise is more noticeable when spark plugs are shorted out on either side of a main bearing, that main bearing may be at fault.

2. A loose connecting rod bearing usually produces a rapid, metallic knock which is most noticeable when accelerator pedal is released immediately following acceleration of engine and at speeds of 40 to 50 mph. Find faulty bearing by shorting out spark plugs--one at a time. If noise quiets down or disappears, when a particular spark plug is shorted out, connecting rod bearing at that point is probably responsible for noise.

3. A piston noise or piston "slap" may be classified as a hot or cold slap. Noise caused by a cold piston is not harmful. If a piston slap continues after engine reaches operating temperature, it is an indication that there is excessive piston clearance.

4. Valves - If valve noise is evident, check valve tappet clearance. After checking clearance, inspect valve stem ends, valve guides, valve tappet adjusting screw, and cam lobes for wear. Also inspect for weak or broken valve springs.

5. Fuel Pump - An air leak on intake side of fuel pump will increase diaphragm movement and result in noise. Inspect inlet lines for tightness.

HIGH OIL PRESSURE

1. Make sure plunger of oil pressure relief valve is not sticking in closed position. Spring should not be backed up with washers or other such material.

2. Make sure that recommended oil is used in crankcase. A heavy oil will not flow as rapidly as a light oil and high oil pressure may result.

OIL CONSUMPTION

Blue smoke escaping from tail pipe immediately after engine is accelerated or decelerated is an indication that oil is being drawn past piston rings or past valves in guides and into combustion chambers. If no smoke escapes from tail pipe when engine is running, yet oil consumption exists, check for external leakage.

To determine if piston rings or valves are faulty, perform a compression test.

EXCESSIVE FUEL CONSUMPTION

Accurate fuel tests should be made under controlled conditions. Make two test runs (one with, and one against wind) at a constant speed of 30 miles an hour over a level road. An average of these two test runs will indicate mileage the car is capable of delivering under these controlled conditions.

If results indicate excessive fuel consumption, the following items should be checked:

1. Check ignition timing at various operating speeds. Check vacuum advance unit.

2. Check spark plugs for fouled electrodes, cracked insulators and improper gap.

3. Check for high float level and for dirt in air cleaner. Test for excessive fuel pump pressure.

4. Choke must be wide open with engine at operating temperature.

5. Slightest amount of brake drag will tend to increase fuel consumption. Inspect for tight wheel bearings. Check front wheel toe-in. Inflate tires to recommended pressure. Check lubrication of rear axle and transmission.

DRIVING METHODS AND WEATHER CONDITIONS

1. City Driving - To obtain maximum fuel mileage in city traffic, avoid frequent use of low gears as much as possible. Fast starts and resulting excessive brake applications will greatly increase fuel consumption.

2.   Highway driving requires more fuel per mile to operate car at 70 miles an hour than at 35 miles an hour. At high speeds, wind resistance must be overcome and friction on moving parts increases.

At freezing temperatures, tests show that a car must be driven approximately 8 miles before maximum mileage can be obtained. At lower temperatures, car must be driven even greater distances to secure maximum fuel mileage.

Not only does engine have to be warmed up during cold weather, but also units of drive train, to reduce chassis friction.

3.   Overloading - Pulling Heavy Loads - When operating with excessive loads, engine must deliver extra power and more fuel will be burned.

4.   With Automatic Stick Shift transmission: Use Driving Range 1 for city traffic; Driving Range 2 for highway driving. Shift from Range 1 to Range 2 at about 20 mph for best economy.

5.   With Automatic Transmission: Use Driving Range 3 for most conditions, allowing transmission to automatically shift from 1 to 2 and from 2 to 3.

BRAKES

SPONGY PEDAL

If brake pedal, when depressed, feels like a "cushion," condition is generally termed "spongy pedal."

1.   Air - Check for air in lines. Air can enter system when brake fluid is low in master cylinder or when any part of system has been disconnected. Air may be left in system if bleeding operation is not properly performed; or air bubbles may develop in a tightly sealed system when an inferior type brake fluid is used.

2.   Heel contact - Heavy heel contact of brake shoe may cause a "spongy pedal" on light brake application.

3.   Defective and swollen flexible brake hose.

DRAGGING BRAKES

Major causes of dragging brakes are:

1.   Adjustment - Perform a major brake adjustment.

2.   Brake Shoe Return Springs - Check for weak return springs.

3.   Master Cylinder - Remove filler plug and check relief port with a tag wire to be sure it is not partially blocked. A swollen primary cup, incorrect pedal free play, scoring or rust between piston and piston stop, may also partially restrict return of fluid to master cylinder reservoir.

4.   Wheel Cylinders - Check for swollen cups which can slow up return of pistons. Check inside of wheel cylinders for scoring or corrosion.

5.   Brake Hose - Inspect for plugging or swelling which could restrict return flow of fluid in lines.

LOCKED BRAKES

1. Master Cylinder - Make sure relief port is free of dirt. It may also be blocked by a swollen primary cup, incorrect free pedal travel, scoring or rust between piston and piston stop.
2. Flexible Hose - Inspect for plugging or swelling.
3. Brake Shoe Anchors - Check for loose brake shoe anchor bolts.
4. Brake Shoe Return Springs - Check for broken return spring.

GRABBING BRAKES

1. Adjustment - Check for improper adjustment of brake shoe cams.
2. Brake Lining - Inspect linings. If lining has become soaked with brake fluid, oil or grease, it will cause brakes to grab.
3. Brake Drum - Inspect for scoring, cracks or an out-of-round condition.
4. Anchor Pins - Inspect fit of brake shoes on anchor pins. Looseness at this point will cause heavy toe contact and may result in grabbing brakes.
5. Disc Brakes - Check for dirty caliper, rust in cylinder, pistons turned in cylinders.

PEDAL GOES TO FLOOR

If no braking action results when brake pedal is pushed to floor, and pressure cannot be built up by pumping pedal, the following causes may be responsible:
1. Brake Fluid - Check brake fluid level in master cylinder reservoir. Inspect all connections and flexible hose. Check wheel cylinder rubber cups for scoring or damage. Also there may be a complete break in brake line or stoplight switch may be ruptured.
2. Free Play - Check adjustment of push rod.
3. Air in Lines - Check for air in system. Flush and refill systems with high quality brake fluid.
4. Brake Pedal Goes to Floor but Can be Pumped Up - Look for following conditions:
   (a) Adjustment - Adjust brake shoe cams.
   (b) Master Cylinder - A scored or damaged primary cup will not hold pressure due to leakage of fluid past cup.
   (c) External Leakage - Inspect for leaks at wheel cylinders, all brake lines and connections.
   (d) Disc Brakes - Friction pads worn, disc runout excessive, disc too thin, piston seal damaged.

HARD PEDAL

If excessive effort is required when applying brakes, condition is usually referred to as "hard pedal."

1. Linings - Inspect linings for evidence of oil, grease, brake fluid or a heavy glaze.
2. Shoe Adjustment - Check for proper shoe adjustment, indicated by heavy heel, toe or uneven contact.
3. Master Cylinder - Relief port may be partially restricted.
4. Disc Brakes - Friction pads worn and plates contact spreader springs.

BRAKE NOISE

1. Brake Shoe Adjustment - Inspect heal and toe clearance.
2. Loose Parts - Determine if anchor bolts, brake support to steering knuckle bolts, brake support to axle flange bolts, wheel cylinder cap screws, are properly tigntened. Check fit of shoes on anchors.
3. Brake Shoe Adjustment - Check straightness of brake shoes and support plate.
4. Lining Contact - Inspect lining to determine if it is contacting brake drum over entire surface.
5. Brake Drums - Inspect brake drums for evidence of heavy scoring or cracks. Determine if drums are out-of-round or bell-mouthed.
6. Linings - Inspect for oil, grease, dirt or brake fluid on linings.
7. Dust - Blow dust from linings and backing plates.
8. Disc Brakes - Inferior or incorrect pads, pistons have turned in cylinders, disc not running parallel to caliper. Also loose caliper, disc too thin or run-out excessive.

STEERING

HARD STEERING

Hard steering is usually due to binding in steering assembly and may be accompanied by wander. Make sure tires are inflated to recommended pressure, front wheel alignment is correct and steering system properly lubricated. Test steering action with weight of car on front wheels and front wheels on turntables. If hard steering is evident, inspect following:
1. Steering Knuckle Bushings or Ball Joints - First take weight of car off front wheels. Wheels should turn easily from right to left with hand pressure. If wheels do not turn freely, bushings or ball joints may be too tight or scored.
2. Place thumb on steering knuckle thrust bearings and turn wheels from right to left with weight of car on wheels. If roughness is felt, raise front wheels and repeat test. If roughness diminishes, it indicates worn or damaged thrust bearings.
3. Lubricate tie rod ends and check alignment. Sockets should rotate freely on ball studs. Tie rod and sockets on same tie rod should be parallel with each other. If one socket is level and one is at an angle, a binding action may occur on extreme turns.

Late model Volkswagen Beetles feature new 60 hp engine, extensively improved by use of magnesium alloy block. Also introduced is flow-through ventilation from fresh air vent in instrument panel to vents behind rear side windows.

4. Turn steering wheel from right to left through center position. If binding is evident at center position, cross shaft adjustment is too tight.

5. Worm and Tube Assembly - Inspect for binding near extreme right or left position of steering wheel. If binding is evident, bearings are damaged, or are adjusted too tightly.

6. Jacket and Jacket Bushing - Loosen instrument panel bracket and check free position of steering column. If jacket does not line up with center of bracket, binding may occur.

LOOSE STEERING

If any part of steering system is unusually loose, wander, excessive road shock, or wheel shimmy may result. Excessively worn king pin bushings or ball joints could be cause. To check for looseness, jack up front end of car and move wheels in and out.

FRONT SUSPENSION SYSTEM

CAR PULLS TO ONE SIDE

Be sure to determine that condition is not due to driving on highly crowned roads or under-inflated tires.

1. Camber and Caster - If camber and caster are not equal on each side, car will pull to one side on a level road. Car may pull to the side which has highest camber. If caster is not equal, car may pull to side having lowest caster.

2. Tires - Unequal tire pressure will cause car to pull to side having lowest pressure.

3. Frame and Suspension Units - Bent suspension parts, or shifted axle may cause car to pull to one side. To check for these conditions, measure wheelbase, center-to-center, between front and rear wheels on both sides.

4. Brakes - Inspect adjustment of each front and rear wheel brake for "Dragging."

5. Steering Tube and Worm Assembly - A bent steering tube and worm assembly will cause hard steering and may result in car pulling to one side. Check by jacking up front end of car and turn steering wheel to extreme right and left. If intermittent drag is felt, tube may be bent.

WANDER

Term "wander" means tendency of car to drift slightly to one side, then to other.

1. King Pin Bushings or Ball Joints and Steering Connections - To check for looseness, jack up front end of car and move wheels in and out.

2. Steering Wheel - An improperly centered steering wheel will give effect of wander. Steering wheel is correctly centered when spokes are equally positioned, with front wheels pointing straight ahead.

3. Tires - A smooth tread on front tires may cause wander when car is driven over gravel, or "black-top" roads. Under-inflation of both front or rear tires may cause unstable steering and result in wander.

4. Caster - Bent front wheel suspension parts or unequal wheel base may cause car to wander.

WHEEL TRAMP

Wheel tramp usually develops at high speeds and is caused by excessive looseness of king pin bushings, ball joints, or wheel bearings, lack of control in shock absorbers, or out-of-balance front wheels.

EXCESSIVE TIRE WEAR

Different types of tire wear are classified as "Spotty Wear," "Under-inflation Wear," "Toe-in and Toe-out Wear" and "Camber Wear." Tires wear at a different rate on all four wheels due to driving conditions, distribution of car's weight, power on rear wheels, and crown of road. For this reason, it is recommended that tires be rotated every 3,000 miles to equalize wear and to obtain maximum tire life.

1. Spotty Wear - This condition occurs on front tires but does not progress to any great extent before first 3,000 miles of driving. To keep such wear at a minimum, keep tires inflated to recommended pressure and rotate them every 3,000 miles.

2. Under-inflation wear can be recognized by excessive wear on two tread ribs adjacent to inner and outer shoulder ribs.

3. Over-inflation wear can be recognized by excessive wear on center of tread and little wear on outer edges of tire.

4. Amount of toe-in or toe-out of front wheels affects rate of tire wear more than any other factor of front wheel alignment. Toe-in wear produces a feather-like edge at inside edges of tread ribs and can usually be felt when hand is rubbed over face of tread.

Toe-out wear produces same condition as toe-in wear, except that feather-like edge is formed on outside edges of tread ribs.

5. Excessive positive camber will cause noticeable wear on outer ribs of tire. Excessive negative camber will develop wear on inner ribs of tire.

6. Out-of-round tires and unbalanced wheel assemblies will cause flat spots to be worn on tire tread.

GENERATING SYSTEM

AMMETER TEST SHOWS DISCHARGE

(Engine Running at Fast Idle)

1. Generator or Regulator Defective.

2. Battery - Test for a weak or discharged battery. Inspect cables in charging circuit for looseness and battery terminals for corrosion.

3. Fan Belt - Make sure fan belt is tight and in good condition.

4. Wiring - Inspect wiring for frayed or worn insulation in generating circuit.

EXCESSIVE LOSS OF BATTERY FLUID

If battery is continually low on fluid or will not hold fluid, look for following possible causes:

1. Inspect for a cracked battery.
2. Inspect for an improperly adjusted voltage regulator.

CONTINUAL LOSS OF BATTERY CHARGE

If battery can be fully charged but will not retain charge, one of following conditions may exist:

1. Inspect for a short circuit in wiring system. Make sure top surface of battery is clean.
2. Inspect for sulfation of battery plates.

STARTING SYSTEM

STARTER TURNS SLOWLY OR DOES NOT OPERATE

1. Test for weak or discharged battery. Inspect terminals for corrosion or looseness.

2. If solenoid switch fails to "click" when ignition key is turned, connect a jumper wire from positive battery post to small terminal on solenoid. If this causes solenoid to "click," check for loose connections at small terminal on solenoid switch and ignition-starter switch. If solenoid switch fails to "click" when energized with a jumper wire, install a new solenoid.

3. If test indicates that starter motor is at fault, it should be removed and inspected for repair. A heavy arc, appearing when battery terminal is touched to starter terminal, indicates a grounded condition in starter. If no arcing occurs, there is probably a poor brush contact or an open circuit in starter windings.

STARTER FAILS TO ENGAGE

When starter motor pinion fails to engage flywheel ring gear (with the battery fully charged), trouble is in starter motor.

1. Inspect for heavy oil, dirt or ice on threads of drive.

STARTER LOCKS IN ENGAGEMENT

If starter locks in engagement, it can be freed by pushing car back and forth with transmission in high gear.

1. Another way to free a locked starter is to loosen starter mounting, pull starter out slightly and then retighten bolts.
2. Flywheel Ring Gear or Pinion - Examine for burrs or chipped teeth. If ring gear is damaged, replace both gear and starter drive unit.

LIGHTING SYSTEM

DIM HEADLIGHTS

(Engine Idling or Shut Off)
1. Test for a weak or discharged battery, loose or defective cables, or for corroded battery terminals.
2. Test wiring and switches in lighting circuit for voltage drop.

DIM HEADLIGHTS

(Engine Running Above Idle With Battery Fully Charged)
1. Test wiring and switches in lighting circuit for voltage drop.
2. Test for low output or high resistance in generator brushes.

LIGHTS FAIL

1. Test battery. Inspect for loose or defective cables and for corroded battery terminals.
2. Wiring - Inspect for poor grounds, or for a short circuit in lighting circuit.
3. Install a new head light switch if stop light operates and all other lights fail.

CLUTCH

SLIPPING

To test for a slipping clutch, start engine, set hand brake and shift into high gear. Then engage clutch and accelerate engine slowly. Engine should stall if clutch is not slipping.
1. Pedal Free Play - Inspect for insufficient pedal free play.
2. Clutch Disc - Inspect for burned, worn, or oil soaked clutch disc facings.
3. Pressure Plate Springs - Inspect for weak or broken pressure plate springs.

CHATTERING

This condition can be determined by vibration that may occur during clutch engagement.
1. Clutch Disc - Inspect for oil or grease on facings.
2. Pressure Plate - Inspect for a cocked pressure plate.

DRAGGING

This condition exists when clutch is slow in disengaging, or will not completely release. When this occurs, gears may be difficult to shift without clashing.

1. Pedal Free Play - Inspect for excessive pedal free play.
2. Clutch Disc - Inspect for a bent clutch disc.
3. Clutch Release Levers - Inspect adjustment of clutch release levers.
4. Clutch Disc Hub - Make sure clutch disc hub does not bind on drive pinion shaft.
5. Return Springs - Inspect for broken or weak return springs.

PEDAL STIFF OR BINDING

1. Clutch Linkage - Inspect clutch linkage, cable and tube for rust or corrosion and for bent or misaligned linkage.

NOISES

1. Release Bearing - A high-pitched noise, occurring only with engine running, transmission in NEUTRAL, and clutch pedal down, usually indicates that release bearing should be replaced.
2. Release Levers - A rattling noise may develop when an uneven release lever causes release bearing to shuffle on its sleeve.
3. Pilot Bearing - A high-pitched noise occuring only with engine running, transmission in gear, and clutch pedal down, may indicate that pilot bushing or bearing is tight, worn or dry.
4. Pressure Plate Assembly - A whining noise heard when engine is accelerated and clutch disengaged may be due to excessive clearance between pressure plate lugs and openings in stamped cover.

A squeaky noise heard while clutch pedal is being operated, may be due to pressure plate release levers, or drive lugs rubbing on cover.

TRANSMISSION

NOISES

Noise present in all gear positions may be due to worn or damaged bearings. Noise present in only one gear position can usually be traced to particular gear involved.

1. A worn or damaged low and reverse sliding gear will be noisy only while transmission is in either of these two gears. If sliding gear is in good condition, and a noise is heard when low gear is used, it indicates that cluster gear is at fault. If noise is heard when reverse gear is used, reverse idler or mating cluster gear may be worn or damaged.
2. A mainshaft bearing noise can usually be determined by driving

car in high gear at a speed where noise is more apparent, and then shifting into neutral, shutting off engine and coasting.

3. Noise made by a worn drive pinion pilot bushing or bearing (in rear end of crankshaft) is usually apparent while coasting in low or second gear at moderate speeds, with transmission in gear and clutch disengaged.

4. Noises caused by excessive backlash or end play are similar. To determine which condition exists, it will be necessary to check backlash or end play.

REAR AXLE

LEAKAGE OF LUBRICANT

When there is an excessive amount of lubricant in differential, high pressure will build up and force lubricant out through seals and gasket.

1. Axle Shaft Oil Seals - Grease may leak out around brake support plate. Grabbing brakes may also indicate leakage at oil seal.

NOISES

Rear axle noises are often confused with sounds that originate in other parts of car. Always make a careful inspection of other units before condemning rear axle.

1. Tires - Tire noise will vary, depending upon type of road surface and condition of tire tread. Road test car on smooth pavement at a speed where noise is most audible. Then, disengage clutch and apply brakes. If noise increases, it can be assumed that tires are causing noise.

2. Wheel Bearings - To determine if wheel bearings are worn or damaged, road test car and apply brakes. Noise, if present, will diminish, indicating that bearings may be at fault.

3. Exhaust - Test for exhaust system noise by slowing and increasing engine speed with car standing still. Noise should be apparent as long as engine speed is steady. But, will fade when engine speed is increased or decreased. A bent tail pipe will cause rattling noise.

4. Clutch - Noise resulting from a faulty clutch disc unit may be heard when car is accelerating at speeds of 25 to 30 miles an hour, or while coasting down from 45 to 38 miles an hour.

5. Differential and Carrier Assembly - Main difference between an axle bearing noise and a gear noise is in duration and sound. Bearing noise is continuous and may change slightly in volume only as speed changes. Slightly worn or damaged bearings cause a "sizzling" noise. Badly worn or broken bearings will make a rough grating sound.

A continuous whine may be produced by a pinion and ring gear which are set up too tightly. Gear noise comes in when car is being driven under load, on coast, or on both pull and coast. Gear noise changes in volume and in pitch as car speed changes. There can also be a combination bearing and gear noise.

Volkswagen Trouble Shooting

(a) Steady Noise on Pull - Loss of lubricant, use of improper lubricant or improper mesh of gear teeth will cause a steady hum. Do not confuse with tire noise.

(b) Steady Noise on Coast - Gear teeth that are badly scored due to excessive end play in pinion bearings, or because of improper adjustment of bearings, will cause a steady hum.

(c) Bearing Noise on Pull and Coast - When pinion or differential bearings are scored, chipped, cracked, or badly worn, a noise will be heard when accelerating, or coasting down to lower speeds.

(d) Ring Gear and Pinion - A sharp, metallic sound, heard when shifting from reverse into a forward speed, may indicate that ring gear is creeping on case, or that its mounting bolts are loose. A thumping sound, heard when car is turning a corner, may be due to a broken tooth, or a large nick in a differential side gear.

6. Axle Shafts - Excessive end play in rear axle shafts will cause a thump or chucking noise when driving on a rough road, also when turning a corner.

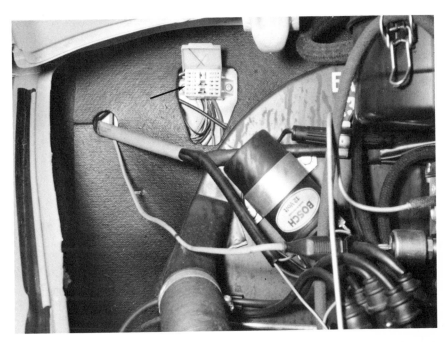

Since June, 1971, all VWs have been fitted with a special receptacle (arrow) for computer diagnosis checks. A single plug from the computer picks up pulses from various systems and the computer prints out a program card covering at least 66 separate items.

VOLKSWAGEN "BEETLE" SPECIFICATIONS

	Jan. Aug. 1954-1960	1961-1965	1966	1967	1968-1969	1970
Engine Type	Air cooled, four cycle, four cylinder					
Cylinder Arrangement	Two pairs, horizontally opposed					
Valve Arrangement	Overhead					
Bore of Cylinders	3.031 in.	3.031 in.	3.031 in.	3.27 in.	3.27 in.	3.36 in.
Stroke of Engine	2.52 in.	2.52 in.	2.72 in.	2.72 in.	2.72 in.	2.72 in.
Displacement of Engine	72.74 cu. in.	72.74 cu. in.	78.42 cu. in.	91.10 cu. in.	91.10 cu. in.	96.66 cu. in.
Compression Ratio	6-1**	7-1	7.3-1	7.5-1	7.5-1	7.5-1
HP Rating at RPM	36-3700	40-3900	50-4600	53-4200	53-4200	57-4400
Inlet Valve Clearance	.004 C	.008 C	.004 C*	.004 C	.004 C	.004 C
Exhaust Valve Clearance	.004 C	.012 C	.004 C*	.004 C	.004 C	.004 C
Inlet Valve Opens (deg.)	2-1/2 B	6 B	7-1/2 B	7-1/2 B	7-1/2 B	7-1/2 B
Breaker Timing (deg.)	7-1/2 B	10 B	7-1/2 B	7-1/2 B	TDC	TDC
Breaker Point Gap (in.)	.016	.016	.016	.016	.016	.016
Spark Plug Type (Bosch)	W175T1***	W175T1	W175T1	W175T1	W145T1	W145T1
Spark Plug Gap	.024 to .028 in.			.028 in.	.028 in.	.028 in.
Fuel Pump (Solex)	Diaphragm type-mechanically operated					
Carburetor (Solex)	28PC1	28PICT	30PICT1	30PICT1	30PICT2	30PICT3
Air Cleaner	Oil bath	Oil bath	Oil bath	Oil bath	Oil bath	Oil bath
Lubrication System	Pressure lubrication with oil cooler					
Cooling System	Thermostatically controlled air					
Battery	6-volt	6-volt	6-volt	12-volt	12-volt	12-volt
Starter (Bosch)	Solenoid operated					
Generator (Bosch)	Voltage controlled					
Clutch	Single disc, dry					
Transmission	Four forward speeds and reverse					
Synchromesh Gears	2-3-4	1-2-3-4	1-2-3-4	1-2-3-4	a 1-2-3-4	a 1-2-3-4
Gear Ratio, First	3.60-1	3.80-1	3.80-1	3.80-1	3.80-1	3.80-1

Gear Ratio, Second	1.88-1	2.06-1	2.06-1	2.06-1	2.06-1	2.06-1
Gear Ratio, Third	1.23-1	1.32-1	1.32-1	1.26-1	1.26-1	1.26-1
Gear Ratio, Fourth	0.82-1	0.89-1	0.89-1	0.89-1	0.89-1	0.89-1
Gear Ratio, Reverse	4.63-1	3.88-1	3.88-1	3.88-1	3.61-1	3.61-1
Final Drive	Swing axles from transaxle housing			b	b	b
Gear Type	Spiral bevel					
Gear ratio	4.4-1	4.375-1	4.375-1	4.125-1	4.125-1	4.375-1
Front Axle	Trailing link independent suspension			c	c	c
Rear Axle	Trailing link independent suspension			c	c	c
Front Springs	Two transverse torsion bars					
Rear Springs	Two torsion bars					
Shock Absorbers	Double acting telescoping type					
Brakes	Lockheed hydraulic					
Tires	5.60-15					
Wheelbase	94.5 in.					
Track, Front	51.4 in.	51.6 in.	51.6 in.		51.6 in.	51.6 in.
Track, Rear	50.7 in.	51.2 in.		53.5 in.	53.3 in.	53.3 in.
Turning Circle	Approximately 36 feet					
Overall Car Length	160.6 in.			158.6 in.	158.6 in.	158.6 in.
Overall Car Width	60.6 in.			61.0 in.	61.0 in.	61.0 in.
Overall Car Height	59.1 in.					
Fuel Tank Capacity	10.5 gallons including 1.3 reserve			10.6	10.6	10.6
Engine Oil Capacity	5.3 pints					
Transaxle Capactiy	6.3 pints total or 5.3 pints refill			d	d	d

B – Before top dead center.

C – Cold.

Deg. – Degrees.

In. – Inches.

Cu. In. – Cubic inches.

HP – Horsepower.

RPM – Revolutions per minute.

TDC – Top dead center.

* – "Tagged" engines. Untagged = inlet
.008, exhaust .012.

** – 1956-1960, 6.6-1.

*** – 1956-1960, W225T1.

a – 3-speed "Automatic Stick Shift" option.

b – Double-jointed rear axles.

c – Trailing and diagonal arms.

d – Auto. Stick Shift – 6.3 pints oil.
Torque converter – 7.6 pints ATF.

251

1971 VOLKSWAGEN SPECIFICATIONS COMPARED

	Beetle Sedan, 111	Super Beetle, 113	Type 3 - Squareback	Type 4, 411
Engine Type	Air cooled, 4 cycle, 4 cylinder			
Cylinder Arrangement	Two pairs, horizontally opposed			
Valve Arrangement	Overhead			
Bore of Cylinders	3.36 in.	3.36 in.	3.36 in.	3.54 in.
Stroke of Engine	2.72 in.	2.72 in.	2.72 in.	2.60 in.
Displacement of Engine	96.66 cu. in.	96.66 cu. in.	96.66 cu. in.	102.5 cu. in.
Compression Ratio	7.5-1	7.5-1	7.7-1	8.2-1
HP Rating at RPM	60-4400	60-4400	65-4600	85-5000
Firing Order	1-4-3-2	1-4-3-2	1-4-3-2	1-4-3-2
Inlet Valve Clearance	.004 in. C	.004 in. C	.004 in. C	.006 in. C
Exhaust Valve Clearance	.004 in. C	.004 in. C	.004 in. C	.006 in. C
Inlet Valve Opens	7-1/2 B	7-1/2 B	7-1/2 B	12 B
Breaker Timing	5A	5A	TDC	27 BD
Breaker Point Gap	.016 in.	.016 in.	.016 in.	.016 in.
Fuel Pump	Diaphragm type-mechanically operated		Electric	Electric
Carburetor (Solex)	34 PICT 3	34 PICT 3	*	*
Air Cleaner	Oil bath, with thermostat		Oil bath	Oil bath
Lubrication System	Pressure feed with oil cooler			
Cooling System	Thermostatically controlled air			
Battery	12-volt	12-volt	12-volt	12-volt
Starter	Solenoid operated			
Generator	Voltage controlled			Alternator
Clutch	Single Disc, dry	Disc	Disc	
Transmission	Four forward speeds and reverse	4-Speed	4-Speed	Automatic
Synchromesh Gears	1-2-3-4	1-2-3-4	1-2-3-4	
Gear Ratio, First	3.80-1	3.80-1	3.80-1	2.65-1

Gear Ratio, Second	2.06-1	2.06-1	2.06-1	1.59-1
Gear Ratio, Third	1.26-1	1.26-1	1.26-1	1.0-1
Gear Ratio, Fourth	0.89-1	0.89-1	0.89-1	
Gear Ratio, Reverse	3.61-1	3.61-1	3.61-1	1.80-1
Final Drive	Double-Jointed axles from transaxle housing			
Gear Ratio	4.125-1	4.125-1	4.125-1	3.91-1
Front Axle	Twin cranked link arms	Link arms	Torsion arms	Link arms
Rear Axle	Trailing arms and diagonal links			
Front Springs	Torsion bars	Coil	Torsion bars	Coil
Rear Springs	Torsion bars	Torsion bars	Torsion bars	Coil
Shock Absorbers	Double acting telescoping type			
Brakes, Front	Drum-Dual circuit	Drum-Dual	Disc-Dual	Disc-Dual
Brakes, Rear	Drum-Dual circuit			
Tires	5.60-15	5.60-15	6.00-15L	155 SR 15**
Wheelbase	94.5 in.	95.3 in.	94.5 in.	98.4 in.
Track, Front	51.6 in.	54.3 in.	51.6 in.	54.7 in.
Track, Rear	53.3 in.	53.3 in.	53.1 in.	52.8 in.
Turning Circle	36 ft.	31.5 ft.	36.5 ft.	37 ft.
Overall Car Length	158.6 in.	161.8 in.	170.9 in.	179.2 in.
Overall Car Width	61.0 in.	62.4 in.	63.2 in.	64.9 in.
Overall Car Height	59.1 in.	59.1 in.	57.9 in.	58.5 in.
Fuel Tank Capacity	10.6 gals.	11.1 gals.	10.6 gals.	13.2 gals.
Engine Oil Capacity	5.3 pts.	5.3 pts.	5.3 pts.	7.4 pts.
Transaxle Capacity	6.3 pts. total or 5.3 pts. refill***			5.3 pts. total or 4.2 pts. refill

Cu. In. – Cubic inches
In. – Inches
HP – Horsepower
RPM – Revolutions per minute
* – Electronic fuel injection

** – 3-Door – 165 SR 15
*** – Auto, Stick Shift – 6.3 pints oil
Torque Conv. – 7.6 pints ATF
Automatic Trans. – 6 pints ATF (Refill)
Final Drive – 2 pints oil

A – After top dead center
B – Before top dead center
C – Cold
D – At 3500 rpm

1972 VOLKSWAGEN SPECIFICATIONS COMPARED

	Beetle Sedan, 111	Super Beetle, 113	Type 3 - Squareback	Type 4, 411
Engine Type	Air cooled, 4 cycle, 4 cylinder			
Cylinder Arrangement	Two pairs, horizontally opposed			
Valve Arrangement	Overhead			
Bore of Cylinders	3.36 in.	3.36 in.	3.36 in.	3.54 in.
Stroke of Engine	2.72 in.	2.72 in.	2.72 in.	2.60 in.
Displacement of Engine	96.66 cu. in.	96.66 cu. in.	96.66 cu. in.	102.5 cu. in.
Compression Ratio	7.3-1	7.3-1	7.3-1	7.8-1
HP Rating at RPM	60-4400	60-4400	65-4600	85-5000
Firing Order	1-4-3-2	1-4-3-2	1-4-3-2	1-4-3-2
Inlet Valve Clearance	.006 in. C	.006 in. C	.006 in. C	.006 in. C
Exhaust Valve Clearance	.006 in. C	.006 in. C	.006 in. C	.006 in. C
Inlet Valve Opens	7-1/2 B	7-1/2 B	7-1/2 B	12 B
Breaker Timing	5A	5A	5 B	27 B D
Breaker Point Gap	.016 in.	.016 in.	.016 in.	.016 in.
Fuel Pump	Diaphragm type-mechanically operated		Electric	Electric
Carburetor (Solex)	34 PICT 3	34 PICT 3	*	*
Air Cleaner	Oil bath, with thermostat		Oil bath	Oil bath
Lubrication System	Pressure feed with oil cooler			
Cooling System	Thermostatically controlled air			
Battery	12-volt	12-volt	12-volt	12-volt
Starter	Solenoid operated			
Generator	Voltage controlled			Alternator
Clutch	Single Disc, dry	Disc	Disc	Automatic
Transmission	Four forward speeds and reverse	4-Speed	4-Speed	Automatic
Synchromesh Gears	1-2-3-4	1-2-3-4	1-2-3-4	
Gear Ratio, First	3.80-1	3.80-1	3.80-1	2.65-1

Gear Ratio, Second	2.06-1	2.06-1	2.06-1	1.59-1
Gear Ratio, Third	1.26-1	1.26-1	1.26-1	1.0-1
Gear Ratio, Fourth	0.89-1	0.89-1	0.89-1	
Gear Ratio, Reverse	3.61-1	3.61-1	3.61-1	1.80-1
Final Drive	Double-Jointed axles from transaxle housing			
Gear Ratio	4.125-1	4.125-1	4.125-1	3.67-1
Front Axle	Twin cranked link arms	Link arms	Link arms	Link arms
Rear Axle	Trailing arms and diagonal links	Torsion bars	Torsion bars	Torsion arms
Front Springs	Torsion bars	Coil	Torsion bars	Coil
Rear Springs	Torsion bars	Torsion bars	Torsion bars	Coil
Shock Absorbers	Double acting telescoping type			
Brakes, Front	Drum-Dual circuit	Drum-Dual	Disc-Dual	Disc-Dual
Brakes, Rear	Drum-Dual circuit	Drum-Dual	Disc-Dual	Disc-Dual
Tires	5.60-15	5.60-15	6.00-15L	155 SR 15**
Wheelbase	94.5 in.	95.3 in.	94.5 in.	98.4 in.
Track, Front	51.6 in.	54.3 in.	51.6 in.	54.7 in.
Track, Rear	53.3 in.	53.3 in.	53.0 in.	52.8 in.
Turning Circle	36 ft.	31.5 ft.	36 ft.	37 ft.
Overall Car Length	158.6 in.	161.8 in.	170.9 in.	179.2 in.
Overall Car Width	61.0 in.	62.4 in.	63.2 in.	64.9 in.
Overall Car Height	59.1 in.	59.1 in.	57.9 in.	58.5 in.
Fuel Tank Capacity	10.6 gals.	11.1 gals.	10.6 gals.	13.2 gals.
Engine Oil Capacity	5.3 pts.	5.3 pts.	5.3 pts.	7.4 pts.
Transaxle Capacity	6.3 pts. total or 5.3 pts. refill***		5.3 pts. total or 4.2 pts. refill	

Cu. In. – Cubic inches
In. – Inches
HP – Horsepower
RPM – Revolutions per minute
* – Electronic fuel injection

** – 3-Door – 165 SR 15
*** – Auto. Stick Shift – 6.3 pints oil
Torque Conv. – 7.6 pints ATF
Automatic Trans. – 6 pints ATF (Refill)
Final Drive – 2 pints oil

A – After top dead center
B – Before top dead center
C – Cold
D – At 3500 rpm with vacuum hoses off

1973 VOLKSWAGEN SPECIFICATIONS COMPARED

	Basic Beetle Sedan, 111	Super Beetle, 113	Type 3 – Squareback	Type 4, 412
Engine Type	Air cooled, 4 cycle, 4 cylinder			
Cylinder Arrangement	Two pairs, horizontally opposed			
Valve Arrangement	Overhead			
Bore of Cylinders	3.37 in.	3.37 in.	3.37 in.	3.54 in.
Stroke of Engine	2.72 in.	2.72 in.	2.72 in.	2.59 in.
Displacement of Engine	96.66 cu. in.	96.66 cu. in.	96.66 cu. in.	102.5 cu. in.
Compression Ratio	7.5-1	7.5-1	7.5-1	8.2-1
HP Rating at RPM	46-4000	46-4000	52-4000	76-4900
Firing Order	1-4-3-2	1-4-3-2	1-4-3-2	1-4-3-2
Inlet Valve Clearance	.006 in. C	.006 in. C	.006 in. C	.006 in. C
Exhaust Valve Clearance	.006 in. C	.006 in. C	.006 in. C	.006 in. C
Inlet Valve Opens	7-1/2 B	7-1/2 B	7-1/2 B	12 B
Breaker Timing	5A	5A	5B	27 B D
Breaker Point Gap	.016 in.	.016 in.	.016 in.	.016 in.
Fuel Pump	Diaphragm type-mechanically operated			
Carburetor (Solex)	34 PICT 3	34 PICT 3	Electric *	Electric *
Air Cleaner	Oil bath, with thermostat	Oil bath	Oil bath	Oil bath
Lubrication System	Pressure, feed with oil cooler			
Cooling System	Thermostatically controlled air			
Battery	12-volt	12-volt	12-volt	12-volt
Starter	Solenoid operated			
Generator	Voltage controlled			Alternator
Clutch	Single Disc, dry/diaphragm plate	Disc	Disc	
Transmission	4-Speed manual Stick shift	4-Speed	4-Speed	Automatic
Synchromesh Gears	1-2-3-4	1-2-3-4	1-2-3-4	
Gear Ratio, First	3.78-1 2.25-1	3.78-1	3.78-1	2.65-1

	(1)	(2)	(3)	(4)
Gear Ratio, Second	1.59-1	2.06-1	2.06-1	1.26-1
Gear Ratio, Third	1.0-1	1.26-1	1.26-1	0.88-1
Gear Ratio, Fourth		0.88-1	0.93-1	
Gear Ratio, Reverse	1.80-1	3.61-1	3.78-1	3.07-1
Final Drive				Double-Jointed axles from transaxle housing
Gear Ratio	3.73-1	4.125-1	3.875-1	3.875-1
Front Axle	Struts and Arms	Torsion arms	Torsion arms	Torsion arms
Rear Axle				Trailing arms and diagonal links
Front Springs	Coil	Torsion bars	Coil	Torsion bars
Rear Springs	Coil	Torsion bars	Torsion bars	Torsion bars
Shock Absorbers				Double acting telescoping type
Brakes, Front	Disc-Dual	Disc-Dual	Drum-Dual	Drum-Dual circuit
Brakes, Rear	Disc-Dual	Disc-Dual	Drum-Dual	Drum-Dual circuit
Tires	155 SR 15**	6.00-15L	6.00-15L	6.00-15L
Wheelbase	98.4 in.	94.5 in.	95.3 in.	94.5 in.
Track, Front	54.2 in.	51.6 in.	54.6 in.	52.1 in.
Track, Rear	52.7 in.	53.0 in.	53.6 in.	53.6 in.
Turning Circle	37.4 ft.	36.7 ft.	31.5 ft.	36.1 ft.
Overall Car Length	180.4 in.	172.0 in.	163.0 in.	159.8 in.
Overall Car Width	65.9 in.	64.6 in.	62.4 in.	61.0 in.
Overall Car Height	58.1 in.	57.9 in.	59.1 in.	59.1 in.
Fuel Tank Capacity	13.2 gals.	10.6 gals.	11.1 gals.	10.6 gals.
Engine Oil Capacity	6.3 pts.	5.3 pts.	5.3 pts.	5.3 pts.
Transaxle Capacity	12.7 pts.***** (Auto.)	12.7 pts.**** (Auto.)	6.3 pts.***	6.3 pts.***

Cu. In. - Cubic inches
In. - Inches
HP - Horsepower
RPM - Revolutions per minute

* - Electronic fuel injection
** - Wagon - 165 SR 15
*** - Auto. Stick Shift - 7.6 ATF
**** - Basic Compact - 6.3 pts. oil
***** - 2-Door - 7.4 pts. oil

A - After top dead center
B - Before top dead center
C - Cold
D - At 3500 rpm

YEAR IDENTIFICATION
"BEETLE" MODELS

Prior to 1955, models were produced according to calendar year. The 1955 Volkswagen and later models start on the preceding August 1st. Chassis numbers are the only sure model identification.

1949 CHASSIS NUMBERS: 91922-138554
1950 CHASSIS NUMBERS: 138555-220471
1951 CHASSIS NUMBERS: 220472-313829
1952 CHASSIS NUMBERS: 313830-428156
1953 CHASSIS NUMBERS: 428157-575414
1954 CHASSIS NUMBERS: 575415-722934
1955 CHASSIS NUMBERS: 722935-929745
1956 CHASSIS NUMBERS: 929746-1246618
1957 CHASSIS NUMBERS: 1246619-1600439
1958 CHASSIS NUMBERS: 1600440-2007615

Brake drums and shoes widened. Flat accelerator replaces roller pedal. Rear window and windshield enlarged. Front turn signals moved to top of front fenders.

1959 CHASSIS NUMBERS: 2007616-2528667

Stronger clutch springs adopted. Frame structure reinforced. Fan belt improved.

1960 CHASSIS NUMBERS: 2528668-3192506

Steering wheel dished. Steering damper added. Push button door handles replace pull-out lever type handles. Padded sun visor replaces transparent plastic type visor. Generator output increased from 160 to 180 watts. Anti-sway bar added.

1961 CHASSIS NUMBERS: 3192507-4010994

Engine horsepower increased from 36 to 40. Transmission synchronized in all forward speeds. Automatic choke and anti-icing air supply added with new carburetor. Transparent brake fluid reservoir adopted. Push-on connectors fitted throughout electrical system. Pump-type windshield washer adopted. Non-repeat starter switch installed.

1962 CHASSIS NUMBERS: 4010995-4846835

Worm and roller steering gear replaces worm and sector type. Gasoline gauge adopted. Spring loading added to hood. Sliding covers added to heat outlets. Pneumatic windshield washer replaces pump-type. Permanently lubricated tie rod ends adopted.

1963 CHASSIS NUMBERS: 4846836-5677118

Nylon window guides added. Fresh air heating adopted along with fan and housing changes. Wolfsburg hood crest dropped. Folding handle installed for sunroof models.

1964 CHASSIS NUMBERS: 5677119-6502399

Crank-operated sliding steel sunroof replaces fabric sunroof. Two thumb buttons replace horn half-ring. Panel truck and station wagon rear doors widened.

1965 CHASSIS NUMBERS: 115000001-115979202

Windshield and window glass area enlarged. Flexible blade windshield wipers park on left side. Heating system capacity increased. Push-button release replaced T-handle on engine lid.

Year Identification "Beetle" Models

1966 CHASSIS NUMBERS: 116000001-1161021298

Engine horsepower increased from 40 to 50, displacement from 1200 to 1300 cc. No. 1300 appears on engine lid. Accelerator linkage improved. Ball joint front suspension introduced; also emergency warning flasher and safety locks on front seat backrests. Wheel slots ventilate brakes.

1967 CHASSIS NUMBERS: 117000001-117844892

Larger displacement (1493 cc), higher horsepower (53) engine featured. Twelve volt electrical system has 36 amp. hr. battery, early cut-in generator, more powerful starter, 2-speed windshield wiper motor and added fuses. Oil bath air cleaner has air preheater. Brakes have dual hydraulic circuit.

1968 CHASSIS NUMBERS: 118000001-1181016098

Exhaust emission control system installed. Gas tank filler located outside. Collapsible steering column standard. Fresh air ventilation system built into top of dash. Optional Automatic Stick Shift transmission introduced.

1969 CHASSIS NUMBERS: 119000001-1191093704

Rear suspension has trailing arms and diagonal links; double-jointed half axles with constant velocity joints. Engine has closed crankcase ventilation; heated air to carburetor. Rear window is "laced" with heating wires for defogging.

1970 CHASSIS NUMBERS: 1102000001-1103096945

More powerful 57 hp, 96.6 cu. in. engine introduced. New carburetor has air bypass port and improved throttle positioner. California cars have evaporative control fuel system. Engine lid has 10 air intake slots to aid engine-cooling. Side marker lights and side reflectors are incorporated in turn signal/parking light housings. Buzzer signals warning if key is left in ignition lock. Glove compartment has a lock.

1971 CHASSIS NUMBERS: 1112000001-1113143118

New 60 hp engine has larger carburetor, thermostat in air cleaner and evaporative control fuel system. Featured is diagonal arm axle at rear with double-jointed driveshafts.

1972 CHASSIS NUMBERS: 1122000001-1122961362

Improvements include: safety steering wheel with 4 in. collapsible hub, plus energy-absorbing column; larger rear window; windshield wiper and washer control arm is mounted on right side of steering column. Compression ratio is reduced from 7.5 to 1 to a ratio of 7.3 to 1 to permit use of lead free gasoline.

YEAR IDENTIFICATION
TYPE 3 MODELS

Fastback and Squareback models were put on the U. S. market in August, 1965, to supplement the Beetle. Beginning with 1971 models, the designation "Fastback" was dropped in favor of "Type 3."

1966 CHASSIS NUMBERS: 316000001-316316238

Front bucket seats adjust to seven different positions fore and aft. Backrests adjust to seven different angles and lock in place. Emergency flasher is standard. Headlight dimmer is built into turn signal lever. Squareback has auxiliary spring in rear; Fastback has hingeless rear side windows.

1967 CHASSIS NUMBERS: 317000001-317233853

Dual braking system is standard. A 12-volt electrical system introduced with early cut-in generator and dual back-up lights. All models use softer rear torsion bars. Auxiliary rear spring added to Fastback.

1968 CHASSIS NUMBERS: 318000001-318235387

Electronic fuel system replaces twin carburetors. System maintains metered flow of fuel and air to cylinders under varying operating conditions. Built-in front seat headrests, collapsible steering column and brake system warning device are used.

1969 CHASSIS NUMBERS: 319000001-369264032

Fully automatic transmission becomes optional equipment. Diagonal-arm rear suspension with double-jointed half axle featured. Rear window defogger and locking steering wheel added. Front hood release lever in glove compartment.

1970 CHASSIS NUMBERS: 3102000001-3602274094

Fuel injection system is improved, as are starting and lighting systems. Engine has more oil passages, an additional oil pressure relief valve and altered oil pump housing. Modifications in torque converter promotes cooling of automatic transmission to permit towing of trailers. California cars have evaporative control fuel system. Buzzer signals warning if key is left in ignition lock. Windshield wiper attachments are splined.

1971 CHASSIS NUMBERS: 3112000001-3612277190

All models have flow-through ventilation. In addition, Type 3 has 2-speed fan. Ignition switch turns off headlights if driver forgets. Engine crankcase is made of modified magnesium alloy; exhaust valve stems are chrome plated. Towing eyes are welded to front axle beam and rear bumper bracket.

1972 CHASSIS NUMBERS: 3122000001-3222166114

Features include: energy-absorbing steering wheel with collapsible hub; fingertip controls at steering column for windshield wiper/washer; test light for dual braking system; improved air intake preheating system for better exhaust emission control.

1973 CHASSIS NUMBERS: 3132000001-

Model changes are described and illustrated on page 8.

YEAR IDENTIFICATION
TYPE 4 MODELS

Type 4, Model 411 4-Door Sedans and Wagons were introduced in U. S. in April, 1971.

1971 CHASSIS NUMBERS: 4212000001-4612068020

Standard equipment includes a "1700" electronic fuel injection engine and a 3-speed fully automatic transmission. Both models are set on a 98.4 in. wheel base and are suspended by coil springs front and rear.

1972 CHASSIS NUMBERS: 4222000001-4222064917

Modifications were made in "1700" engine for fewer emissions and improved cold running. Engine has new temperature and vacuum-controlled air intake preheating systems. Larger warm air outlets are incorporated in heating system.

1973 CHASSIS NUMBERS: 4132000001-

Model changes are described and illustrated on page 8.

INDEX

Index